Teen Finance Series

Debt Information For Teens,
Third Edition

Debt Information For Teens,
Third Edition

Tips For A Successful Financial Life

Including Facts About The Economy And Personal Finances,
Money Management, Interest Rates, Loans, Credit Cards, Predatory
Lending Practices, And Resolving Debt-Related Problems

OMNIGRAPHICS
615 Griswold, Ste. 901
Detroit, MI 48226

Bibliographic Note
Because this page cannot legibly accommodate all the copyright notices, the Bibliographic Note portion of the
Preface constitutes an extension of the copyright notice.

* * *

OMNIGRAPHICS
John Tilly, *Managing Editor*

* * *

Copyright © 2018 Omnigraphics

ISBN 978-0-7808-1569-8
E-ISBN 978-0-7808-1570-4

Library of Congress Cataloging-in-Publication Data

Title: Debt information for teens: tips for a successful financial life including facts about the
economy and personal finances, money management, interest rates, loans, credit cards,
predatory lending practices, and resolving debt-related problems.

Description: Third Edition. | Detroit, MI: Omnigraphics, [2018] | Series: Teen finance series |
Audience: Grade 9 to 12. | Revised edition of Debt information for teens, c2012. | Includes
bibliographical references and index.

Identifiers: LCCN 2017061014 (print) | LCCN 2018000429 (ebook) | ISBN 9780780815704 (eBook)
| ISBN 9780780815698 (hardcover: alk. paper)

Subjects: LCSH: Teenagers--Finance, Personal--Juvenile literature. | Consumer credit--Juvenile
literature.

Classification: LCC HG179 (ebook) | LCC HG179.D379 2018 (print) | DDC 332.024/020835--dc23

LC record available at https://lccn.loc.gov/2017061014

Table Of Contents

Preface

Part One: The Economy And Your Wallet

Part Two: Personal Money Management

Part Three: Establishing And Using Credit

Part Four: Credit Cards

Part Five: Identifying And Resolving Debt-Related Problems

Part Six: If You Need More Information

Preface

About This Book

According to a recent survey conducted by the Programme for International Student Assessment (PISA), about 1 in 5 children in the United States don't meet baseline levels for financial literacy proficiency. Only 10 percent of U.S. children are considered "top performers" capable of analyzing complex financial products and problems. There are about 64 percent of parents who discuss finance with their children at least once a week and say their children are smart about managing money.

Debt Information for Teens, Third Edition offers updated information about economic fundamentals that impact personal finances and ways to manage money. It explains how to develop a personal budget, save for future goals, and make purchasing decisions. It also discusses establishing and using credit, the basics of borrowing, the purposes of credit reports and credit scores, and some of the most frequently encountered types of loans, including installment, vehicle, and education loans. A special section on credit cards explains the different types of credit cards, how fees are calculated, the perils of making minimum payments, and tactics sometimes used by credit card companies that can be costly for consumers. Another section provides information about resolving debt-related problems, and the book concludes with a list of online tools and a directory of resources for additional information.

How To Use This Book

This book is divided into parts and chapters. Parts focus on broad areas of interest; chapters are devoted to single topics within a part.

Part One: The Economy And Your Wallet explains the relationship between global financial issues and personal finances. The latest annual report to congress on student banking featuring information on bank accounts and debit and credit cards is present. It reviews basic fundamentals about money, monetary policy, and interest rates and explains how these issues affect people—even teens—on a day-to-day basis.

Part Two: Personal Money Management describes important concepts and tools that can help teens handle the funds under their control. It discusses the importance of making a budget, using good decision-making regarding spending, and building wealth by saving. It also explains how banks work, how to avoid costly mistakes in managing checking accounts, and steps that can be taken to help minimize risks associated with identify theft.

Part Three: Establishing And Using Credit explains credit comprehensively. It details the process by which credit reputations are formed and how credit history can impact the ability to borrow money, rent an apartment, or even get a job. It explains credit reports and credit scores, and it offers details about the types of loans most commonly encountered by teens—installment loans, car loans, and education loans.

Part Four: Credit Cards offers a look at credit cards. The advantages and disadvantages associated with credit cards and important differences between credit cards and debit cards are discussed. Tips for evaluating and comparing credit card terms are included along with explanations regarding interest, fees, and practices that may lead to increased consumer costs. Measures to take in case of inability to repay credit on time and rebuilding credit history is discussed.

Part Five: Identifying And Resolving Debt-Related Problems talks about situations that can occur when debt gets out of control. Options for repaying student and credit card debt by consolidation is detailed. It explains the legal protections available to consumers and provides facts about related issues, such as vehicle repossession and bankruptcy. Deceptive tactics and illegal practices sometimes used by companies that prey on people with financial difficulties are also described.

Part Six: If You Need More Information provides a list of interactive financial tools, online calculators, and other web-based resources along with a directory of financial organizations.

Bibliographic Note

This volume contains documents and excerpts from publications issued by the following government agencies: Board of Governors of the Federal Reserve System; Consumer Financial Protection Bureau (CFPB); Federal Deposit Insurance Corporation (FDIC); Federal Student Aid; Federal Trade Commission (FTC); International Trade Administration (ITA); Office of the United States Trade Representative (USTR); TreasuryDirect; U.S. Bureau of Economic Analysis (BEA); U.S. Bureau of Engraving and Printing (BEP); U.S. Department of Education (ED); U.S. Department of Justice (DOJ); U.S. Department of the Treasury (USDT); U.S. Government Publishing Office (GPO); USA.gov; and Youth.gov.

It may also contain original material produced by Omnigraphics.

The photograph on the front cover is © sirtravelalot.

Part One
The Economy And Your Wallet

Chapter 1

Overview Of American Currency

History Of The BEP And U.S. Currency

The U.S. Bureau of Engraving and Printing (BEP) had its foundations in 1862 with workers signing, separating, and trimming sheets of United States Notes in the Treasury building. Gradually, more and more work, including engraving and printing, was entrusted to the organization. Within a few years, the BEP was producing Fractional Currency, revenue stamps, government obligations, and other security documents for many federal agencies. In 1877, the BEP became the sole producer of all United States currency. The addition of postage stamp production to its workload in 1894 established the BEP as the nation's security printer, responding to the needs of the U.S. government in both times of peace and war. Today, the BEP no longer produces government obligations or postage stamps, but it still holds the honor of being the largest producer of government security documents with production facilities in Washington, DC, and in Fort Worth, Texas.

The centrality of the BEP to the financial, monetary, postal, and printing developments of the United States since the Civil War has made it a repository of numerous invaluable historic items. At the same time, the BEP's history reflects and provides a unique perspective on the development of modern America. These facts have long been recognized by the BEP, which is devoted to the preservation and exploration of its own past. Some of the work of the curatorial, archival, and historical efforts of the BEP and its Historical Resource Center (HRC) is presented on this website.

About This Chapter: Text under the heading "History Of The BEP And U.S. Currency" is excerpted from "History Of The BEP And U.S. Currency," U.S. Bureau of Engraving and Printing (BEP), February 6, 2016; Text under the heading "American Money" is excerpted from "United States Currency," USA.gov, November 29, 2017.

Colonial Notes

1690

The Massachusetts Bay Colony, one of the 13 original colonies, issues the first paper money to cover costs of military expeditions. The practice of issuing paper notes spread to the other colonies.

Franklin's Unique Counterfeit Deterrent

1739

Benjamin Franklin's printing firm in Philadelphia prints colonial notes with nature prints—unique raised impressions of patterns cast from actual leaves. This process added an innovative and effective counterfeit deterrent to notes, not completely understood until centuries later.

Continental Currency

1775

The Continental Congress issues paper currency to finance the Revolutionary War. Continental currency was denominated in Spanish milled dollars. Without solid backing and easily counterfeited, the notes quickly lost their value, giving rise to the phrase "not worth a Continental."

Monetary System

1792

The Coinage Act of 1792 creates the U.S. Mint and establishes a federal monetary system, sets denominations for coins, and specifies the value of each coin in gold, silver, or copper.

Greenbacks

1861

The first general circulation of paper money by the federal government occurs. Pressed to finance the Civil War, Congress authorizes the U.S. Treasury to issue noninterest-bearing Demand Notes. All U.S. currency issued since 1861 remains valid and redeemable at full face value.

First $10 Bills–Demand Notes

1861

The first $10 notes are Demand Notes, issued in 1861 by the U.S. Department of the Treasury (USDT). A portrait of President Abraham Lincoln is included on the face of the notes.

Treasury Department Authorization

1862

The Treasury Secretary is authorized to engrave and print notes at the Treasury Department; the design of which incorporates fine-line engraving, intricate geometric lathe work patterns, a Treasury seal, and engraved signatures to aid in counterfeit deterrence.

Spencer Clark

1862

Spencer M. Clark, Chief Clerk in the Treasury Department's Bureau of Construction, obtains presses for the Treasury's Loan Branch for overprinting seals on notes. About the same time, Clark experiments with two hand-crank machines for trimming and separating. Later that year, Treasury Secretary Salmon Chase directs Clark to proceed with trials using steam-powered machines to trim, separate, and seal $1 and $2 United States Notes.

National Banknotes

1863

Congress establishes a national banking system and authorizes the U.S. Treasury to oversee the issuance of National Banknotes. This system sets federal guidelines for chartering and regulating "national" banks and authorizes those banks to issue national currency secured by the purchase of United States bonds. These notes are printed by private companies and finished by the BEP until 1875, when the BEP begins printing the faces.

Fractional Currency

1863

Fractional Currency notes, in denominations of 5, 10, 25, and 50 cents, are issued. This is the first currency produced entirely at the Treasury Department.

1864

The 5-cent note of the second issue of Fractional Currency features the portrait of Spencer Clark, causing a public uproar. It is unclear how Clark's portrait ended up on the note, but in 1866, Congress prohibits the portrait or likeness of any living person on currency notes, bonds, or securities.

1865

The United States Secret Service is established as a bureau of the Treasury for the purpose of deterring counterfeiters whose activities are destroying the public's confidence in the nation's currency. The Secret Service is now part of the U.S. Department of Homeland Security (DHS).

Gold Certificates

1865

Gold Certificates, backed by gold held by the Treasury, are first issued. Along with Fractional Currency, Gold Certificates are one of the first currency issues produced entirely by the BEP.

Revenue Stamps

1866

The BEP begins producing revenue stamps to be placed on boxes of imported cigars.

United States Notes

1869

The BEP begins engraving and printing the faces and seals of United States Notes, Series 1869. Prior to this time, United States Notes were produced by private banknote companies and then sent to the BEP for sealing, trimming, and cutting.

U.S. Bureau of Engraving and Printing

1874

For the first time, Congress allocates money specifically to a "U.S. Bureau of Engraving and Printing" for fiscal year 1875.

1876

Congress passes an appropriation bill that directs the Internal Revenue Service to procure stamps engraved and printed at the BEP—provided costs do not exceed that of private firms. As a result, the BEP begins producing almost all revenue stamps in fiscal year 1878.

1877

The BEP begins printing all United States currency.

Silver Certificates

1878

Silver Certificates are first issued. Backed by silver held by the Treasury, the certificates are authorized by legislation directing an increase in the purchase and coinage of silver.

First Facility

1880

The first building constructed specifically for BEP operations is completed at the corner of 14th Street and B Street (Independence Avenue).

Treasury Coin Notes

1890

Treasury Notes, also known as Treasury Coin Notes, are first issued as part of legislation requiring the Treasury Secretary to increase government purchases of silver bullion.

Postage Stamps

1894

The BEP begins printing postage stamps. The first BEP-printed stamp issued is the 6 cent President Garfield.

1900

The first issue of postage stamps in small booklets is produced.

Paper Currency With Background Color

1905

The last United States paper money printed with background color is the $20 Gold Certificate, Series 1905, which had a golden tint and a red seal and serial number.

Offset Printing

1912

Offset printing is first used in the BEP for the production of checks, certificates, and other miscellaneous items.

Federal Reserve Act

1913

The Federal Reserve Act of 1913 establishes the Federal Reserve as the nation's central bank and provides for a national banking system that is more responsive to the fluctuating financial needs of the country. Federal Reserve Bank Notes are authorized by the Federal Reserve Act and used as a form of emergency currency in the early twentieth century. The Board of Governors of the Federal Reserve System then issues new notes called Federal Reserve notes.

The First $10 Federal Reserve Notes

1914

The first $10 Federal Reserve notes are issued. These notes are larger than today's notes and feature a portrait of President Andrew Jackson on the face.

New DC Facility

1914

The BEP moves into a new, larger facility, later known as the "main" building.

Federal Reserve Note Standardized Design

1929

The first sweeping change to affect the appearance of all paper money occurs in 1929. In an effort to lower manufacturing costs, all Federal Reserve notes are made about 30 percent smaller. The reduced size enables the BEP to convert from eight to 12 notes per sheet. In addition, standardized designs are instituted for each denomination across all classes of currency, decreasing the number of different designs in circulation. This standardization makes it easier for the public to distinguish between genuine and counterfeit notes.

Annex Building

1938

BEP operations begin in the "annex" building. The building is officially dedicated in November 1938.

Food Stamps

1939

The BEP begins printing Food Order and Surplus Food Order stamps. The Cotton Order and Surplus Cotton Order stamps follow in 1940. The stamps encourage consumption of surplus farm commodities while providing assistance to low-income consumers.

Hawaii Overprints

1942

The BEP receives an order for special $1, $5, $10, and $20 notes overprinted with the word "Hawaii." The overprinted notes replace regular currency in Hawaii. In the event of enemy occupation of the islands, the overprinted currency can be declared worthless.

Allied Military Currency

1943

The War Department places an order for Allied Military Currency (AMC). The first AMCs are used by Allied forces in Italy. Production begins in July, 1943.

Military Payment Certificates

1946

The BEP begins work on Military Payment Certificates for use by U.S. troops.

Congressional Appropriations

1951

The BEP begins operating on a reimbursable basis in accordance with a legislative mandate to convert to business-type accounting methods. As a result, annual Congressional appropriations cease.

18-Subject Sheets

1952

The BEP begins conversion from 12- to 18-subject sheets in currency production. The use of larger sheets is made possible by new nonoffsetting ink. By reducing wetting and drying operations, distortion of paper is decreased. By September 1953, all currency is produced from 18-subject plates.

In God We Trust

1957

Following a 1955 law that requires "In God We Trust" on all currency, the motto first appears on paper money on series 1957 $1 silver certificates, then on 1963 series Federal Reserve notes.

32-Subject Sheets

1957

The BEP begins producing currency on high-speed rotary presses that print notes via the dry intaglio process. Paper distortion caused by wetting is now completely eliminated and sheet sizes increase from 18- to 32-subjects. The first notes printed by this process are the series 1957 silver certificates.

Barr Notes

1968

Joseph W. Barr served as Secretary of the Treasury from December 21, 1968 to January 20, 1969. There are fewer notes bearing his facsimile signature than notes imprinted with signatures of other Secretaries of the Treasury because of his short tenure in that office.

High-Denomination Notes

1969

The Treasury Secretary announces that currency in denominations larger than $100 will no longer be issued. Last printed in 1945, the high-denomination notes had been used mainly by banking institutions, but advances in bank transfer technologies preclude their further use.

$2 Federal Reserve Note

1976

The $2 Federal Reserve note is re-introduced on the 233rd anniversary of Thomas Jefferson's birth. Issuance of the $2 United States Note had been halted in 1966 as United States Notes were phased out of existence.

Security Thread And Microprinting

1990

A security thread and microprinting are introduced to deter counterfeiting by advanced copiers and printers. The features first appear in Series 1990 $100 notes. By Series 1993, the features appeared on all denominations except $1 and $2 notes.

Western Currency Facility

1990

The BEP's Western Currency Facility in Fort Worth, Texas begins producing currency. It is the first government facility outside Washington, DC to print United States paper money. The facility is intended to better serve the currency needs of the western half of the nation and to act as a contingency operation in case of emergencies at the DC facility.

Currency Redesign

1996

In the first significant design change in 67 years, United States currency is redesigned to incorporate a series of new counterfeit deterrents. The new notes are issued beginning with the $100 note in 1996, followed by the $50 in 1997, the $20 in 1998, and the $10 and $5 notes in 2000.

Redesigned $20 Note

2003

For the first time since the Series 1905 $20 Gold Certificate, the new currency features subtle background colors, beginning with the redesigned $20 note in October 2003. The redesigned $20 note features subtle background colors of green, peach and blue, as well as images of the American eagle.

Redesigned $50 Note

2004

The currency redesigns continue with the $50 note, issued on September 28, 2004. Similar to the redesigned $20 note, the redesigned $50 note features subtle background colors and highlights historical symbols of Americana. Specific to the $50 note are background colors of blue and red, and images of a waving American flag and a small metallic silver-blue star.

Final Postage Stamp Run

2005

The BEP produces its final run of postage stamps, printing the 37-cent Flag on the Andreotti gravure press.

Redesigned $10 Note

2006

A redesigned Series 2004A $10 note is issued on March 2, 2006. The A in the series designation indicates a change in some feature of the note, in this case, a change in the Treasurer's signature. Like the redesigned $20 and $50 notes, the redesigned $10 note features subtle shades of color and symbols of freedom. Specific to the $10 note are background colors of orange, yellow and red, and images of the Statue of Liberty's torch and the words, We the People, from the United States Constitution.

Redesigned $5 Note

2008

A redesigned Series 2006 $5 note is issued on March 13, 2008. The redesigned $5 note retains two of the most important security features first introduced in the 1990s: the watermark and embedded security thread.

Redesigned $100 Note

2013

On October 8, the Board of Governors of the Federal Reserve System issues the redesigned $100 note. Complete with advanced technology to combat counterfeiting, the new design for the $100 note retains the traditional look of U.S. currency.

50-Subject Printing

2014

On February 14, the BEP ushers in a new era by completing its first $1 note 50-subject production order. Fifty-subject and 32-subject notes are distinguishable by one minor technical change. On a 50-subject produced note, the letter and number of the alphanumeric note-position identifier, is the same font size and smaller than the alpha letter of the 32-subject note. In comparison, on the 32-subject note, the number is a smaller font size compared to the letter.

American Money

The United States issues paper currency and coins to pay for purchases, taxes, and debts.

Paper Money

American paper currency is issued in several denominations: $1, $2, $5, $10, $20, $50, and $100. The Bureau of Engraving and Printing manufactures paper money. It also redesigns money, with new appearances and enhanced security features to prevent counterfeiting. You can purchase commemorative or bulk versions of American currency through the Bureau's Money Store.

The United States no longer issues bills in larger denominations, such as $500, $1,000, $5,000, and $10,000 bills. However, they are still legal tender and may still be in circulation.

Coins

The United States issues several denominations, with the most common being: 1¢, 5¢, 10¢, 25¢, 50¢, and $1. The U.S. Mint is responsible for manufacturing and circulating coins to pay for goods and services. It also issues collectible and commemorative coins that honor a person, place, or event and are available for purchase.

Mutilated Money

If you have paper money that is extremely damaged, you can redeem it with the BEP. Examples of damaged paper money include bills that are less than one half of the bill, or in such a condition that you are unable to tell the denomination of the bill. If you have paper money that is dirty, defaced, torn or more than half of the original size, you can take it to your local bank to exchange it for a bill that is in better shape.

The U.S. Mint has suspended its exchange program for coins that are fused, melted, or mutilated in any other way. Visit your local bank to exchange other coins that aren't severely damaged.

Chapter 2

Financial Capability And Literacy

Financial capability and literacy is "the capacity, based on knowledge, skills, and access, to manage financial resources effectively." This set of skills can help youth achieve financial well-being, which happens when they can fully meet current and ongoing financial obligations, feel secure in their financial future, and are capable of making decisions that allow them to enjoy life. Financial education is how youth can learn these skills through a variety of resources and programming.

At present, youth face a financial marketplace that is more complex than the one faced by previous generations. A recent study found that millennials have greater financial concerns than older generations:

- 55 percent of millennials with student debt worry that they will not be able to pay off their debt, and

- almost 50 percent are concerned that they have too much debt in general (i.e., credit cards).

Financial capability is knowing how to spend wisely, manage credit, and plan for the future. Financial capability is an effective way to help youth, no matter their circumstances, avoid common financial vulnerabilities, and build economic stability. Youth should be educated about finances early in life and at pivotal points in their development and financial lives. Having a higher financial literacy early in life is associated with:

- less credit card debt,

- higher savings rates,

About This Chapter: This chapter includes text excerpted from "Financial Capability And Literacy," Youth.gov, April 28, 2016.

- and fewer personal bankruptcies.

As they approach high school graduation, students and their caregivers will make important decisions about whether to pursue higher education and if so, how to face the reality of paying for it. Additionally, youth who do not attend college or trade school directly after high school will more quickly face financial responsibilities as adults. These early choices can have a long-lasting impact on their financial well-being.

Financial Capability Activities For Schools

Financial institutions around the country often work with their local governments, local community groups, and community leaders to participate in financial literacy and education activities. For schools they provide:

- School savings programs and savings clubs in elementary schools.
- Educational programs that progress in complexity as students get older.
- Field trips to banks, guest speakers, investment clubs, stock market simulation games.
- School-based bank savings programs.

(Source: "Fact Sheet—Financial Capability," Office of the Comptroller of the Currency (OCC).)

Facts About Youth Financial Knowledge And Capability

Teaching financial capability is important because youth are increasingly facing higher levels of debt:

- The average debt of students when they graduated from college rose from $18,550 (in 2004) to $28,950 (in 2014), an increase of 56 percent.

- From 2004–2009, the median credit card debt among college students increased 74 percent.

Unfortunately, many youths have not received either formal or informal guidance on financial matters. So, they may not be ready to make sound financial choices:

- A survey of 15-year-olds in the United States found that 18 percent of respondents did not learn fundamental financial skills that are often applied in everyday situations, such as building a simple budget, comparison shopping, and understanding an invoice.

- A report on the results of a financial literacy exam found that high school seniors scored on average 48 percent correct, showing a strong need for more comprehensive financial education for youth in high school.

- According to the 2008 wave of the National Longitudinal Survey of Youth (NLSY), only 27 percent of youth knew what inflation was and could do simple interest rate calculations.

Financial illiteracy is more common among low-income individuals because they typically do not have wide access to accurate financial information. With such illiteracy, youth in low-income households can fall victim later as adults to scams, high-interest rate loans, and increasing debt. Training low-income individuals in financial management can be an effective way to improve their knowledge in five areas:

- predatory lending practices,

- public and work-related benefits,

- banking practices,

- savings and investing strategies,

- and credit use and interest rates.

Young people often learn about money informally through socialization, such as observing and listening to their caregivers, influential adults, and peers. Youth are not consistently introduced to more formal instruction on money matters—for example, through a classroom curriculum or other training on saving, spending, allowances, and the importance of focusing on short-term goals (i.e., purchasing an item, saving money, paying off a debt) to be able to get to long-term financial goals (i.e., saving for college, buying a house).

Distinguishing what youth do not understand about financial topics is important. It is also beneficial to understand the specific concerns that youth have when it comes to money.

A survey of a diverse group of youth and adults regarding what they wanted to learn about finance, found that concerns among youth differed within youth groups depending on their background. The survey also found a disconnect between what adults thought youth should learn and what youth prioritized, for example:

- Pregnant or parenting teens and teens in the juvenile justice system or on probation were most concerned about learning how to save money for a home; whereas migrant teens and teens in school were most interested in learning how to save money for college.

- Almost 70 percent of adults in the survey felt that teens should learn about how to complete and file a tax return form, but only 39 percent of the teens were interested in learning about this topic.

- However, more than half of the teens in the juvenile justice system or on probation and almost half of the migrant teens showed an interest in learning how to complete and file a tax return.

- Although a majority of teens wanted to learn about money, more than half wanted to learn in an easy way. This could include strategies that are convenient, utilize technology, and are not time consuming for youth.

Chapter 3

The American Experience With Money

The first system of "money" in North America was not coins or bills but the exchange of commodities. For thousands of years, Native Americans used the barter system, trading goods like furs, tobacco, indigo, rice, wheat, and corn with each other and with neighboring tribes. Eventually they introduced the first actual money in North America, called wampum, composed of beads made from shells and strung together to exchange for food, tools, weapons, and other useful items. When European settlers began arriving, they too mostly used the barter system, but some also adopted wampum as a means of exchange.

The earliest gold and silver coins used by the settlers were from European countries, including Great Britain, Portugal, France, and Spain. The first coins actually produced in the English colonies were issued in the Massachusetts Bay Colony in 1652, and America's first paper currency was also printed there in 1690. Other colonies followed suit, and a variety of paper money came into use. To help finance the Revolutionary War, the Continental Congress issued about $240 million in paper currency called Continentals, which were supposed to be redeemable for an agreed amount of gold or silver after the war.

This became the first paper currency issued by the United States government. Unfortunately, individual states continued to print their own money, which caused a great deal of confusion and resulted in Continentals becoming virtually worthless. To keep this from happening in the future, states were forbidden to issue paper money by the new U.S. Constitution.

About This Chapter: "The American Experience With Money," © 2017 Omnigraphics.

Timeline Of The Gold Standard In The United States

1865: After the Civil War, the government keeps its promise to exchange "greenbacks" for gold, tying the value of the U.S. dollar to gold.

1879: The United States adopts the gold standard, in which a standard amount of gold defines the value of U.S. currency, and the amount of gold for which currency can be redeemed.

1900: Congress passes the Gold Standard Act, officially establishing gold as the only standard for redeeming paper money.

1913: The Federal Reserve Act mandates that every U.S. dollar must be backed by 40 cents worth of gold in the treasury.

1933: In response to the Great Depression, Congress ends the gold standard, bans private ownership of gold, and declares that currency can no longer be exchanged for gold. (However, for the purposes of international trade, U.S. dollars could still be redeemed for gold.)

1943: Representatives from the United States and 43 other countries agree that all currency would be linked to the U.S. dollar, which was still redeemable in gold for international trade. At the time, the United States held about 75 percent of the world's gold reserves.

1971: President Richard Nixon announces that the United States would temporarily stop exchanging U.S. dollars for gold for purposes of international trade.

1974: President Gerald Ford signs a law that once again legalizes the private ownership of gold.

1976: The government redefines the U.S. dollar, officially severing all its links to gold, effectively removing the international monetary system from a gold standard. Today, very few countries tie their currency to gold, silver, or other metals.

The Bank Of The United States

Alexander Hamilton, the first secretary of the U.S. Treasury, convinced Congress to establish the Bank of the United States. Part of the reason for its creation was to help pay off the debt from the American Revolution by holding, controlling, and disbursing the country's money. But it also issued a national currency (the dollar) that would be accepted in all states, created money by borrowing as needed, loaned money to the government, and eventually oversaw the regulation of private banks that were chartered by various states.

From the beginning, the bank was a major source of controversy in the new country. Hamilton and his Federalist Party, who believed in a strong, financially sound national government, were opposed by Thomas Jefferson and the Democratic-Republicans, who advocated for states' rights and a primarily agrarian economy. The debate centered on the two parties' different interpretations of the Constitution. The Preamble gave Congress the right to make laws that were "right and proper" in order to carry out its part in the governing of the nation. But the Tenth Amendment said that any powers not specifically granted to Congress were given to the individual states. Hamilton's party thought the Bank of the United States was necessary for the economic health of the country, while Jefferson's party felt it would give too much power to the federal government. In the end, President Washington was convinced by the Federalists, and signed the bank into law in 1791.

But that didn't end the controversy. The two factions kept the argument going and continued to make the Bank of the United an example of their political beliefs and their interpretations of the Constitution. The bitter debate resulted in the bank's charter failing to be renewed in 1811. It was revived in 1816, but the partisan factions wouldn't drop their feud over the issue. In the early 1830s, President Andrew Jackson and his Democratic Party took up opposition to the bank, while the new Whig Party, led by Henry Clay, decided to make its mark by defending the institution in what became known as the "Bank Wars" during the presidential campaign of 1832, in which Jackson defeated Clay. Jackson vetoed the renewal of the bank's charter amid strong opposition, but the veto held, and the bank dissolved after its charter ran out in 1836. It was rechartered as a commercial bank in Pennsylvania, where it continued to operate until it failed in 1841.

The United States Mint

In addition to urging Congress to create the Bank of the United States, Alexander Hamilton also championed the establishment of the United States Mint. On April 2, 1792, Congress passed the Coinage Act, which created the Mint and authorized construction of a building to house it in Philadelphia, the nation's capital at the time. The Act also specified the salary of the Mint's director, as well as those of other Mint employees. President Washington appointed David Rittenhouse, a highly regarded scientist, inventor, and mathematician, as the first director of the Mint, a position he held until 1795.

The Coinage Act mandated that coins produced by the Mint must bear the words "United States of America," "Liberty," and the year of coinage, but Rittenhouse believed the coins should also be works of art, and he personally consulted on the design. He hand-struck the first coins himself to test the Mint's new equipment and presented them to Washington as gift. Legend has it that those first "pattern" or sample coins were made from Martha Washington's silverware. The first coins authorized by Congress were made of copper (the half-cent, cent), silver (half-dime, dime, quarter, half-dollar, dollar), and gold (quarter-eagle, half-eagle, eagle), and the first ones to enter mass production were the copper half-cent and one-cent coins in 1793.

> The Constitution did not specify the degree to which the federal government could become involved in the country's monetary system. It only specified that Congress could mint metal coins, set the percentage of precious metal in those coins, and officially determine the amount of precious metal of any foreign coins circulating in the United States.

But controversy soon erupted again. This time the issue was that the Mint was unable to supply enough coins to satisfy the country's need, in part because of a shortage of the metals needed for their production. Hamilton and other Federalists argued that the Mint should be closed and the Bank of the United States take over responsibility for minting coins, because it had better access to precious metals and could run the operation more efficiently. Congress took up the debate, but after several close votes the Mint remained open. In 1803, Elias Boudinot, then director of the Mint, submitted a report to Congress outlining his plan to improve efficiency and increase the Mint's production. A bill was passed that year authorizing the Mint's continued operations, and no serious challenge to its work has been mounted since that time. As more states joined the Union, more Mints were added throughout the country. Today the Mint operates facilities in Philadelphia, Denver, San Francisco, and West Point, New York, in addition to its headquarters in Washington, D.C.

The Free Banking Era

The period from 1836, when the Bank of the United States was dissolved, to 1863 is sometimes called the Free Banking Era. During this time, there was no central federal bank, and the individual states ran their own banking systems. State-chartered banks were free to issue paper currency against their gold and silver reserves, and regulations about interest rates, loan terms, and the amount of coin or precious metal reserves they were required to maintain were set by the states, not by the federal government. In addition, some states passed free banking acts, which allowed banks to open and run like any other business, with almost no legislative oversight.

The result was chaos. Banks operated with less regulation than at any other time in U.S. history, with the result that almost anyone could open a bank, many were severely underfunded, and a lot of their currency became worthless. About half the banks failed, with many of them going out of business because they were unable to redeem their banknotes in specie (gold and silver coins), leaving depositors with loads of useless paper. Some of the problems were caused the inherent lack of regulation, some by crooks who opened banks and defrauded the public by intentionally issuing more currency than they ever planned to redeem, and others were simply the result of poor management by inexperienced business people.

> The counterfeiting of American money goes back to the earliest European settlers who began dying common white shells to resemble the rarer blue-black shells used by native tribes as wampum. When copper, silver, and gold coins came into use, their designs became more and more elaborate in an attempt to foil counterfeiters. Early paper money proved even easier to fake than coins, so through the years its design and printing techniques have become increasingly sophisticated. Some of the latest bills employ anti-counterfeiting measures like watermarks, interwoven security threads, and even ink that changes color as the bill is held at different angles.

National Banks

In the United States, a national bank is a commercial bank that is a member of the Federal Reserve System and the Federal Deposit Insurance Corporation (FDIC), which insures bank deposits against loss. These banks are chartered and overseen by the Office of the Comptroller of the Currency (OCC), part of the U.S. Department of the Treasury (USDT), and are required to have the word "national" or the letters "NA" (for national association) in their names. To become a national bank, a bank must prove the competence and experience of its senior managers and board of directors and must demonstrate its stability by having sufficient capital reserves to withstand a certain amount of economic fluctuation.

Currently there are more than 350 national banks in the United States. Some of the largest, with more than 1,000 locations, include familiar names like Bank of America, Citizens Bank, Chase, PNC Bank, Regions Bank, SunTrust, U.S. Bank, and Wells Fargo. But not all national banks have so many branches or subsidiaries around the country. Some operate in just one region, state, or city. Whatever their size, national banks manage the process for buying and selling U.S. Treasury bonds, handle daily transactions with their local Federal Reserve Bank, and perform many of the same functions as any other bank, including maintaining savings and checking accounts for customers.

References

1. "About The United States Mint," USmint.gov, 2016.

2. "Bank Of The United States," Encyclopaedia Britannica, September 12, 2016.

3. Flaherty, Edward. "A Brief History Of Central Banking In The United States," Letrug.nl, n.d.

4. Hendrik, Rhab. "The Free Banking Era," ArticlesFactory.com, January 5, 2011. Hill, Andrew T. "The First Bank of the United States," Federalreservehistory.org, December 4, 2015.

5. Hunt, Steve. "History Of The United States Mint," SBCgold.com, September 17, 2015.

6. "Money Matters: The American Experience With Money," Federal Reserve Bank of Chicago, 1996.

7. Paige, Joseph. "Native American Money," Native American Cultural Center, 2006.

8. Sanches, Daniel. "The Free Banking Era: A Lesson For Today?" Federal Reserve Bank of Philadelphia, third quarter, 2016.

9. "What Are The Major National Banks Of The United States?" Reference.com, n.d.

Chapter 4

The State Of The Economy In The United States

U.S. Bureau of Economic Analysis (BEA) produces some of the most closely watched economic statistics that influence decisions of government officials, business people, and individuals. These statistics provide a comprehensive, up-to-date picture of the U.S. economy. The data on this chapter are drawn from featured BEA economic accounts.

National Economic Accounts

Gross Domestic Product (GDP)

Quarterly data: Real gross domestic product (GDP) increased at an annual rate of 3.2 percent in the third quarter of 2017, according to the "third" estimate released by the U.S. Bureau of Economic Analysis (BEA). In the second quarter, real GDP increased 3.1 percent.

What Is GDP?

GDP is the value of the goods and services produced by the nation's economy less the value of the goods and services used up in production. GDP is also equal to the sum of personal consumption expenditures, gross private domestic investment, net exports of goods and services, and government consumption expenditures and gross investment.

(Source: "National Income And Product Accounts Gross Domestic Product: First Quarter 2017 (Advance Estimate)," U.S. Bureau of Economic Analysis (BEA).)

About This Chapter: This chapter includes text excerpted from "U.S. Economy At A Glance," U.S. Bureau of Economic Analysis (BEA), November 16, 2017.

Personal Income

Monthly data: In November 2017, real disposable personal income increased 0.1 percent.

What Is Personal Income?

Personal income is the income received by, or on behalf of, all persons from all sources: from

participation as laborers in production, from owning a home or business, from the owner-ship of financial assets, and from government and business in the form of transfers. It includes income from domestic sources as well as the rest of world. It does not include realized or unre-alized capital gains or losses.

(Source: "National Income And Product Accounts Gross Domestic Product: First Quarter 2017 (Advance Estimate)," U.S. Bureau of Economic Analysis (BEA).)

Industry Economic Accounts

Quarterly Industry Accounts: GDP By Industry

Quarterly Data: Finance and insurance; durable goods manufacturing; and information services were the leading contributors to the increase in U.S. economic growth in the third quarter of 2017. According to GDP by industry statistics released by the BEA, 18 of 22 indus-try groups contributed to the overall 3.2 percent increase in real GDP in the third quarter.

International Economic Accounts

U.S. Balance Of Payments (BOP) (International Transactions)

Quarterly data: The U.S. current-account deficit decreased $23.8–$100.6 billion (prelimi-nary) in the third quarter of 2017.

International Investment Position

Quarterly data: The U.S. net international investment position increased to -$7,768.7 bil-lion (preliminary) at the end of the third quarter of 2017 from -$8,004.1 billion (revised) at the end of the second quarter, according to statistics released by the BEA.

International Trade In Goods And Services

Monthly: Total November exports of $200.2 billion and imports of $250.7 billion resulted in a goods and services deficit of $50.5 billion.

New Foreign Direct Investment In The United States

Annual Data: Expenditures by foreign direct investors to acquire, establish, or expand U.S. businesses totaled $373.4 billion in 2016. Spending was down 15 percent from $439.6 billion in 2015, but was above the annual average of $350.0 billion for 2014–2015, and was well above the annual average of $226.0 billion for 2006–2008. As in previous years, expenditures to acquire existing businesses accounted for a large majority of the total.

Regional Economic Accounts

Gross Domestic Product (GDP) By State

Quarterly Data: Real GDP increased in 48 states and the District of Columbia in the second quarter of 2017. Real GDP by state growth ranged from 8.3 percent in North Dakota to -0.7 percent in Iowa.

Gross Domestic Product (GDP) By Metropolitan Area

Annual data: Real gross domestic product (GDP) increased in 267 out of 382 metropolitan areas in 2016. Real GDP by metropolitan area growth ranged from 8.1 percent in Lake Charles, LA and Bend-Redmond, OR to −13.3 percent in Odessa, TX. Real GDP for U.S. metropolitan areas grew 1.7 percent in 2016, led by growth in professional and business services; information services; and finance, insurance, real estate, rental, and leasing.

State Personal Income (SPI)

Quarterly data: State personal income increased 0.7 percent on average in the third quarter of 2017. In the second quarter, state personal income increased 0.6 percent. Increases in earnings and personal current transfer receipts were the leading contributors to the acceleration in personal income in the third quarter.

Local Area Personal Income

Local area data: Personal income grew in 2016 in 2,285 counties, fell in 795, and was unchanged in 33. On average, personal income rose 2.5 percent in 2016 in the metropolitan portion of the United States and rose 1.0 percent in the nonmetropolitan portion. Personal income growth in 2016 ranged from -40.8 percent in Kenedy County, Texas to 27.1 percent in Tillman County, Oklahoma.

Real Personal Income For States And Metropolitan Areas

State and Metropolitan area data: Real state personal income grew on average 4.1 percent in 2015, after increasing 3.6 percent in 2014. Growth of real state personal income ranged from -2.3 percent in North Dakota to 7.0 percent in Delaware. Across metropolitan areas, growth ranged from -10.1 percent in Midland, TX to 9.9 percent in Carson City, NV.

Personal Consumption Expenditures By State

Annual data: State personal consumption expenditures (PCE) grew on average 4.0 percent in 2016, the same rate as in 2015. In 2016, PCE growth ranged from 0.2 percent in North Dakota to 6.2 percent in Utah.

Chapter 5

A Look At The U.S. Economy

Constituting less than 5 percent of the world's population, Americans generate and earn more than 20 percent of the world's total income. America is the world's largest national economy and leading global trader. The process of opening world markets and expanding trade, initiated in the United States in 1934 and consistently pursued since the end of the Second World War, has played an important role in the development of American prosperity. According to the Peterson Institute for International Economics (PIIE), American real incomes are 9 percent higher than they would otherwise have been as a result of trade liberalizing efforts since the Second World War. In terms of the U.S. economy in 2013, that 9 percent represents $1.5 trillion in additional American income.

Such gains arise in a number of ways. Expanding the production of America's most competitive industries and products, through exports, raises U.S. incomes. Shifting production to the most competitive areas of our economy helps raise the productivity of the average American worker and through that the income they earn. With the ability to serve a global market, investment is encouraged in expanding export sectors and the rising scale of output helps lower average production costs. Such effects help strengthen America's economic growth rate. Moreover, imports increase consumer choice, and help keep prices low raising the purchasing power for consumers. Imports also provide high quality inputs for American businesses helping companies and their U.S. employees become or remain highly competitive in both domestic and foreign markets.

About This Chapter: Text in this chapter begins with excerpts from "Economy And Trade," Office of the United States Trade Representative (USTR), January 27, 2015; Text beginning with the heading "U.S. Trade In 2016" is excerpted from "U.S. Trade Overview 2016," International Trade Administration (ITA), April 2017.

The potential economic gains from trade for America are far from exhausted. Roughly three quarters of world purchasing power and over 95 percent of world consumers are outside America's borders. The Peterson Institute analysis also estimated that elimination of remaining global trade barriers would increase the benefit America already enjoys from trade by another 50 percent. Trade remains an engine of growth for America. The negotiation of further reductions in global barriers and effective enforcement of existing agreements are the tools to reap those additional benefits.

Benefits Of Trade Expansion

Trade expansion benefits families and businesses by:

- Supporting more productive, higher paying jobs in export sectors
- Expanding the variety of products for purchase by consumers and business
- Encouraging investment and more rapid economic growth

Trade keeps economy open, dynamic, and competitive, and helps ensure that America continues to be the best place in the world to do business.

(Source: "Benefits Of Trade," Office of the United States Trade Representative (USTR)

As policy actions taken in the United States and countries around the globe continue to restore economic and job growth, an important part of the recovery will be the restoration of trade expansion. Over the past 5 and one quarter years of recovery (from the 2nd quarter of 2009 to the 3rd quarter of 2014), U.S. real GDP is up 2.3 percent at an annual rate, and exports have contributed one-third (0.7 percentage points) to this growth. Jobs supported by U.S. exports of goods and services are up an estimated 1.6 million since 2009, to an estimated 11.3 million in 2013.

Rapid trade growth may well act as a transmitter of economic stimulus around the globe and a vehicle of continued recovery, particularly if enhanced by additional efforts to reduce barriers and expand trading opportunities further. Recognition of the long-term benefits of expanded trade, as well as the positive role trade can play in the current economic recovery are central factors reflected in the Administration's trade policy.

U.S. Trade In 2016

- U.S. exports of goods and services decreased 2.3 percent in 2016 to $2.21 trillion, reflecting a decrease in both goods and services exports.

- Imports decreased 1.8 percent to $2.71 trillion reflecting a decrease in goods imports; services imports increased.

- In 2016, the U.S. goods and services trade deficit totaled $502.3 billion, a 0.4 percent increase from the $500.4 billion trade deficit in 2015.

- Goods account for the majority of U.S. trade, generally driving both exporting and importing activity.

- Exports as a share of GDP fell again in 2016, due to increased personal consumption playing a larger role in U.S. GDP.

- The trade deficit accounted for -2.7 percent of GDP in 2016, its lowest share since 2009.

Top U.S. Export Markets

- Canada was the top U.S. goods export market in 2016, led by sales of vehicles and parts and machinery.

- U.S. goods exports were a record high to 18 countries in 2016.

- Goods exports to Vietnam showed the largest dollar growth, up by $3.1 billion in 2016.

- Since 2006, U.S. goods exports have grown 42 percent, with most of this growth occurring with Mexico and China.

- Among the top 30 export markets, goods exports to Vietnam have grown the fastest over the past 10 years, up by more than 800 percent.

U.S. Goods Trade

- Goods exports totaled $1.46 trillion in 2016, led by sales of capital goods.

- Lower global commodity prices continued to play a significant role in the decline in U.S. exports in 2016. In addition, U.S. exporters faced headwinds from overall weak global demand and a worldwide trade slowdown.

- Although U.S. goods exports declined in nominal (price included) values, in real terms (adjusted to remove the impact of prices) they remained flat, with exports of petroleum products, semiconductors, soybeans, natural gas liquids, and corn showing the largest growth.

- U.S. imports of crude oil, by value, decreased 19.5 percent in 2016 to $101.3 billion, entirely due to a decrease in price.

- The average price of a barrel of crude oil was 23.6 percent less than the 2015 average. This was the lowest annual price since 2004.

U.S. Services Trade

- Services exports totaled $750.0 billion in 2016, down slightly from the previous year. U.S. services imports increased 2.7 percent to $501.8 billion.

- Major services export categories in 2016 were travel, for all purposes (a record $207.9 billion); other business services (a record $139.9 billion); charges for the use of intellectual property ($120.3 billion); financial services ($95.1 billion); and transport ($84.7 billion).

- The U.S. had record exports in several services categories in 2016 including other business services; travel, for all purposes; maintenance and repairs; telecommunications, computer, and information services; and insurance services.

- The U.S. maintained a surplus in services trade in 2016. However, this surplus decreased by 5.5 percent, largely due to higher imports, such as increased travel imports, and lower exports of charges for the use of intellectual property and financial services.

U.S. Exporters

- Nearly 295,000 U.S. companies exported and almost 197,000 imported goods in 2015

- Nearly 98 percent of these exporters were small- or medium-sized with fewer than 500 employees. Small and medium-sized enterprises (SMEs) accounted for 97 percent of identified importers in 2015.

- SMEs were responsible for a third of goods trade (by value) in 2015.

- Most SMEs (59%) only export to a single market, while 74 percent of large firms export to multiple countries.

- The majority of exporters are nonmanufacturing firms such as wholesalers.

- California is home to more than 70,000 SME exporters, the highest among the 50 states. Other top states are Florida, Texas, New York, and Illinois.

Chapter 6

Understanding U.S. Monetary Policy And Interest Rates

What Is The Difference Between Monetary Policy And Fiscal Policy, And How Are They Related?

Monetary policy is a term used to refer to the actions of central banks to achieve macroeconomic policy objectives such as price stability, full employment, and stable economic growth. In the United States, the Congress established maximum employment and price stability as the macroeconomic objectives for the Federal Reserve; they are sometimes referred to as the Federal Reserve's dual mandate. Apart from these overarching objectives, the Congress determined that operational conduct of monetary policy should be free from political influence. As a result, the Federal Reserve is an independent agency of the federal government. Fiscal policy is a broad term used to refer to the tax and spending policies of the federal government. Fiscal policy decisions are determined by the Congress and the Administration; the Federal Reserve plays no role in determining fiscal policy.

The Federal Reserve uses a variety of policy tools to foster its statutory objectives of maximum employment and price stability. Its main policy tools is the target for the federal funds rate (the rate that banks charge each other for short-term loans), a key short-term interest rate. The Federal Reserve's control over the federal funds rate gives it the ability to influence the general level of short-term market interest rates. By adjusting the level of short-term interest rates in response to changes in the economic outlook, the Federal Reserve can influence

---

About This Chapter: This chapter includes text excerpted from "Money, Interest Rates, And Monetary Policy," Board of Governors of the Federal Reserve System, March 1, 2017.

longer-term interest rates and key asset prices. These changes in financial conditions then affect the spending decisions of households and businesses.

The monetary policymaking body within the Federal Reserve System is the Federal Open Market Committee (FOMC). The FOMC currently has eight scheduled meetings per year, during which it reviews economic and financial developments and determines the appropriate stance of monetary policy. In reviewing the economic outlook, the FOMC considers how the current and projected paths for fiscal policy might affect key macroeconomic variables such as gross domestic product growth, employment, and inflation. In this way, fiscal policy has an indirect effect on the conduct of monetary policy through its influence on the aggregate economy and the economic outlook. For example, if federal tax and spending programs are projected to boost economic growth, the Federal Reserve would assess how those programs would affect its key macroeconomic objectives—maximum employment and price stability—and make appropriate adjustments to its monetary policy tools.

What Is The Statement On Longer-Run Goals And Monetary Policy Strategy And Why Does The Federal Open Market Committee Put It Out?

In January 2012, the FOMC first published a "Statement on Longer-Run Goals and Monetary Policy Strategy." The Committee has reaffirmed the Statement each January since then. The publication of a statement on longer-run goals helps hold the Fed accountable; it also helps the public understand how the FOMC interprets its statutory mandate to promote maximum employment and stable prices.

In the statement, the FOMC says that it judges that inflation at the rate of 2 percent, as measured by the annual change in the price index for personal consumption expenditures, is most consistent over the longer run with the Federal Reserve's statutory mandate. The Committee states that it would be concerned if inflation were running persistently above or below the 2 percent objective. In addition, the document notes that the FOMC's policy decisions will be informed by its assessments of the maximum level of employment, recognizing that such assessments are necessarily uncertain and subject to revision. In setting monetary policy, the FOMC seeks to mitigate deviations of inflation from its longer-run goal and deviations of employment from the FOMC's assessments of its maximum level.

What Is The Basic Legal Framework That Determines The Conduct Of Monetary Policy?

The Congress established a basic legal framework for the conduct of monetary policy that involves three key pillars:

1. statutory long-run economic objectives for the conduct of monetary policy—maximum employment and stable prices

2. a structure for the Federal Reserve System that provides for a significant degree of operational independence in the conduct of monetary policy

3. mechanisms to ensure appropriate transparency and accountability of the Federal Reserve in the conduct of monetary policy

This basic framework of statutory objectives, operational independence, and mechanisms to ensure transparency and accountability now governs the conduct of monetary policy by all major central banks around the world and is commonly viewed as a best practice for central banking.

What Are The Federal Reserve's Objectives In Conducting Monetary Policy?

The Congress established the statutory objectives for monetary policy—maximum employment, stable prices, and moderate long-term interest rates—in the Federal Reserve Act.

The FOMC is firmly committed to fulfilling this statutory mandate. In pursuing these objectives, the FOMC seeks to explain its monetary policy decisions to the public as clearly as possible. Clarity in policy communications facilitates well-informed decision making by households and businesses, reduces economic and financial uncertainty, increases the effectiveness of monetary policy, and enhances transparency and accountability, which are essential in a democratic society.

The maximum level of employment is largely determined by nonmonetary factors that affect the structure and dynamics of the job market. These factors may change over time and may not be directly measurable. As a result, the FOMC does not specify a fixed goal for maximum employment; rather, the FOMC's policy decisions must be informed by its members' assessments of the maximum level of employment, though such assessments are necessarily uncertain and subject to revision. In the FOMC's December 2017 Summary of Economic Projections, Committee participants' estimates of the longer-run normal rate of unemployment ranged from 4.3–5.0 percent and had a median value of 4.6 percent.

How Does Monetary Policy Influence Inflation And Employment?

In the short run, monetary policy influences inflation and the economy-wide demand for goods and services—and, therefore, the demand for the employees who produce those goods and services—primarily through its influence on the financial conditions facing households and firms. During normal times, the Federal Reserve has primarily influenced overall financial conditions by adjusting the federal funds rate—the rate that banks charge each other for short-term loans. Movements in the federal funds rate are passed on to other short-term interest rates that influence borrowing costs for firms and households. Movements in short-term interest rates also influence long-term interest rates—such as corporate bond rates and residential mortgage rates—because those rates reflect, among other factors, the current and expected future values of short-term rates. In addition, shifts in long-term interest rates affect other asset prices, most notably equity prices and the foreign exchange value of the dollar. For example, all else being equal, lower interest rates tend to raise equity prices as investors discount the future cash flows associated with equity investments at a lower rate.

In turn, these changes in financial conditions affect economic activity. For example, when short- and long-term interest rates go down, it becomes cheaper to borrow, so households are more willing to buy goods and services and firms are in a better position to purchase items to expand their businesses, such as property and equipment. Firms respond to these increases in total (household and business) spending by hiring more workers and boosting production. As a result of these factors, household wealth increases, which spurs even more spending. These linkages from monetary policy to production and employment don't show up immediately and are influenced by a range of factors, which makes it difficult to gauge precisely the effect of monetary policy on the economy.

Monetary policy also has an important influence on inflation. When the federal funds rate is reduced, the resulting stronger demand for goods and services tends to push wages and other costs higher, reflecting the greater demand for workers and materials that are necessary for production. In addition, policy actions can influence expectations about how the economy will perform in the future, including expectations for prices and wages, and those expectations can themselves directly influence current inflation.

In 2008, with short-term interest rates essentially at zero and thus unable to fall much further, the Federal Reserve undertook nontraditional monetary policy measures to provide additional support to the economy. Between late 2008 and October 2014, the Federal Reserve purchased longer-term mortgage-backed securities and notes issued by certain government-sponsored enterprises, as well as longer-term Treasury bonds and notes. The primary purpose of these purchases was to help to lower the level of longer-term interest rates, thereby improving financial conditions. Thus, this nontraditional monetary policy measure operated through the same broad channels as traditional policy, despite the differences in implementation of the policy.

What Is Inflation? How Does The Federal Reserve Evaluate Changes In The Rate Of Inflation?

Inflation occurs when the prices of goods and services increase over time. Inflation cannot be measured by an increase in the cost of one product or service, or even several products or services. Rather, inflation is a general increase in the overall price level of the goods and services in the economy.

Federal Reserve policymakers evaluate changes in inflation by monitoring several different price indexes. A price index measures changes in the price of a group of goods and services. The Fed considers several price indexes because different indexes track different products and services, and because indexes are calculated differently. Therefore, various indexes can send diverse signals about inflation.

(Source: "FAQs Economy, Jobs, And Prices," Board of Governors of the Federal Reserve System.)

Why Did The Federal Reserve Begin Raising Interest Rates After Seven Years Of Keeping Them Near Zero?

In March 2015, the FOMC indicated in its post-meeting statement that it anticipated that it would be appropriate to raise the target range for the federal funds rate when it had seen further improvement in the labor market and was reasonably confident that inflation would move back to its 2 percent objective over the medium term. In December 2015, the Committee judged that both of those tests had been met. Given the outlook for the economy and the fact that it takes time for policy actions to affect future economic outcomes, the Committee decided to raise its target for policy interest rates. The Committee noted in its statement that monetary policy remains accommodative, thereby supporting further improvement in labor market conditions and a return to 2 percent inflation.

The Federal Reserve pursues policy to promote the goals of maximum employment and stable prices set forth by the Congress in the Federal Reserve Act. During the global financial crisis, the FOMC cut short-term interest rates to nearly zero. To promote economic recovery, the FOMC then undertook a series of large-scale asset purchase programs and used its communications about the path of future policy rates (known as forward guidance). Since October 2009, the unemployment rate has fallen from its peak of 10–5 percent in November 2015. Inflation—as measured by the increase in the price index for personal consumption expenditures—has generally run somewhat below the FOMC's objective of 2 percent, averaging about 1–1/2 percent since the recession began in late 2007. Inflation was especially low in 2015, held down by declines in energy prices and in prices of nonenergy imports. However, with the economy having strengthened considerably, the FOMC is reasonably confident that inflation will move back to 2 percent as energy and import prices stabilize and the economic expansion continues.

What Does The Federal Reserve Mean When It Says Monetary Policy Remains "Accommodative"?

In general, monetary policy is considered to be "accommodative" when it aims to make interest rates sufficiently low to spur strong enough economic growth to reduce unemployment or to prevent unemployment from rising. For example, toward the end of 2008, in the midst of the global financial crisis and Great Recession, with unemployment above 6–1/2 percent and rising, and inflation below 2 percent and expected to decline, the FOMC pushed short-term interest rates to nearly zero. The FOMC then embarked on a series of large-scale asset purchase programs to reduce longer-term interest rates.

By December 2015, the unemployment rate had come down to 5 percent and there had been considerable improvement in a broad range of indicators of labor market conditions. The Committee projected further improvement, and it was reasonably confident that inflation would rise to 2 percent over the medium term after prices of energy and imported goods stop declining. Considering the economic outlook and the fact that policy actions take time to affect the economy, the FOMC decided to increase its target range for the federal funds rate by 1/4 percentage point. The stance of monetary policy remains accommodative after this increase in the sense that interest rates remain low enough to support further strengthening in labor market conditions and a return to 2 percent inflation.

What Does The Federal Reserve Mean When It Talks About The "Normalization Of Monetary Policy"?

The global financial crisis that began in 2007 had profound effects on the U.S. economy and other economies around the world. To support a return to the Federal Reserve's statutory goals of maximum employment and price stability, the FOMC reduced short-term interest rates to nearly zero and held them at that exceptionally low level for seven years. The FOMC also undertook large-scale open-market purchases of longer-term U.S. Treasury securities and mortgage-backed securities (MBS) to put downward pressure on longer-term interest rates. The term "normalization of monetary policy" refers to plans for returning both short-term interest rates and the Federal Reserve's securities holdings to more normal levels.

In September 2014, the FOMC published a statement of Policy Normalization Principles and Plans describing the overall strategy it intends to follow in normalizing the stance of monetary policy following the period of extraordinarily accommodative policies taken in the aftermath of the 2008–09 recession. These plans were further elaborated in the minutes of the March 2015 FOMC meeting.

At its December 2015 meeting, the FOMC decided to begin the normalization process by modestly raising its target range for the federal funds rate.

Policy Normalization Plan

The FOMC indicated that there would be two main components to policy normalization: gradually raising its target range for the federal funds rate to more normal levels and gradually reducing the Federal Reserve's securities holdings.

(Source: "Policy Normalization—FOMC Communications Related To Policy Normalization," Board of Governors of the Federal Reserve System.)

Why Is The Federal Reserve Paying Banks Interest?

The payment of interest on banks' reserve balances is a common monetary policy tool at the disposal of major central banks. The Congress authorized the Federal Reserve to pay interest on balances that banks hold at the Fed, effective late in 2008. Since then, the Federal Reserve has paid interest on balances that banks hold to meet reserve requirements and on amounts in excess of required reserves. The Board of Governors sets the interest rate the Federal Reserve pays on reserve balances to help implement the FOMC's monetary policy decisions.

During the monetary policy normalization process, the Federal Reserve intends to raise the interest rate it pays on reserve balances in line with increases in the main monetary policy rate—the target that the FOMC sets for the federal funds rate. Doing so will help control the federal funds rate and keep it in the target range set by the FOMC. When the Federal Reserve raises the Interest Rate On Excess Reserves (IOER) rate, banks will take this new, higher rate into account when making decisions about lending funds and would be unlikely to loan funds for an interest rate that is below the IOER rate.

More broadly, as the Federal Reserve increases rates, banks will also have to pay higher rates on their sources of funding—that includes paying more to depositors. And that process will help to boost incomes for savers, many of whom have experienced low returns for quite a few years.

The IOER rate is not the only policy tool at the Federal Reserve's disposal.

What Is Forward Guidance And How Is It Used In The Federal Reserve's Monetary Policy?

In today's interconnected world, many central banks communicate regularly and frequently with the public about the state of the economy, the economic outlook, and the likely future course of monetary policy. Communication about the likely future course of monetary policy is known as "forward guidance."

When central banks provide forward guidance about the future course of monetary policy, individuals and businesses will use this information in making decisions about spending and investments. Thus, forward guidance about future policy can influence financial and economic conditions today.

The FOMC began using forward guidance in its post-meeting statements in the early 2000s. Before increasing its target for the federal funds rate in June 2004, the FOMC used a sequence of changes in its statement language to signal that it was approaching the time at which a tightening of monetary policy was warranted.

In the aftermath of the global financial crisis, the FOMC reduced its federal funds rate target nearly to zero, and then used forward guidance to provide information about likely future monetary policy. For example, the post-meeting statement issued in December 2008 noted that the Committee anticipated that weak economic conditions were "likely to warrant exceptionally low levels of the federal funds rate for some time." The FOMC's forward guidance has evolved over time; eventually, the Committee's guidance indicated that the future path of the federal funds rate would depend upon how future economic conditions changed. In addition, the FOMC used forward guidance language about the flow-based asset purchase program that it undertook in September 2012.

In December 2015, when the Committee decided to begin raising the target range for the federal funds rate from nearly zero—the first change in seven years—it indicated in its post-meeting statement that the timing and size of future adjustments in the policy target range would depend on "realized and expected economic conditions relative to its objectives of maximum employment and 2 percent inflation." Moreover, the FOMC noted that it expected that economic conditions would evolve in a manner that was consistent with only gradual increases in interest rates.

What Economic Goals Does The Federal Reserve Seek To Achieve Through Its Monetary Policy?

The Federal Reserve works to promote a strong U.S. economy. The Congress has directed the Fed to conduct the nation's monetary policy to support three specific goals: maximum sustainable employment, stable prices, and moderate long-term interest rates. These goals are sometimes referred to as the Fed's "mandate."

Why Do Interest Rates Matter?

Interest rates matter in many different ways that affect the U.S. economy. One way that interest rates matter is they influence borrowing costs. Lower interest rates, for example, would encourage more people to obtain a mortgage for a new home or to borrow money for an automobile or for home improvement. Lower rates also would encourage businesses to borrow funds to invest in expansion such as purchasing new equipment, updating plants, or hiring more workers. Higher interest rates would restrain such borrowing by consumers and businesses.

The Fed seeks to set interest rates to help set the backdrop for promoting the conditions that achieve the mandate set by the Congress—namely, maximum sustainable employment, low and stable inflation, and moderate long-term interest rates.

Chapter 7

U.S. Public Debt

Have You Ever Borrowed Money?

Have you ever wanted to buy something, but didn't have quite enough money? If you've borrowed money from friends, family, or anyone else and promised to repay them, then you are "indebted" to pay it back. This is called "debt."

Debt is money one person, organization, or government owes to another person, organization, or government. Typically, the person who borrows the money has a limited amount of time to pay back that money with interest (an additional amount you pay to use borrowed money).

Why Do People, Organizations And Businesses Have Debt?

People and businesses have debt because they need or want to buy something, but they don't have enough money to pay for it at the time. Adults sometimes borrow a large amount of money to pay for a house, a car, college tuition, medical bills, or home repairs.

Credit cards are also a form of debt. If you purchase a pair of shoes by charging it on a credit card, you are in debt to the credit card company until you pay your bill. Businesses borrow money to help pay their employees and buy expensive items such as buildings, computers, and other large purchases.

About This Chapter: This chapter includes text excerpted from "What Is Debt?—Have You Ever Borrowed Money?" TreasuryDirect, U.S. Department of the Treasury (USDT), August 11, 2010.

Why Does The U.S. Government Have Debt?

The U.S. Government is just like a business. The Government has to provide services for the people of the United States such as military protection, education and health programs, the space program, and social services programs. It also needs money to buy supplies and equipment.

The Government's main source of money is the taxes it collects from individuals and businesses. There are different kinds of taxes. Here are some examples:

- Income tax (money people pay to the Government based on how much they earn from their jobs)

- Sales and excise tax (money people pay to the Government when they buy things)

- Corporate tax (money businesses pay to the Government based on their earnings)

However, the amount of money the Government spends to pay for the services it provides is often more than the taxes it collects. To make up the difference, the Government borrows money—in other words, it goes into "debt."

The Beginning Of U.S. Debt

1775—Paying for the American Revolutionary War was the start of the country's debt.

1781—The Department of Finance was created.

1783—The U.S. debt totaled $43 million. Congress was given the power to raise taxes to cover the Government's costs.

1789—The U.S. Department of the Treasury (USDT) was created to help the country borrow money and manage debt.

(Source: "The History Of U.S. Public Debt," TreasuryDirect, U.S. Department of the Treasury (USDT).)

How Does The U.S. Government Borrow Money?

Here's where the Government is different from individual people and businesses. When the Government borrows money, it doesn't go to the bank and apply for a loan. It "issues debt." This means the Government sells Treasury marketable securities such as Treasury bills, notes, bonds, and Treasury inflation-protected securities (TIPS) to other federal government agencies, individuals, businesses, state and local governments, as well as people, businesses and governments from other countries. Savings bonds are sold to individuals, corporations, associations, public and private organizations, fiduciaries, and other entities.

Here is how Treasury securities—such as savings bonds—generally work. People lend money to the Government so it can pay its bills. Over time, the Government gives that money, plus a bit extra, back to those people as payment for using the borrowed money. That extra money is "interest."

Savings Bonds

Unlike the other types of Treasury securities, savings bonds can be owned by kids. Also, savings bonds are nonmarketable, which means they are registered to a specific owner and cannot be bought and sold to other people in the "secondary market" by brokers and dealers.

(Source: "The Basics Of Treasury Securities—Savings Bonds," TreasuryDirect, U.S. Department of the Treasury (USDT).)

This is how the U.S. system of debt works:

- The U.S. Treasury issues or creates the debt.

- The Bureau of the Fiscal Service manages the Government's debt. That means it keeps records, takes care of selling the debt, and handles paying back people who loaned the Government money.

- The U.S. Treasury and the Bureau of the Fiscal Service do not decide how the money is spent. The legislative branch of Government (Congress) decides how the money is spent.

- There is a maximum amount of debt the Government can have. This is known as the "debt ceiling." To raise that amount, the U.S. Treasury must get Congress to approve a new and higher limit.

Chapter 8

Federal Borrowing And Debt

Debt is the largest legally and contractually binding obligation of the Federal Government. At the end of 2016, the Government owed $14,168 billion of principal to the individuals and institutions who had loaned it the money to fund past deficits. During that year, the Government paid the public approximately $284 billion of interest on this debt. At the same time, the Government also held financial assets, net of financial liabilities other than debt, of $1,699 billion. Therefore, debt held by the public net of financial assets was $12,469 billion.

In addition, at the end of 2016 the Treasury had issued $5,372 billion of debt to Government accounts. As a result, gross Federal debt, which is the sum of debt held by the public and debt held by Government accounts, was $19,539 billion. Interest on the gross Federal debt was $430 billion in 2016. Gross Federal debt is discussed in more detail later in the chapter.

The $14,168 billion debt held by the public at the end of 2016 represents an increase of $1,051 billion over the level at the end of 2015. This increase is the result of the $585 billion deficit in 2016 and other financing transactions that increased the need to borrow by $466 billion.

Debt held by the public increased from 73.3 percent of gross domestic product (GDP) at the end of 2015 to 77.0 percent of GDP at the end of 2016. Meanwhile, financial assets net of liabilities grew by $464 billion in 2016, so that debt held by the public net of financial assets increased by $587 billion during 2016. Debt held by the public net of financial assets was 66.4 percent of GDP at the end of 2015 and 67.7 percent of GDP at the end of 2016. The deficit is estimated to increase to $603 billion, or 3.1 percent of GDP, in 2017, and then to decrease

About This Chapter: This chapter includes text excerpted from "Federal Borrowing And Debt," U.S. Government Publishing Office (GPO), December 26, 2013.

to $440 billion, or 2.2 percent of GDP, in 2018. The deficit is projected to increase temporarily in 2019, but then to decrease in nominal terms and as a percent of GDP in each of the subsequent years, reaching surplus in 2027. Debt held by the public is projected to grow to 77.4 percent of GDP at the end of 2017 and then to fall in each of the subsequent years, falling to 59.8 percent of GDP in 2027.

Debt held by the public net of financial assets is expected to similarly grow to 68.2 percent of GDP at the end of 2017, then to decline in the following years, falling to 52.2 percent of GDP at the end of 2027.

Trends In Debt Since World War II

Federal debt peaked at 106.1 percent of GDP in 1946, just after the end of the war. From that point until the 1970s, Federal debt as a percentage of GDP decreased almost every year because of relatively small deficits, an expanding economy, and unanticipated inflation. With households borrowing large amounts to buy homes and consumer durables, and with businesses borrowing large amounts to buy plant and equipment, Federal debt also decreased almost every year as a percentage of total credit market debt outstanding. The cumulative effect was impressive.

From 1950 to 1975, debt held by the public declined from 78.5 percent of GDP to 24.5 percent, and from 53.3 percent of credit market debt to 17.9 percent. Despite rising interest rates, interest outlays became a smaller share of the budget and were roughly stable as a percentage of GDP.

Federal debt relative to GDP is a function of the Nation's fiscal policy as well as overall economic conditions. During the 1970s, large budget deficits emerged as spending grew faster than receipts and as the economy was disrupted by oil shocks and rising inflation. The nominal amount of Federal debt more than doubled, and Federal debt relative to GDP and credit market debt stopped declining for several years in the middle of the decade. Federal debt started growing again at the beginning of the 1980s, and increased to almost 48 percent of GDP by 1993. The ratio of Federal debt to credit market debt also rose during this period, though to a lesser extent. Interest outlays on debt held by the public, calculated as a percentage of either total Federal outlays or GDP, increased as well. The growth of Federal debt held by the public was slowing by the mid-1990s. In addition to a growing economy, three major budget agreements were enacted in the 1990s, implementing spending cuts and revenue increases and significantly reducing deficits. The debt declined markedly relative to both GDP and total credit market debt, with the decline accelerating as budget surpluses emerged from 1997–2001. Debt fell from 47.8 percent of GDP in 1993 to 31.4 percent of GDP in 2001. Over that same period, debt fell from 26.3 percent of total credit market debt to 17.4 percent. Interest as a share of outlays peaked at 16.5 percent in 1989 and then fell to 8.9 percent by 2002; interest as a percentage of GDP fell by a similar proportion.

The progress in reducing the debt burden stopped and then reversed course beginning in 2002. A decline in the stock market, a recession, the attacks of September 11, 2001, and two major wars, and other policy changes all contributed to increasing deficits, causing debt to rise, both in nominal terms and as a percentage of GDP. Following the most recent recession, which began in December 2007, the deficit began increasing rapidly in 2008 and 2009, as the Government acted to rescue several major corporations and financial institutions as well as enact a major stimulus bill. Since 2008, debt as a percent of GDP has grown rapidly, increasing from 35.2 percent at the end of 2007 to 77.0 percent at the end of 2016.

Under the proposals in the Budget, the deficit is projected to increase to $603 billion in 2017, and then generally fall in subsequent years, reaching a $16 billion surplus in 2027. Gross Federal debt is projected to increase slightly to 106.2 percent of GDP in 2017 and then decrease in each of the years thereafter. Debt held by the public as a percent of GDP is estimated to be 77.4 percent at the end of 2017, after which it falls in each of the subsequent years.

Debt held by the public net of financial assets as a percent of GDP is estimated to grow to 68.2 percent at the end of 2017 and then fall in the following years, to 52.2 percent of GDP by the end of 2027.

Part Two
Personal Money Management

Chapter 9

Managing Money In The Real World

As a teen, you're beginning to make some grown-up decisions about how to save and spend your money. That's why learning the right ways to manage money—right from the start—is important. Here are suggestions:

- **Save some money before you're tempted to spend it.** When you get cash for your birthday or from a job, automatically put a portion of it—at least 10 percent, but possibly more—into a savings or investment account. This strategy is what financial advisors call "paying yourself first." Making this a habit can gradually turn small sums of money into big amounts that can help pay for really important purchases in the future.

Also put your spare change to use. When you empty your pockets at the end of the day, consider putting some of that loose change into a jar or any other container, and then about once a month put that money into a savings account at the bank.

"Spare change can add up quickly," said Luke W. Reynolds, Chief of the Federal Deposit Insurance Corporation's (FDIC) Community Affairs Outreach Section. "But don't let that money sit around your house month after month, earning no interest and at risk of being lost or stolen."

If you need some help sorting and counting your change, he said, find out if your bank has a coin machine you can use for free. If not, the bank may give you coin wrappers.

Some supermarkets and other nonbanking companies have self-service machines that quickly turn coins into cash, but expect to pay a significant fee for the service, often close to

---

About This Chapter: This chapter includes text excerpted from "How To Ace Your First Test Managing Real Money In The Real World," Federal Deposit Insurance Corporation (FDIC), June 12, 2014.

10 cents for every dollar counted, plus you still have to take the cash to the bank to deposit it into your savings account.

- **Keep track of your spending.** A good way to take control of your money is to decide on maximum amounts you aim to spend each week or each month for certain expenses, such as entertainment and snack food. This task is commonly known as "budgeting" your money or developing a "spending plan." And to help manage your money, it's worth keeping a list of your expenses for about a month, so you have a better idea of where your dollars and cents are going.

"If you find you're spending more than you intended, you may need to reduce your spending or increase your income," Reynolds added. "It's all about setting goals for yourself and then making the right choices with your money to help you achieve those goals."

- **Consider a part-time or summer job.** Whether it's babysitting, lawn mowing or a job in a "real" business, working outside of your home can provide you with income, new skills, and references that can be useful after high school or college. Before accepting any job, ask your parents for their permission and advice.

- **Think before you buy.** Many teens make quick and costly decisions to buy the latest clothes or electronics without considering whether they are getting a good value.

"A $200 pair of shoes hawked by a celebrity gets you to the same destination at the same speed as a $50 pair," said Reynolds. "Before you buy something, especially a big purchase, ask yourself if you really need or just want the item, if you've done enough research and comparison-shopping, and if you can truly afford the purchase without having to cut back on spending for something else."

Identity Theft

Identity (ID) theft is a crime where a thief steals your personal information, such as your full name or social security number, to commit fraud. The identity thief can use your information to fraudulently apply for credit, file taxes, or get medical services. These acts can damage your credit status, and cost you time and money to restore your good name. You may not know that you are the victim of ID theft until you experience a financial consequence (mystery bills, credit collections, denied loans) down the road from actions that the thief has taken with your stolen identity.

(Source: "Scams And Frauds—Identity Theft," USA.gov.)

- **Protect yourself from crooks who target teens.** Even if you're too young to have a checking account or credit card, a criminal who learns your name, address, and Social Security number may be able to obtain a new credit card using your name to make purchases.

One of the most important things you can do to protect against identity theft is to be very suspicious of requests for your name, Social Security number, passwords or bank or credit card information that come to you in an e-mail or an Internet advertisement, no matter how legitimate they may seem.

"Teens are very comfortable using e-mail and the Internet, but they need to be aware that criminals can be hiding at the other end of the computer screen," said Michael Benardo, manager of the FDIC's financial crimes section. These types of fraudulent requests can also come by phone, text message or in the mail.

- **Be smart about college.** If you're planning to go to college, learn about your options for saving or borrowing money for what could be a major expense—from tuition to books, fees, and housing. Also consider the costs when you search for a school. Otherwise, when you graduate, your college debts could be high and may limit your options when it comes to a career path or where you can afford to live.

Avoid Borrowing Money

Understand that borrowing money comes with costs and responsibilities. When you borrow money, you generally will repay the money monthly and pay interest. Always compare offers to borrow money based on the Annual Percentage Rate (APR). The lower the APR, the less you will pay in interest. And, the longer you take to repay a debt, the more you will pay in interest. If you miss loan payments, you can expect to pay fees and have a hard time borrowing money at affordable rates for some time into the future.

(Source: For Young Adults And Teens: Quick Tips For Managing Your Money," Federal Deposit Insurance Corporation (FDIC).)

- **Be careful with cards.** Under most state laws, you must be at least 18 years old to obtain your own credit card and be held responsible for repaying the debt. If you're under 18, though, you may be able to qualify for a credit card as long as a parent or other adult agrees to repay your debts if you fail to do so.

An alternative to a credit card is a debit card, which automatically deducts purchases from your savings or checking account. Credit cards and debit cards offer convenience, but they also come with costs and risks that must be taken seriously.

Chapter 10

Budgeting Basics

A financial plan that helps you track your money, make informed spending decisions, and plan for your financial goals. As you create and maintain your budget, you'll want to keep some important tips and suggestions in mind.

What Is A Budget? Do I Need One?

A budget is a plan you write down to decide how you will spend your money each month. A budget helps you make sure you will have enough money every month. Without a budget, you might run out of money before your next paycheck.

A budget shows you:

- how much money you make
- how you spend your money

A budget helps you decide:

- what you must spend your money on
- if you can spend less money on some things and more money on other things

For example, your budget might show that you spend $100 on clothes every month. You might decide you can spend $50 on clothes. You can use the rest of the money to pay bills or to save for something else.

(Source: "Making A Budget," Consumer.gov, Federal Trade Commission (FTC).)

About This Chapter: Text in this chapter begins with excerpts from "Budgeting Tips," Federal Student Aid, U.S. Department of Education (ED), December 19, 2017; Text under the heading "Creating Your Budget" is excerpted from "Creating Your Budget," Federal Student Aid, U.S. Department of Education (ED), December 19, 2017.

Get Started

Here are some important points to keep in mind as you build your budget and identify what goes into your income and expenses.

- **Overestimate your expenses.** It's better to overestimate your expenses and then under-spend and end up with a surplus.

- **Underestimate your income.** It's better to end up with an unexpected cash surplus rather than a budget shortfall.

- **Involve your family in the budget planning process.** Determine how much income will be available from family sources such as parents or your spouse. Discuss how financial decisions will be made.

- **Prepare for the unexpected by setting saving goals to build your emergency fund.** Budgeting will help you cover unusual expenses and plan for changes that may happen while you're in school.

- Planning to move off campus? Short-term budgeting goals for the year can include saving for the rent deposit and furniture for your new apartment.

- Starting an internship next semester? Adjust your budget to save for buying new clothes to wear to work and paying increased transportation costs.

- Finishing school in the next year? Budget to include job search expenses such as résumé preparation, travel to interviews and job fairs, and professional exam fees. Also, you may need to think about how you will manage your money between leaving school and finding a job—this is a time when an emergency fund can really help out.

Differentiate Between Needs And Wants

One benefit of budgeting is that it helps you determine if you have the resources to spend on items that you want versus those you need.

- Start by making a list of things you'd like to save up for.

- Identify whether each item on the list is something you absolutely need or is really a want.

- If you decide you want something, ask yourself if you will still be happy you bought the item in a month.

- Next, prioritize each item on the list.

- Once you have set your priorities, you can then determine whether you should incorporate each item into your budget.

Table 10.1. Difference Between Needs And Wants

First Step: My Needs And Wants	Second Step: Need Or Want?	Third Step: Priority Importance? 1=must have 2=really want 3=would be nice
Save for a vacation	Want	3
Buy a new computer	Want	2
Go to college	Need	1
Buy a better car	Want	2
Save for an emergency fund	Need	1
Save money for a down payment on a house	Need	3
Pay off credit cards	Need	1

Pay Yourself First!

Include "Savings" as a recurring expense item in your monthly budget. Small amounts that you put away each month **do** add up.

Manage Your Budget

Keeping track of all of your spending may seem like a lot of work. But if you're organized, keep good records, and use some of the following tips, you'll find it's easier than you may think. And, don't be too hard on yourself if you slip up.

- **Record your actual expenses.** Have you noticed how fast your cash disappears? To get a handle on where your cash is going, carry a small notebook or use a phone app to record even the smallest expenditures such as coffee, movie tickets, snacks, and parking. Some expenses that are often ignored include music downloads, charges for extra cell phone usage, and entertainment expenses. Search for an online tool to assist you—many are free!

- **Organize your records.** Decide what system you're going to use to track and organize your financial information. There are mobile apps and computer-based programs that work well, but you can also track your spending using a pencil and paper. Be sure to be consistent and organized, and designate a space to store all your financial information. Good record-keeping saves money and time!

- **Create a routine.** Manage your money on a regular basis, and record your expenses and income regularly. If you find that you can't record your expenses every day, then record them weekly. If you wait longer than two weeks to record information, you may forget some transactions and be overwhelmed by the amount of information you need to enter.

- **Include a category in your budget called "Unusual."** There will be some expenses every month that won't fall neatly into one category or that you couldn't have planned for. An "Unusual" category will help you budget for these occasional expenses.

- **Review your spending for little items that add up to big monthly expenditures.** The daily cup of coffee and soda at a vending machine will add up. Consider packing your lunch rather than eating out every day. Spending $10 a day eating out during the week translates to $50 a week and $200 a month. A $5 packed lunch translates into a savings of $1,200 a year. Save even more by looking for ways to manage and reduce your transportation and entertainment expenses.

- **Make your financial aid credit balance refund last.** If your school applies your financial aid to your tuition and fees and there's money left over, the school will refund that money to you so you can use it for other education-related expenses (textbooks, transportation, food, etc.). Remember that your financial aid is supposed to help you cover your cost of attendance for the whole semester or term, so be sure to make that refund stretch over time rather than spending it all as soon as you get it.

- **Comparison shop.** Comparison shopping is simply using common sense to compare products in an attempt to get the best prices and best value. This means doing a little research before running out to buy something, especially when it comes to more expensive items. Make the most of tools like phone apps for comparing prices and value.

- **Use credit cards wisely.** Think very carefully before you decide to get your first credit card. Is a credit card really necessary, or would another payment option work just as well? If you receive a credit card offer in the mail, don't feel obligated to accept it. Limit the number of cards you get.

- **Don't spend more on your credit card than you can afford to pay in full on a monthly basis.** Responsible use of credit cards can be a shopping convenience and help you establish a solid credit rating and avoid financial problems. Consider signing up for electronic payment reminders, balance notices, and billing statement notifications from your credit card provider.

Expect The Unexpected

Your emergency fund should be used for expenses that fall outside the categories of annual and periodic bills. Unexpected expenses are the result of life events such as job loss, illness, or car repairs. Redefine your notion of "unexpected" bills to encompass these unforeseen events rather than more common but infrequent expenses. The good news is that if you do not use your emergency fund, you will have savings—which should always be a priority when managing your finances. And, if you have to use your emergency fund, you may avoid unnecessary borrowing.

Why Should I Save Money?

It can be hard to save money. It is very hard when your expenses go up and your income does not. Here are some reasons to try to save money even when it is not easy.

- Emergencies. Saving small amounts of money now might help you later. Everyone has expenses they do not expect.

- Expensive things. Sometimes, we have to pay for expensive things—like a car, a trip, or a security deposit on an apartment. You will have more choices if you have money to pay for those expensive things.

- Your goals. You might want to pay for college classes. Maybe you need to visit family in another country. You can plan for these goals and save money. then you might not have to use a credit card or borrow money to pay.

(Source: Making A Budget," Consumer.gov, Federal Trade Commission (FTC).)

Creating Your Budget

Creating a budget may sound complicated, but all you need to do to get started is set aside some time and get organized—the benefits will make the effort worthwhile. The following steps will help you set up your budget and manage your finances by helping you track your income and expenses.

Determine A Time Span For Your Budget

You can create your budget for a month, academic year, or calendar year. If you are currently attending college or career school, you may want to consider creating a monthly budget for an academic term, such as your fall semester. Keep in mind that your income may vary from month to month, and not all of your expenses will be the same each month. Larger expenses (such as car insurance and books) and seasonal expenses (such as a trip home at the holidays or a higher electricity bill in summer when the air conditioning is on) need to be incorporated into your budget.

Choose A Tool To Help You Manage Your Budget

To create a budget, you'll want to use a tool for tracking your income and expenses. You can use pen and paper, a simple automated spreadsheet, or a budgeting app. Many banks offer budgeting tools, so see what works best for you.

Review Your Monthly Income

First, estimate how much money you will have coming in each month. Here are some tips for assessing your income:

- Your income may come from sources such as your pay from work, financial contributions from family members, or financial aid (scholarships, grants, work-study, and loans).

- If you're working while in school, review your records to determine how much your take-home pay is each month. If you earn most of your money over the summer, you may want to estimate your yearly income then divide it by 12.

- Include income from any financial aid credit balance refunds—money that may be left over for other expenses after your financial aid is applied toward tuition and fees.

Monthly Income Tracking Example

Table 10.2. Monthly Income Tracking Example

Income Source	Monthly Income
Income from work	$1,200
Tax refund ($360 total divided by 12)	$30
Estimated financial aid credit balance refund ($2,100 total divided by 12)*	$175
Monthly support from parents and/or family member	$250
Other income	
Total Monthly Income	**$1,655**

*Note: If you are getting ready to attend school, you'll want to estimate your federal aid credit balance by taking your estimated financial aid and subtracting your expected tuition and fees. If you have not yet received an aid offer from your school, you can use FAFSA4caster to get an early estimate of your eligibility for federal student aid.

Identify And Categorize Your Expenses

To estimate your monthly expenses, you'll want to start by recording everything you spend money on in a month. This may be a bit time-consuming but will definitely be worthwhile in helping you understand where your money is going and how to better manage it. After that, gather your bank records and credit card statements that will show you other expenditures that may be automatically paid.

If you are currently attending college or career school or getting ready to go, you'll also need to estimate your college costs. In addition to tuition and fees (unless covered by financial aid), you'll want to make sure to include books and supplies, equipment and room materials, and travel expenses. Find details on what's included in the cost of college and tips on how to reduce college costs.

If you are still researching your school options, keep in mind that college and career school costs can vary significantly from school to school.

Once you've identified your expenses, you should group them into two categories—fixed expenses and variable expenses.

- Fixed expenses stay about the same each month and include items such as rent or mortgage payments, car payments, and insurance. These obligations are generally non-negotiable until you realize that you are spending too much money on rent and take steps to find a cheaper place! When creating a monthly budget, divide the amount due by the number of months the bill covers. For example, take your yearly $1,200 insurance bill that's paid in two $600 installments six months apart, and divide it by 12 to know you need to set aside $100 per month.

- Variable expenses are those that are flexible or controllable and can vary from month to month. Examples of variable expenses include groceries, clothing, eating out, and entertainment. You'll want to examine these expenses to make sure they stay under control and don't bust your budget at the end of the month.

Monthly Expenses Tracking Example

Table 10.3. Monthly Expenses Tracking Example

Fixed Expenses	Projected Cost
Rent or dorm fee	$500
Books	$70

Table 10.3. Continued

Fixed Expenses	Projected Cost
Electricity	$35
Gas and water	$22
Cable and Internet	$50
Car insurance ($600 divided by 12 months)	$50
Parking fee ($84 divided by 12)	$7
Car maintenance and repairs ($480 divided by 12 months)	$40
Cell phone (basic charges)	$60
Car loan payment	$125
Money set aside for savings	$50
Total Fixed Expenses	**$1,009**
Variable Expenses	**Projected Cost**
Groceries	$250
Dining out	$50
Entertainment (example: concerts)	$50
Music downloads	$20
Movies (theater and downloads)	$48
Medical (including prescriptions)	$40
Hair and nails	$40
Clothing	$50
Laundry and dry cleaning	$10
Health club	$40
Credit card monthly payment	$25
Public transportation	$25
Gas for car	$60
Total Variable Expenses	**$708**
Total Expenses	**$1,717**

Save For Emergencies

Include "Savings" as a fixed expense in your monthly budget. Pay yourself first every month! Your savings can be used as an emergency fund to help you deal with unexpected expenses. The ideal amount of an emergency fund typically covers three to six months of your expenses.

Balance Your Budget

Now that you've identified your sources of income and expenses, you'll want to compare the two to balance your budget. To do so, you simply subtract your expenses from your income.

Table 10.4. Balance Your Budget

Total Monthly Income	$1,655
Minus Total Expenses	$1,717
(= + / - Difference)	-$62

If you have a positive balance, then your income is greater than your expenses. In other words, you're earning more money than you're spending. If you have a positive balance, you shouldn't start looking at new ways to spend your money. Instead, focus on putting the extra money toward your savings to cover your emergency fund or to support future goals such as buying a car. Also, if you have a positive balance but you've borrowed student loan funds, pay back some of your loans and consider borrowing less in the future.

If you have a negative balance, then you are spending more money than you have. You'll want to balance your budget and make sure your expenses don't exceed your income. Balancing your budget may include monitoring your variable expenses, reducing your expenses, and/or finding ways to increase your income. Spending less can be a lot easier than earning more. Consider eating out less frequently and making your own lunch. Rent books rather than buying them, or buy books to download to your computer. Use a shopping list when grocery shopping, and buy only what you need. Ask yourself before buying anything, "Do I really need this?"

Maintain And Update Your Budget

Now that you've created your budget, you'll want to make sure it remains a living document and you update it over time. Here are some smart practices to keep in mind:

- **Review your budget on a monthly basis.** Regular review and maintenance of your budget will keep you on top of things and may help you avoid being blindsided by something unexpected.

- **Forgive yourself for small spending mistakes and get back on track.** Most people overspend because they buy things on impulse. The next time you're tempted to make an impulse buy, ask yourself the following questions:

  - What do I need this for?

  - Can I afford this item?

- If I buy this item now, will I still be happy that I bought it a month from now?

- Do I need to save this money for a financial goal?

- Will this item go on sale? Should I wait to buy it?

- Does it matter if I buy brand-name or can I get by with generic?

If you take a moment to think about what you're buying, you're more likely to make a choice that fits your budgeting goals.

Chapter 11

Spending Money Wisely

Do you want to find ways to stretch your money, so it goes farther and is there when you really need it?

Here are some suggestions for knowing how much money you have, how much you need for expenditures, and how to reach your goals by cutting back on what you spend.

1. **Practice self-control.** To avoid making a quick decision to buy something just because you saw it featured on display or on sale:

    *   Make a shopping list before you leave home and stick to it.

    *   Before you go shopping, set a spending limit (say, $5 or $10) for "impulse buys"-items you didn't plan to buy but that got your attention anyway. If you are tempted to spend more than your limit, wait a few hours or a few days and think it over.

    *   Limit the amount of cash you take with you. The less cash you carry, the less you can spend and the less you lose if you misplace your wallet.

2. **Research before you buy.** To be sure you are getting a good value, especially with a big purchase, look into the quality and the reputation of the product or service you're considering. Read "reviews" in magazines or respected websites. Talk to

About This Chapter: Text in this chapter begins with excerpts from "Start Smart: Money Management For Teens," Federal Deposit Insurance Corporation (FDIC), August 29, 2006; Text under the heading "Spending Tracker" is excerpted from "Your Money, Your Goals—A Financial Empowerment Toolkit For Social Services Programs," Consumer Financial Protection Bureau (CFPB), April 2015.

knowledgeable people you trust. Check other stores or go online and compare prices. Look at similar items. This is known as "comparison shopping," and it can lead to tremendous savings and better quality purchases. And if you're sure you know what you want, take advantage of store coupons and mail-in "rebates."

3. **Keep track of your spending.** This helps you set and stick to limits, what many people refer to as budgeting. "Maintaining a budget may sound scary or complicated, but it can be as simple as having a notebook and writing down what you buy each month," said Janet Kincaid, Federal Deposit Insurance Corporation (FDIC) Senior Consumer Affairs Officer. "Any system that helps you know how much you are spending each month is a good thing."

How Do I Make A Budget?

Write down your expenses. Expenses are what you spend money on. Expenses include:

Bills:

- bills that are the same each month, like rent
- bills that might change each month, like utilities
- bills you pay once or twice a year, like car insurance

Other expenses, like:

- food
- gas
- entertainment
- clothes
- school supplies
- money for family
- unplanned expenses, like car repairs or medical bills
- credit card bills

You might have bills that change every month. Look at what you paid for the same month last year. You might need $200 for your gas bill in January, but $30 in July.

(Source: "Making A Budget," Consumer.gov, Federal Trade Commission (FTC).)

Also pay attention to small amounts of money you spend. "A snack here and a magazine there can quickly add up," said Paul Horwitz, an FDIC Community Affairs Specialist. He suggested that, for a few weeks, you write down every purchase in a small notebook. "You'll probably be amazed at how much you spend without even thinking."

4. **Think "used" instead of "new."** Borrow things (from the library or friends) that you don't have to own. Pick up used games, digital video discs (DVD), and music at "second-hand" stores around town.

5. **Take good care of what you buy.** It's expensive to replace things. Think about it: Do you really want to buy the same thing twice?

Spending Tracker

Many people cannot tell you exactly how they get and spend their money during a month. Whether they have a lot of money to spend or are struggling to make ends meet, most people cannot account for all of the ways they use their money.

Before you think about making any changes, it's a good idea to understand how you use your money now.

How can you do this? It takes three steps and commitment. The three steps are:

1. Keep track of everything you spend money on for a week, two weeks, or one month. A month is best, because all of your income and your bills will be included. But, keeping up with the tracking for a month may be a challenge.

2. Analyze your spending. See how much you spend in each category. Notice trends. Identify areas you can eliminate or cut back on.

3. Use this information for figuring out where you can make changes.

It takes commitment, because this is a lot of work. But, it's important work. Many people are actually able to find money to save for emergencies, unexpected expenses, and goals by doing this work. Others are able to make their budgets balance.

Get a simple plastic case or envelope. Every time you spend money, get a receipt and put it into the case or envelope. If the receipt doesn't list what you purchased, take a few seconds and write it down on the receipt. If you don't get a receipt, write one out on scrap paper.

Analyze your spending. Analyze your spending for each week of the month. Go through your receipts. Record the total you spent that makes most sense to you. Be sure to write it in on for every date. See how much you spend and at the end of each week, add the amounts. Once you have these totals, add them together to get a total spending for the week. You can track your spending for one week, two weeks, or an entire month.

Notice trends. Circle those items that are the same every month (for example, rent, car payment, cell phone payment). These are often your needs and obligations. This will make creating your budget easier. Identify areas you can eliminate or cut back on—these will generally be wants.

Here is a list of the categories that are used in the spending tracker:

Table 11.1. Categories In Spending Tracker

Savings	Saving for goals, for emergencies, for children's education, for retirement, for holiday purchases, for back-to-school shopping
Debt payments	Credit card, installment loan, payday loan, pawn loan, and car title loan payments; other loan payments
Housing	Rent, mortgage, insurance, property taxes
Utilities	Electricity, gas, water, sewage, phone, television, internet service, cell phone
Household supplies and expenses	Things for your home like cleaning supplies, kitchen appliances, furniture, other equipment
Groceries	Food and beverages you bring into the home to prepare, including baby food and formula
Eating out (meals and beverages)	Any meals or beverages purchased outside of the home
Pets	Food, healthcare costs, and other costs associated with caring for your pets
Transportation	Gas, car payment, insurance payment, repairs, public transportation
Healthcare	Copayments, medication, eye care, dental care, healthcare premiums
Personal care	Haircuts, hygiene items, dry cleaning
Child care and school expenses	Child care costs, diapers, school supplies, school materials fees, field trip, and other activity fees

Table 11.1. Continued

Entertainment	Going to the movies, concerts, or sporting events; sports equipment/fees, lottery tickets, memberships, alcohol, books/CDs, subscriptions
Court-ordered obligations	Child support, alimony, restitution, etc.
Gifts, donations, and other	Donations to religious organizations or other charities, gifts, other expenses

Chapter 12

Saving Money

Saving money may not be as much fun as spending money, but it's still important to do. When you save your money, you can use it later to buy fun things (DVDs, video games, clothes) as well as pay for serious things like college or a car.

> Saving is a key principle. People who make a habit of saving regularly, even saving small amounts, are well on their way to success. It's important to open a bank or credit union account so it will be simple and easy for you to save regularly. Then, use your savings to plan for life events and to be ready for unplanned or emergency needs.
>
> *(Source: "Save And Invest," MyMoney.gov, Financial Literacy and Education Commission (FLEC).)*

Why is the Federal Deposit Insurance Corporation (FDIC), a government agency best known for protecting bank accounts, publishing a money guide for teens? It's because consumer education is a big part of what the FDIC does to protect the public.

The more people understand how to save and manage money, the more likely they are to make smart decisions that affect their finances and their future.

Although the FDIC's financial education programs are mostly for adults, this special guide will help you learn how to make good decisions about your money, right from the start.

About This Chapter: Text in this chapter begins with excerpts from "Start Smart: Money Management For Teens," Federal Deposit Insurance Corporation (FDIC), August 29, 2006; Text under the heading "It's Never Too Early—Or Too Late—To Save" is excerpted from "It's Never Too Early—Or Too Late—To Save," Federal Trade Commission (FTC), April 2014.

Teens have access to more money than ever before, thanks to allowances and gifts and, for many, income from chores, summer jobs, or part-time jobs. Teens also are becoming more responsible for handling money and making decisions for everything from small, everyday purchases to bigger-ticket items (such as a bike or a camera) to saving for college.

Simple, Everyday Things You Can Do To Save Money

Everyone can use a little guidance on how to save more money. Here are some suggestions for simple things you can do.

- **Set goals.** "Saving money now for use in the future gets easier if you know what you want and how much you'll need," said Janet Kincaid, FDIC Senior Consumer Affairs Officer. It helps to set savings goals you can easily achieve. If you want to buy a $500 item within the next year, plan to save $50 a month for 10 months, which is just $12.50 a week. (We're not including any "interest" you could earn on your savings.)

- **Have a strategy for saving money.** Every time you receive money from your allowance, a gift, a summer job or some other source-try to automatically put some of it into savings instead of spending it. That approach to saving money is known as "paying yourself first."

  Consider putting about 25 percent ($1 out of every $4) or more into savings that you intend to let build for a few years, perhaps for a down payment on your first car. Separately you can save a similar amount of money for clothes, video games, electronics or other items you might want to buy within the next few months. With what's left, keep some handy for spending money (maybe for snacks or a movie) and, also consider donating some of your money to charity.

- **Cut back, not out.** Are you spending $5 a week on snacks? If you save $2 by cutting back, after a year you'll have $104 to put in a savings or investment account that earns interest.

It's Amazing: How A Small Savings Account Can Get Big Over Time

People who put even a small amount of money into a savings account as often as they can and leave it untouched for years may be amazed at how big the account grows. The reason? A combination of saving as much as possible on a regular basis and the impact of interest payments (what the financial world calls "the miracle of compounding").

Here's how you can slowly build a large savings account and experience the miracle of compounding.

Let's say you put money into a savings account that pays you interest every month. After the first month, the interest payment will be calculated based on the money you put in. But the next time the bank pays you interest, it will calculate the amount based on your original deposit plus the interest you received the previous month. Later, that larger, combined amount will earn more interest, and after many years it becomes a much larger sum of money. The earnings are called compound interest.

You can earn even more in compound interest if you make deposits regularly and stretch to put in as much as you can and leave it untouched.

It's Never Too Early—Or Too Late—To Save

Create a budget. The first step toward taking control of your financial life is to evaluate how much money you take in and how much money you spend. Start by listing your income from all sources. Then, list your "fixed" expenses—those that are the same each month—like rent, car payments, and insurance premiums. Next, list the expenses that vary—like entertainment, recreation, and clothing. Writing down all your expenses, even those that seem insignificant, is a helpful way to track your spending patterns, identify necessary expenses, and prioritize the rest.

Pay yourself first. This phrase refers to the practice of automatically making a savings contribution or investment with your income before it can reach your wallet. For example, consider a payroll savings plan where a certain amount goes directly into your savings account each payday. This can help you get used to managing living expenses with what looks like a smaller paycheck, when actually you're building up your own savings.

Get to know the value of compound interest. Setting aside money and watching it grow can be a powerful motivator. Compound interest can be thought of as "interest on interest." It is the interest you earn on your initial investment plus all the interest that has accumulated over time. It makes your investment grow at a faster rate than simple interest, which is interest earned only on your original investment.

Watch your money double with the Rule of 72. The Rule of 72 is an easy way to calculate how long it will take for your investment to double at a given interest rate if you don't make

> ## Compound Interest: Illustrated
>
> if you have $100 and it earns 5 percent interest each year, you'll have $105 at the end of the first year. At the end of the second year, you'll have $110.25. Not only did you earn $5 on the initial $100 deposit, you also earned $0.25 on the $5 in interest. While 25 cents may not sound like much at first, it adds up over time. Even if you never add another dime to that account, in 10 years you'll have more than $162 thanks to the power of compound interest, and in 25 years you'll have almost $340.
>
> *(Source: "What Is Compound Interest?" Investor.gov, Office of Investor Education and Advocacy (OIEA).)*

any further deposits. Take the number 72 and divide it by the interest rate you hope to earn. That number gives you the approximate number of years it will take for your investment to double. For example, say you invest $8,000 in a mutual fund with an average 8 percent rate of return. In about 9 years (72 divided by 8) your savings will have doubled to $16,000.

Keep it going. If you get a raise at work, bank it. If you pay off your car, bank the monthly payments. If you're not sure you'll remember to make the deposits, consider automated transfers from your checking account to your savings or investment account. That way you never even notice it. If you were able to live on less before, you can continue to.

Get creative. Save and have fun. Saving money doesn't have to be boring or a chore. Get your hair done for free or at a discount by searching online for local beauty schools and making an appointment with a student in training. Pack your lunch. Did you know that spending $6 a day on lunch means spending about $800 a year? Instead of buying books, music, and DVDs, dust off your library card or trade favorite reads, music, and movies with friends. Go generic on your favorite grocery, beauty, and healthcare items. Keep your car tires properly inflated, which can increase fuel efficiency, meaning less money spent on gas. The list is endless.

Bottom-line: Everyone has the ability to save. You can start small and save only $10 a week or month. Over time, your deposits will add up. Even small amounts of savings can help you in the future.

Chapter 13

Saving For College

The cost of a four-year college education has increased much faster than the rate of inflation over the past few decades. From 1995 to 2015, for instance, the average cost of tuition and fees at private colleges rose 179 percent to reach $31,200 per year. Meanwhile, the average cost of in-state tuition and fees at public universities rose 296 percent to reach $9,100 per year. For many families, the high cost of college stretches budgets to the limit and forces students to take on ever-increasing amounts of debt.

One approach to dealing with the skyrocketing costs of higher education is to begin saving for college early in your child's life. By investing a small amount of money on a regular basis, you can accumulate enough over time to make a big dent in tuition costs.

> ## Did You Know...
> Putting even $2 per day—the cost of a cup of coffee—into a college savings account that earns 1 percent interest would add up to more than $12,000 over the course of seventeen years.

Some financial planners argue that parents should focus on paying down their own debts and saving for retirement rather than setting aside money for college. After all, scholarships, grants, and loans are available to help pay for college, while you are unlikely to receive assistance toward meeting your other financial goals. But saving money for college offers you a number of important benefits, including the following:

- **You can receive tax benefits**

  Many states offer income-tax deductions for contributions to a 529 college savings plan. In addition, the money you contribute—plus any earnings on your initial

About This Chapter: "Reasons To Save For College," © 2017 Omnigraphics.

investment—can be withdrawn tax-free later to pay for qualified education expenses. If you put that money in a regular investment account instead, you would not receive the state income-tax deduction and any earnings would be taxable.

- **You may not qualify for financial aid**

  Although the U.S. government provides billions of dollars in financial aid to students, your eligibility is based on your family's financial need, which is determined by a complex formula. Many online tools are available to help you estimate the amount of need-based aid you would qualify to receive if your child enrolled in college at the present time. If your child will not enter college for a few years, though, you may not be able to count on that money. Either your income or the financial aid rules could change to make you ineligible by the time your child actually starts college.

- **Savings have a limited impact on financial aid**

  Some people resist saving for college because they believe it will only reduce the amount of financial aid they qualify to receive. In the formula used to calculate financial aid, however, your income affects your Expected Family Contribution (EFC) much more than your savings. The federal government puts more emphasis on income because it wants to encourage families to save for college. As a result, an average family would only reduce their calculated financial need by about $60 for every $1,000 in college savings. In other words, they would still be $940 closer to paying for college.

- **Your student will graduate with less debt**

  Many students have to borrow money in order to afford college. In fact, the average 2016 college graduate owed more than $37,000 in student loans. Repaying these debts can take many years and prevent college graduates from accomplishing other financial goals. Saving for college when your child is young can reduce your family's need for student loans in the future. In addition, it can increase your child's chances of graduating from college debt free.

- **Your student may have more college choices**

  Some of the most selective colleges base their financial awards for prospective students on merit rather than on need. If your child manages to win admission to a dream school, you want them to be able to enroll even without receiving merit-based scholarships or grants. A college savings fund might make up the difference and allow your child to attend their top choice school.

- **College savings offer flexibility**

  Although college savings accounts must be used for qualified education expenses, they do offer some flexibility to adapt to changing circumstances. If your child does not end up needing the money for college, you can designate a new beneficiary for the funds. Your child can also put the money toward graduate school, professional programs, or nontraditional educational opportunities.

- **Family members can contribute as well**

  Once you set up a college savings account, you can invite other family members to contribute to it instead of buying your child birthday and holiday gifts. Relatives who place a high value on education will feel good about supporting your child's future opportunities.

References

1. Becker, Matt. "Five Good Reasons To Use A College Savings Account," Mom and Dad Money, February 16, 2016.

2. Lieber, Ron. "Why It Makes Good Sense To Save For College Now," *New York Times,* October 23, 2015.

3. "Saving Early = Saving Smart," Federal Student Aid, U.S. Department of Education, 2017.

Chapter 14

You And Your Bank

Many parents set up bank savings accounts for their children as soon as they're born, so it's possible that you've been dealing with banks for many years. But perhaps you've never done business with a bank, or if you had an account as a child maybe you're ready to transition to a more adult account of your own. In any case, it pays to learn a bit about the banking system so you can understand your choices and make informed decisions.

What Is A Bank?

No one is sure when and where banking first began, but it's a good bet that it started in ancient times, probably in the area around the Mediterranean Sea, when wealthy individuals would back merchants traveling to distant areas to sell goods. In exchange for paying travel expenses, those individuals would take a percentage of the profits, essentially acting as banks loaning money.

It may seem obvious, but a bank is more than the building on the corner with a drive-through cash machine. Odds are that building houses a branch of a much larger organization that consists of many branches and an overarching corporate structure. In some cases there may be no brick-and-mortar building at all. Some banks strictly operate online, with all transactions taking place via a secure website.

Whatever its structure, a bank is a financial institution that provides a wide variety of functions for businesses and individual customers. But its main purpose is to take in funds, pool

---

About This Chapter: "You And Your Bank," © 2017 Omnigraphics.

them together, and use that money for loans and other investments. The money it earns is then paid to depositors in the form of interest.

Bank Services

Most of the many functions performed by banks probably won't concern you at the moment, but it's worthwhile to understand a few of the more common services they provide, including:

- **Savings accounts.** There are simple savings accounts that pay a relatively small amount of interest on your deposits but allow you to withdraw your money at any time. Then there are other types of accounts that earn a higher rate of interest in exchange for leaving your money in the bank for longer periods, such as money market accounts and certificates of deposit (CDs).

- **Checking accounts.** When you open a checking account you deposit funds and receive a book of checks, slips of paper that are a promise to pay a specified amount of money from your account. These days, writing physical checks is becoming something of a rarity, but checking accounts also let you make deposits and withdrawals from an ATM (automated teller machine), pay bills online, and transfer money between accounts.

- **Debit cards.** When you open a savings or checking account, the bank might issue a debit card to you. This card has a magnetic strip and an embedded microchip that can be scanned by readers at ATMs, restaurants, gas stations, and stores, allowing you to conduct transactions using funds in your accounts at the bank.

- **Loans.** One of the primary ways banks make money is by taking funds it receives from depositors and lending it to people who need it. The bank makes money by charging a higher fee for these loans than it pays out in interest.

- **Credit cards.** Credit cards are, essentially, a type of loan. Unlike with a debit card, money for credit-card purchases doesn't automatically come out of the customer's bank account. Rather, the bank is advancing the funds to a merchant or other payee with the understanding that the customer will pay the money back to the bank.

- **Online and mobile banking.** When you open an account, you're typically given a user ID and password to get access to the bank's secure website. Then, from any computer with an Internet connection, you can check your balances, transfer funds between accounts, and pay bills. Most banks now also have mobile apps that allow you to perform these same functions from your phone or tablet.

Advantages Of Banks

As an informed consumer, it's to your benefit to learn how banks can work for you. Some advantages include:

- **You earn money.** Funds you deposit into a savings account—and some checking accounts—earn interest, which the bank pays you for letting it use your money. Generally, the interest earned on these accounts is not a lot, but it's more than you'd get by keeping it in a drawer.

- **Your money is safe.** The Federal Deposit Insurance Corporation (FDIC), an independent agency created by the U.S. Congress, insures most personal bank deposits up to $250,000. There are some types of bank investments that are not covered, but customers with regular savings and checking accounts know their money is guaranteed to be there.

- **Banks help you budget.** A bank statement, either mailed to you monthly or accessed online, lets you keep track of income and expenses very easily. You can also set up different accounts for different purposes. For example, you might have one savings account where you accumulate money for a car and another for short-term use, such as school expenses.

- **Convenience.** Banks give you option of buying goods and services or paying bills as easily as possible using their various payment methods, including debit cards and online or mobile banking. They also allow you to go to the bank location to make deposits or withdrawals or take advantage of the nearest ATM to perform the same functions.

> Banks are highly regulated by the U.S. government, by individual states, and even by some cities. Among other things, these rules ensure that banks reduce risk to depositors by making sound loans and investments, protect customer confidentiality, and maintain adequate cash reserves to cover a minimum percentage of depositor funds.

Bank Fees

Unsurprisingly, banks charge fees for many of their services. These vary depending on the bank and the type of account, so it's smart to shop around. Some bank fees can include:

- **Checking account fees.** Most banks charge a monthly fee for maintaining your checking account, usually between $10 and $20. This can often be avoided by either keeping a minimum balance in that account or by maintaining a minimum balance in a saving account at the same bank.

- **Overdraft charge.** If you use more money than you have in your checking account—either by writing a check or by using your debit card—and the bank covers the difference, you may be charged an overdraft fee of $20 to $40.

- **Returned check fee.** A returned check fee (also called NSF, for nonsufficient funds) is incurred when you write a check without enough money in your account and the bank doesn't cover the difference. The bank may charge as much as $40 in such a case.

- **ATM fees.** Usually banks don't charge customers for using their own cash machines. But if you use an ATM operated by another bank, the other bank will charge a fee, and in some instances your own bank may add a fee, as well. The average charge is around $3.

Other bank charges can include foreign transaction fees; paper statement fees, charged by some banks if you want hard-copies mailed to you; inactivity fees, which are sometimes incurred if an account lies dormant for a long time; check-printing fees; and lost debit-card fees.

> In 2015, the first year banks were required to provide this information, the three biggest banks in the U.S. made $6 billion from overdraft and ATM fees. Together, all of the nation's biggest banks made over $11 billion in fees.

Choosing A Bank

As with shopping for clothes, a car, or anything else, when selecting a bank it's smart to shop around. Banks vary considerably in such areas as the fees the charge, the amount of interest they pay, and the services they offer, and some are bound to meet your needs better than others. Some factors to consider:

- **Fees.** One of the most important things to learn is how much it's going to cost you to do business with a bank. Ask about account maintenance charges, ATM fees, overdraft fees, and any other charges that may be associated with the accounts you plan to open.

- **Legitimacy.** You want to be sure you're dealing with a reliable, established bank. One of the most important things is to be sure the bank is a member of the FDIC. The bank's website will usually tell you this, but you can also go to FDIC.gov and search their Bank Find tool just to be sure.

- **Location.** Even people who don't actually go to the bank building very often tend to select a bank near where they live or work. If the need arises for a personal visit, you'll appreciate the convenience.

- **Size.** If you travel a lot it could be helpful to do business with a large bank that has branches in several states, or even outside the country.

- **Minimum deposit amount.** Many banks have a minimum amount required to open an account, and this can vary widely.

- **Types of services offered.** Right now, you might only be interested in opening a savings account, but at some point you may want a checking account, credit card, or car loan. It's good to know your options before you begin doing business with a bank.

- **Technology.** If you plan to make regular use of electronic banking, be sure the bank offers what you need. Ask about online fund transfers, remote deposits, text, and e-mail alerts for unusual account activity, and mobile apps.

Finally, when shopping for a bank, use the Internet to your advantage. You can learn a lot about a bank from its website. There you'll find information about interest rates, fees, services they offer, and special promotions they may be running (such as free check-printing for new customers). And, as with pretty much everything these days, you can Google the bank's name and find useful customer reviews and ratings.

References

1. "Banking 101," USTrust.com, 2016.

2. "Banking Basics," Indiana Department of Financial Institutions, n.d.

3. "Banking Basics 101: A Quick Lesson In Banking And Saving," CesiSolutions.org, September 21, 2013.

4. Calonia, Jennifer. "Banking," Learnvest.com, June 1, 2012.

5. Campisi, Natalie. "Banking 101 Guide: Tips And Terms To Know Before Opening Your First Account," GoBankingRates.com, August 19, 2016.

6. Your First Account," GoBankingRates.com, August 19, 2016.

7. "Selecting A Bank," Teensguidetomoney.com, n.d.

Chapter 15

Electronic Banking

For many people, electronic banking means 24-hour access to cash through an automated teller machine (ATM) or Direct Deposit of paychecks into checking or savings accounts. But electronic banking involves many different types of transactions, rights, responsibilities—and sometimes, fees. Do your research. You may find some electronic banking services more practical for your lifestyle than others.

Electronic Fund Transfers

Electronic banking, also known as electronic fund transfer (EFT), uses computer and electronic technology in place of checks and other paper transactions. EFTs are initiated through devices like cards or codes that let you, or those you authorize, access your account. Many financial institutions use ATM or debit cards and personal identification numbers (PINs) for this purpose. Some use other types of debit cards that require your signature or a scan. For example, some use radio frequency identification (RFID) or other forms of "contactless" technology that scan your information without direct contact with you. The federal Electronic Fund Transfer Act (EFT Act) covers some electronic consumer transactions.

Here are some common EFT services:

ATMs are electronic terminals that let you bank almost virtually any time. To withdraw cash, make deposits, or transfer funds between accounts, you generally insert an ATM card and enter your PIN. Some financial institutions and ATM owners charge a fee, particularly

About This Chapter: This chapter includes text excerpted from "Electronic Banking," Federal Trade Commission (FTC), August 2012.

if you don't have accounts with them or if your transactions take place at remote locations. Generally, ATMs must tell you they charge a fee and the amount on or at the terminal screen before you complete the transaction. Check with your institution and at ATMs you use for more information about these fees.

Direct Deposit lets you authorize specific deposits—like paychecks, Social Security checks, and other benefits—to your account on a regular basis. You also may preauthorize direct withdrawals so that recurring bills—like insurance premiums, mortgages, utility bills, and gym memberships—are paid automatically. Be cautious before you pre-authorize recurring withdrawals to pay companies you aren't familiar with; funds from your bank account could be withdrawn improperly. Monitor your bank account to make sure direct recurring payments take place and are for the right amount.

Pay-by-Phone Systems let you call your financial institution with instructions to pay certain bills or to transfer funds between accounts. You must have an agreement with your institution to make these transfers.

Personal Computer Banking lets you handle many banking transactions using your personal computer. For example, you may use your computer to request transfers between accounts and pay bills electronically.

Debit Card Purchase or Payment Transactions let you make purchases or payments with a debit card, which also may be your ATM card. Transactions can take place in-person, online, or by phone. The process is similar to using a credit card, with some important exceptions: a debit card purchase or payment transfers money quickly from your bank account to the company's account, so you have to have sufficient funds in your account to cover your purchase. This means you need to keep accurate records of the dates and amounts of your debit card purchases, payments, and ATM withdrawals. Be sure you know the store or business before you provide your debit card information to avoid the possible loss of funds through fraud. Your liability for unauthorized use, and your rights for dealing with errors, may be different for a debit card than a credit card.

Electronic Check Conversion converts a paper check into an electronic payment in a store or when a company gets your check in the mail.

When you give your check to a cashier in a store, the check is run through an electronic system that captures your banking information and the amount of the check. You sign a receipt and you get a copy for your records. When your check is given back to you, it should be voided or marked by the merchant so that it can't be used again. The merchant electronically sends information from the check (but not the check itself) to your bank or other financial institution, and the funds are transferred into the merchant's account.

When you mail a check for payment to a merchant or other company, they may electronically send information from your check (but not the check itself) through the system; the funds are transferred from your account into their account. For a mailed check, you still should get notice from a company that expects to send your check information through the system electronically. For example, the company might include the notice on your monthly statement. The notice also should state if the company will electronically collect a fee from your account—like a "bounced check" fee—if you don't have enough money to cover the transaction.

Be careful with online and telephone transactions that may involve the use of your bank account information, rather than a check. A legitimate merchant that lets you use your bank account information to make a purchase or pay on an account should post information about the process on its website or explain the process on the phone. The merchant also should ask for your permission to electronically debit your bank account for the item you're buying or paying on. However, because online and telephone electronic debits don't occur face-to-face, be cautious about sharing your bank account information. Don't give out this information when you have no experience with the business, when you didn't initiate the call, or when the business seems reluctant to discuss the process with you. Check your bank account regularly to be sure that the right amounts were transferred.

Not all electronic fund transfers are covered by the EFT Act. For example, some financial institutions and merchants issue cards with cash value stored electronically on the card itself. Examples include prepaid phone cards, mass transit passes, general purpose reloadable cards, and some gift cards. These "stored-value" cards, as well as transactions using them, may not be covered by the EFT Act, or they may be subject to different rules under the EFT Act. This means you may not be covered for the loss or misuse of the card. Ask your financial institution or merchant about any protections offered for these cards.

Disclosures

To understand your rights and responsibilities for your EFTs, read the documents you get from the financial institution that issued your "access device"—the card, code or other way you access your account to transfer money electronically. Although the method varies by institution, it often involves a card and/or a PIN. No one should know your PIN but you and select employees at your financial institution. You also should read the documents you receive for your bank account, which may contain more information about EFTs.

Before you contract for EFT services or make your first electronic transfer, the institution must give you the following information in a format you can keep.

- a summary of your liability for unauthorized transfers

- the phone number and address for a contact if you think an unauthorized transfer has been or may be made, the institution's "business days" (when the institution is open to the public for normal business), and the number of days you have to report suspected unauthorized transfers

- the type of transfers you can make, fees for transfers, and any limits on the frequency and dollar amount of transfers

- a summary of your right to get documentation of transfers and to stop payment on a preauthorized transfer, and how you stop payment

- a notice describing how to report an error on a receipt for an EFT or your statement, to request more information about a transfer listed on your statement, and how long you have to make your report

- a summary of the institution's liability to you if it fails to make or stop certain transactions

- circumstances when the institution will share information about your account with third parties

- a notice that you may have to pay a fee charged by operators of ATMs where you don't have an account, for an EFT or a balance inquiry at the ATM, and charged by networks to complete the transfer.

You also will get two more types of information for most transactions: terminal receipts and periodic statements. Separate rules apply to deposit accounts from which pre-authorized transfers are drawn. For example, pre-authorized transfers from your account need your written or similar authorization, and a copy of that authorization must be given to you. Additional information about preauthorized transfers is in your contract with the financial institution for that account. You're entitled to a terminal receipt each time you initiate an electronic transfer, whether you use an ATM or make a point-of-sale electronic transfer, for transfers over $15. The receipt must show the amount and date of the transfer, and its type, like "from savings to checking." It also must show a number or code that identifies the account, and list the terminal location and other information. When you make a point-of-sale transfer, you'll probably get your terminal receipt from the salesperson.

You won't get a terminal receipt for regularly occurring electronic payments that you've preauthorized, like insurance premiums, mortgages, or utility bills. Instead, these transfers will appear on your statement. If the preauthorized payments vary, however, you should get a notice of the amount that will be debited at least 10 days before the debit takes place.

You're also entitled to a periodic statement for each statement cycle in which an electronic transfer is made. The statement must show the amount of any transfer, the date it was credited or debited to your account, the type of transfer and type of account(s) to or from which funds were transferred, the account number, the amount of any fees charged, the account balances at the beginning and end of the statement cycle, and the address and phone number for inquiries. You're entitled to a quarterly statement whether or not electronic transfers were made.

Keep and compare your EFT receipts with your periodic statements the same way you compare your credit card receipts with your monthly credit card statement. This will help you make the best use of your rights under federal law to dispute errors and avoid liability for unauthorized transfers.

Errors

You have 60 days from the date a periodic statement containing a problem or error was sent to you to notify your financial institution. The best way to protect yourself if an error occurs is to notify the financial institution by certified letter. Ask for a return receipt so you can prove that the institution got your letter. Keep a copy of the letter for your records.

Under federal law, the institution has no obligation to conduct an investigation if you miss the 60-day deadline.

Once you've notified the financial institution about an error on your statement, it has 10 business days to investigate. The institution must tell you the results of its investigation within three business days after completing it, and must correct an error within one business day after determining that the error has occurred. An institution usually is permitted to take more time—up to 45 days—to complete the investigation, but only if the money in dispute is returned to your account and you're notified promptly of the credit. At the end of the investigation, if no error has been found, the institution may take the money back if it sends you a written explanation.

An error also may occur in connection with a point-of-sale purchase with a debit card. For example, an oil company might give you a debit card that lets you pay for gas directly from your bank account. Or you may have a debit card that can be used for various types of retail purchases. These purchases will appear on your bank statement. In case of an error on your account, however, you should contact the card issuer (for example, the oil company or bank) at the address or phone number provided by the company for errors. Once you've notified the company about the error, it has 10 business days to investigate and tell you the results. In this situation, it may take up to 90 days to complete an investigation, if the money in dispute is returned to your account and you're notified promptly of the credit. If no error is found at the end of the investigation, the institution may take back the money if it sends you a written explanation.

Lost Or Stolen ATM Or Debit Cards

If your credit card is lost or stolen, you can't lose more than $50. If someone uses your ATM or debit card without your permission, you can lose much more.

If you report an ATM or debit card missing to the institution that issues the card before someone uses the card without your permission, you can't be responsible for any unauthorized withdrawals. But if unauthorized use occurs before you report it, the amount you can be responsible for depends on how quickly you report the loss to the card issuer.

- If you report the loss within two business days after you realize your card is missing, you won't be responsible for more than $50 of unauthorized use.

- If you report the loss within 60 days after your statement is mailed to you, you could lose as much as $500 because of an unauthorized transfer.

- If you don't report an unauthorized use of your card within 60 days after the card issuer mails your statement to you, you risk unlimited loss; you could lose all the money in that account, the unused portion of your maximum line of credit established for overdrafts, and maybe more.

If an extenuating circumstance, like lengthy travel or illness, keeps you from notifying the card issuer within the time allowed, the notification period must be extended. In addition, if state law or your contract imposes lower liability limits than the federal EFT Act, the lower limits apply.

Once you report the loss or theft of your ATM or debit card to the card issuer, you're not responsible for additional unauthorized use. Because unauthorized transfers may appear on your statements, though, read each statement you receive after you've reported the loss or theft. If the statement shows transfers that you didn't make or that you need more information about, contact the card issuer immediately, using the special procedures it provided for reporting errors.

Overdrafts For One-Time Debit Card Transactions And ATM Cards

If you make a one-time purchase or payment with your debit card or use your ATM card and don't have sufficient funds, an overdraft can occur. Your bank must get your permission to charge you a fee to pay for your overdraft on a one-time debit card transaction or ATM transaction. They also must send you a notice and get your opt-in agreement before charging you.

For accounts that you already have, unless you opt-in, the transaction will be declined if you don't have the funds to pay it, and you can't be charged an overdraft fee. If you open a new account, the bank can't charge you an overdraft fee for your one-time debit card or ATM transactions, either, unless you opt-in to the fees. The bank will give you a notice about opting-in when you open the account, and you can decide whether to opt-in. If you opt-in, you can cancel anytime; if you don't opt-in, you can do it later.

These rules do not apply to recurring payments from your account. For those transactions, your bank can enroll you in their usual overdraft coverage. If you don't want the coverage (and the fees), contact your bank to see if they will let you discontinue it for those payments.

Limited Stop-Payment Privileges

When you use an electronic fund transfer, the EFT Act does not give you the right to stop payment. If your purchase is defective or your order isn't delivered, it's as if you paid cash: It's up to you to resolve the problem with the seller and get your money back.

One exception: If you arranged for recurring payments out of your account to third parties, like insurance companies or utilities, you can stop payment if you notify your institution at least three business days before the scheduled transfer. The notice may be written or oral, but the institution may require a written follow-up within 14 days of your oral notice. If you don't follow-up in writing, the institution's responsibility to stop payment ends.

Although federal law provides limited rights to stop payment, financial institutions may offer more rights or state laws may require them. If this feature is important to you, shop around to be sure you're getting the best "stop-payment" terms available.

Additional Rights

The EFT Act protects your right of choice in two specific situations: First, financial institutions can't require you to repay a loan by preauthorized electronic transfers. Second, if you're required to get your salary or government benefit check by EFT, you can choose the institution where those payments will be deposited.

For More Information And Complaints

If you decide to use EFT, keep these tips in mind:

- Take care of your ATM or debit card. Know where it is at all times; if you lose it, report it as soon as possible.

- Choose a PIN for your ATM or debit card that's different from your address, telephone number, Social Security number, or birthdate. This will make it more difficult for a thief to use your card.

- Keep and compare your receipts for all types of EFT transactions with your statements so you can find errors or unauthorized transfers and report them.

- Make sure you know and trust a merchant or other company before you share any bank account information or preauthorize debits to your account. Be aware that some merchants or companies may process your check information electronically when you pay by check.

- Read your monthly statements promptly and carefully. Contact your bank or other financial institution immediately if you find unauthorized transactions and errors.

If you think a financial institution or company hasn't met its responsibilities to you under the EFT Act, you can complain to the appropriate federal agency. Visit the Consumer Financial Protection Bureau (CFPB) accessible on the Internet at www.consumerfinance.gov or HelpWithMyBank.gov, a site maintained by the Office of the Comptroller of the Currency, for answers to frequently-asked questions on topics like bank accounts, deposit insurance, credit cards, consumer loans, insurance, mortgages, identity theft, and safe deposit boxes, and for other information about federal agencies that have responsibility for financial institutions.

Chapter 16

A Guide To Checking Accounts

People generally use checking accounts to store money in the short term until it is needed for day to day expenses—like gas or groceries—or to pay bills, and they can usually deposit or withdraw any amount of money in their account as many times as they like. Checking accounts also come with convenient ways to deposit and withdraw money from the account, such as checks and automated teller machine (ATM) cards. However, people with checking accounts must be careful when using them, since some banks charge fees for certain actions, such as using another bank's ATM, withdrawing more money from your account than the amount in it, or not maintaining a minimum balance.

On the other hand, a savings account is used to set money aside for use in the future and allow the money to collect interest. Many people regularly place some of their money into savings accounts rather than spending it in order to achieve financial goals, such as buying the latest gadget or game, without having to go into debt to do it.

Compound interest is interest paid on both the money you put into your account and the interest already earned. For example, if you put $100 into an account that earns 10 percent interest, you will initially earn $10, which will result in a total account balance of $110. The next time your account earns 10 percent it will be based on $110 instead of just $100, giving you a total account balance of $121.

You can earn even more in compound interest if you stretch to put as much money as you can into your account and leave it untouched.

About This Chapter: Text in this chapter begins with excerpts from "Learning Bank—Checking And Savings Accounts," Federal Deposit Insurance Corporation (FDIC), January 30, 2018; Text beginning with the heading "Managing Your Checking Account" is excerpted from "Managing Your Checking Account," Consumer Financial Protection Bureau (CFPB), February 3, 2016.

There are many banks that offer special accounts for kids and teens, so talk to your parents if you'd like to open an account of your own and start learning how to manage money. But you don't need a bank account to start the habit of saving—a simple piggy bank will do!

Managing Your Checking Account

To be successful with your checking account, you first need to choose an appropriate product to meet your needs. The Consumer Financial Protection Bureau (CFPB) has a number of resources to help you choose a checking account.

The Importance Of Good Checking Account Management

Once you have your checking account, you need to manage it in order to keep it. Good account management helps you to avoid unnecessary fees and helps you to maintain the account. If you have trouble keeping enough money in your account to cover your payments or withdrawals, your bank or credit union might close the account and report you to a checking account reporting company. If there is a negative report, you could have trouble opening a new checking account with a financial institution for up to 7 years. Checking account reporting companies must comply with the Fair Credit Reporting Act (FCRA). This means, for example, that they must follow reasonable procedures to maximize the accuracy of the information that they provide to banks, and they can't include most information that's more than 7 years old. They can choose a shorter time period, and the checking account reporting companies typically disregard information that's more than five years old.

Tips To Manage Checking Accounts

Here are some tips for reducing the fees on your checking or prepaid account:

Pay Attention To Monthly Service Fees

Many financial institutions waive monthly service fees if you maintain a minimum balance or sign up for direct deposit. Some institutions waive these fees for senior citizens, students, or members of the military. Be sure to ask about these products if you think you might be eligible.

Keep Track Of Your Balance And Any Outstanding Payments

Keep track of your account balance and your account activity to avoid spending more than you have in your account. Keeping track of your balance also helps you to keep the

Do I Have To Pay Fees At My Bank?

Banks and credit unions might charge fees for different services. Ask your bank or credit union if you can avoid paying fees. Sometimes, banks and credit unions charge fees if you:

- go below the minimum balance in your account. The minimum balance is the amount of money the bank wants you to keep in your account
- spend more money than you have. This is called "overdrawing" your account
- use another bank's ATM to get money. Using your bank or credit union's ATM might be free. Using another bank's ATM almost always means you pay a fee.

Sometimes you can avoid paying fees by having your paycheck deposited directly to your account. "Direct deposit" means your employer pays your salary directly into your bank or credit union account. You do not get a paper check to cash. Ask your employer if it offers direct deposit.

(Source: "Opening A Bank Account," Consumer.gov, Federal Trade Commission (FTC).)

minimum balance you need in your account to avoid monthly fees. Some of the steps you can take are:

- Monitor your account online or on your phone.

- Check your balance by phone or online before you withdraw cash at an ATM.

- Check your balance by phone or online before you write a big check or make a big payment.

- Sign up for transaction alerts and low-balance warnings via e-mail or text.

- Don't assume that the money you deposited is available immediately. Find out when the money you deposit will be available for your use. Ask if there is a "hold" on the money you deposit, and if so when the hold will be lifted.

- The payments that you make can be processed very quickly, so don't make a payment from your checking account unless the money to cover it is already in your account and past any hold period.

- Know that your payments and withdrawals are not always processed in the order in which you make them. Be sure that you have enough in your account to cover everything.

- Know when regular electronic transfers, such as a rent payment or utility bills, will be paid.

Avoid Overdraft Fees

An overdraft occurs when you spend or withdraw more money than you have in your account and the bank or credit union pays to cover the shortfall. Overdrafts can be very expensive. Fees are generally charged "per item" and often as high as $35 or more per each overdraft transaction. To resolve an overdraft, you generally have to pay back the amount of the negative balance plus all fees, and you may have to pay additional fees if you do not repay quickly.

To reduce the likelihood that you will overdraft, you can:

- Switch to a checking account that is designed not to allow overdraft. Such "no-overdraft" products can help you manage your spending, but can still charge you a fee if you overspend. For example, if you write a check or try to pay a bill when you don't have enough money in your account, even if the transaction is declined.

- Choose not to "opt-in" to debit overdraft: Your bank or credit union can't charge you a fee for an overdraft with your debit card unless you "opt-in" to overdraft coverage for these transactions. Keep in mind that you could be charged a fee for checks and online or direct debit ("Automated Clearing House (ACH)") overdrafts even if you have chosen not to opt-in.

- Link your accounts: If you link your account, if you run out of money in your checking account, the bank will pull money from the place you've chosen. You can link your checking account to a savings account, if you have one and are able to maintain a balance in it to cover potential shortfalls. You pay a fee for this service, but the fee is usually much lower than an overdraft fee. You may also be able to link your checking account to a credit card or line of credit, if you have one. While the fee you're charged on your checking account may be much lower than an overdraft fee, you may also be charged a fee on the credit card or line of credit.

- Don't let terminology confuse you. "No Overdraft" products are designed to help you manage your spending and reduce the likelihood that you will overdraft. Banks and credit unions also offer overdraft programs, such as "overdraft coverage" and "overdraft protection," that generally do allow overdrafts.

Open And Review All Of The Statements From Your Bank Or Credit Union

Whether you get your account statements by mail, online, or both, review account statements every month to make sure they are correct and report errors immediately. Also watch for changes in your minimum balance requirement, fees, or other account terms.

Spend Only What You Have

Never write a check or authorize an electronic payment for funds unless you know you will have enough money in your account to cover it. If you don't have the funds you will be charged a nonsufficient funds (NSF) fee or an overdraft fee (for debit card payments and ATM withdrawals, only if you have opted into overdraft) from the bank or credit union. Overdrawing your account or not paying fees could severely impact your ability to access financial services in the future.

Use Your Financial Institution's ATMs

When you use ATMs in your bank's or credit union's network, there is generally no charge. However, many banks and credit unions will charge you for using an out-of-network ATM, such as an ATM branded by another bank or credit union. The owner of the out-of-network ATM may also charge you a fee. Some banks and credit unions will reimburse you for fees you pay at ATMs on other networks. Many banks and credit unions offer ATM locator maps on their websites and mobile apps to help you find in-network ATMs.

The CFPB has additional resources to help you decide what types of financial products and services are right for you.

Chapter 17

Protecting Yourself From Overdraft And Bounced-Check Fees

FAQs On Overdraft Fees And Other Fees

Do you know how to avoid overdraft fees and find out what to do if someone took money from your bank account without permission? Learn more about these and other issues in this chapter.

My Bank/Credit Union Charged Me A Fee For Overdrawing My Account Even Though I Never Agreed To Let Them Do So. What Can I Do?

For one-time debit card transactions and automated teller machine (ATM) withdrawals, banks and credit unions cannot charge you an overdraft fee unless you opt in. However, banks and credit unions are allowed to charge you overdraft fees when the bank or credit union pays a check or certain recurring electronic payments that would have overdrawn your account, even if you did not opt in.

Some banks may also allow you to opt-out of overdrafts for checks and other types of payments. However, consumers that decline overdraft coverage for checks or automated clearing house (ACH) transactions may be charged a nonsufficient funds (NSF) fee from the bank or credit union, which is generally the same amount as an overdraft fee. In addition, declined payments to merchants may trigger a returned item fee from the merchant.

About This Chapter: This chapter includes text excerpted from "Bank Accounts And Services," Consumer Financial Protection Bureau (CFPB), April 4, 2015.

If you had an account open as of July 2010, your bank or credit union may have sent you paperwork asking you to opt in to allow overdrafts on debit card transactions and ATM withdrawals. If you opened a new account since then, you may have signed a document authorizing overdraft protection when you opened the account.

If you are enrolled in a fee-based debit overdraft program, you can change your mind at any time. Just notify the bank or credit union that you don't want debit overdraft coverage. If you do not believe you've authorized debit overdraft protection, and the bank or credit union charges you a debit overdraft fee, you may file a complaint.

If you have chosen not to enroll in a debit overdraft program, the bank or credit union will decline ATM or debit card transactions when your account doesn't have enough funds to cover them, and you will not be charged a fee when this happens. Your debit overdraft program enrollment should not affect whether the bank or credit union will allow you to overdraw your account on check or recurring electronic payment transactions, or the overdraft fees you pay when you do.

I Opened A "Free" Checking Account But There Are Fees Charged On My Account. Can My Bank/Credit Union Do That?

If an account is described as "free" or "no cost," it cannot have any monthly service fees, fees for exceeding a specified number of transactions, or any fees to deposit, withdraw, or transfer money. A "free" or "no cost" account also means that the bank or credit union cannot charge you a fee for not meeting a minimum balance.

However, a "free" account may still have certain fees such as ATM fees, overdraft fees, bounced check fees, balance inquiry fees, fees to stop payment on a check, fees on a dormant account, or check-printing fees.

Why Do I Have To Pay The Bank/Credit Union Back If A Check I Deposited Turns Out To Be Fraudulent?

If your bank or credit union credited your account fraudulently, the bank or credit union can remove the funds from your account. It is entitled to recover funds that were fraudulently transferred and to take steps to reverse a fraudulent transaction. If you believe you have been targeted by a scam, you should file a complaint with the Federal Trade Commission (FTC).

Can My Bank/Credit Union Charge Me A Fee To Use Another Bank Or Credit Union's ATM?

Yes. Both your bank or credit union and the owner of the ATM can charge you a fee. Your bank or credit union must disclose its fee in writing when you open your account or when it adds a new fee. The ATM operator must disclose its fee in writing at the ATM itself.

The Bank/Credit Union Is Charging High Service, Activity, Maintenance, Or Other Fees On My Checking Account. Can The Bank/Credit Union Do This?

Yes, but your bank or credit union must disclose any fees associated with a deposit account (like a checking account) when you open the account.

A bank or credit union cannot charge you more than the amount of the fee that has been disclosed to you, but it may give you notice after you have opened the account that the fees are changing. Federal law generally does not otherwise limit the amount of checking account fees. You may want to talk to your bank or credit union to see if there is a different account that is suited to your needs and costs less to maintain.

How Can I Reduce The Costs Of My Checking Account?

You can reduce the cost of using your checking account by taking the following steps:

Pay attention to what transactions or events are triggering fees. Find out whether you might be able to alter your banking behavior to avoid these fees. For example, you may save a few dollars by using your bank's or credit union's ATMs rather than those of another institution or by signing up for account alerts that help you stop from spending more than you have. Talk to your bank or credit union about possible solutions.

Avoid spending more than you have. Bounced check penalties can be significant, and overdraft fees are an especially costly way to borrow money. Keep careful track of the balance in your account and confirm that deposited funds are available before making a payment or withdrawal that might exhaust your account. Check your balance at the ATM before you withdraw cash, and see if you can sign up to get low-balance warnings via e-mail or text. You can also monitor your balance online.

Keep track of your account. Monitor your account online to keep track of what's coming in and going out. If you have questions, ask your bank or credit union for an explanation. Review your account statement every month to make sure it's correct. Report any errors immediately to your bank or credit union. Banks and credit unions must tell you when they change their terms of service, so any time you get a piece of mail from your bank or credit union, read it.

Reduce monthly service charges. Know the minimum balance requirement. Ask if direct deposit or electronic banking can lower the monthly fee. See if the bank or credit union offers a low-fee checking account for you, such as a seniors or students account, or just a basic checking account with a low minimum balance and a limited number of "free" checks and withdrawals. You may also be able to avoid monthly maintenance fees by consolidating accounts and maintaining a higher balance.

Shop around. Get a copy of your bank or credit union's list of account fees, or ask about them, then compare them with account fees at other banks or credit unions. Assess your habits honestly and consider penalty fees, such as overdraft and nonsufficient funds charges, as well as monthly maintenance, ATM surcharge, and other service fees. When comparing banks or credit unions, also consider factors such as the hours of operation, locations, access to public transportation, available products and services, and reputation for customer service.

I Bounced A Check. Will This Show Up On My Credit Report?

It depends on what you wrote the check to pay. If you wrote the check to pay a bill, such as a credit card or mortgage, the creditor may report that you were late in paying your bill to the major credit reporting agencies.

Banks and credit unions usually don't report a bounced check to the credit reporting agencies, but if you often write bad checks, the bank or credit unions may report that to a specialty credit-reporting agency that specializes in checking information. These companies collect information on consumers' bank accounts, and having a bad record may make it harder for you to open a bank account in the future.

I Received A Check And Tried To Cash It At The Bank/credit Union That Holds The Account On Which The Check Is Written. The Bank/Credit Union Charged Me A Fee For Cashing A Check. Can A Bank/Credit Union Do That?

Generally, a bank or credit union can charge you a fee for cashing a check when you don't have an account with that bank or credit union.

However, some states have laws that require employers to pay you in a way that enables you to get your wages without a fee. In those states, you should be able to cash your paycheck at the bank or credit union the check is from without paying a fee. To learn more about the law in your state, contact your state banking department, state Attorney General's office, or for issues related to your paycheck, your state's Labor Department.

How Do I Avoid ATM Fees?

Generally, use your own bank or credit union's ATMs—most banks or credit unions charge no fee for this service. Usually, when you use another bank or credit union's ATM, both the operator of the ATM and your bank or credit union charge you a fee.

Some banks and credit unions offer to rebate ATM fees for customers that maintain high average balances. Check with your bank or credit union to find out what ATMs you can use without an additional fee.

Can I Be Charged More Than One Fee For A Single Overdraft?

You should check your account documents to see how long you have to repay overdrafts before you are charged additional fees. To find out about overdrafts quickly, your bank or credit union may offer a text or e-mail alert to tell you when your account is overdrawn. You can also monitor your balances online. Ask your bank or credit union how to sign up for these alerts.

How Do I Avoid Or Minimize Overdraft Fees?

If you pay overdraft fees regularly, you are paying a lot for very short-term cash advances. Here are some steps to reduce those costs:

Track your balance. To avoid overdraft fees and not-sufficient funds (NSF) fees, you should always track your balance as carefully as you can. It may be possible to sign up for low balance alerts through your bank, credit union, or other service providers. These alerts can help you know when you are at risk of overdrawing your account. If you have regular electronic transfers, such as rent, mortgage payments, or utility bills, make sure you know how much they will be and on what day they occur. You also need to know when the funds you have deposited become available for your use, so you can ensure you have enough money in your account.

Opt out of overdraft coverage. If you are paying a lot of overdraft fees, consider opting out of overdraft coverage for debit purchases or ATM withdrawals. Without overdraft coverage, your card will be declined if you don't have enough money in your account to cover a debit purchase or ATM withdrawal. You won't be able to complete the transaction, but you won't incur an overdraft fee either. If you have chosen a debit card overdraft program, you can change your mind any time. Just let your financial institution know and it must honor your change request as soon as reasonably practicable.

Link to a savings account. To reduce the costs of overdrafting, link your checking account to a savings account. If you overdraw your checking account, money will be taken from your linked savings account to cover the difference as long as you have sufficient funds in your savings account. You may be charged a transfer fee each time this happens, but it is usually much lower than the fee for an overdraft.

Get a line of credit. As an alternative to a linked savings account, ask your bank or credit union if you are eligible for a line of credit or link to a credit card to cover overdrafts. You may have to pay a fee when the credit line is tapped, and you will owe interest on the amount you borrowed, but this is usually a much cheaper way to cover a brief cash shortfall.

I Opened A "Free" Checking Account. I Received A Notice From The Bank/Credit Union Stating That It Had Decided To Start Charging Monthly Fees. Can The Bank/Credit Union Do This?

Yes. A bank or credit union can start charging you fees on your account as long as the bank or credit union notifies you in writing at least 30 days before it starts charging fees and explains the change to your account.

However, once it starts charging these fees, the bank or credit union can no longer advertise that particular account as a "free" checking account.

Banks and credit unions have multiple types of accounts available, so make sure you review your own account terms. If you feel your bank has violated a promise to you, you may file a complaint.

Can The Bank/Credit Union Put A New Fee On My Checking Account?

Yes, except that in most cases, your bank or credit union must give you at least 30 days' notice before adding a new fee or increasing an existing fee. Exceptions include fees related to check printing and the expiration of clearly designated promotional fee waivers. Check your account agreement for more information on fees your bank or credit union can charge.

If I Link My Credit Card To My Checking Account To Cover Overdrafts, Can The Bank/Credit Union Charge Me A Fee Each Time I Use It To Cover An Overdraft?

If you link your credit card to your checking account to cover overdrafts, you can be charged a fee if the fee was disclosed to you.

In addition to the fee, the transaction will probably be considered a cash advance. This means you will be charged interest immediately on the amount charged to the credit card at the interest rate (or APR) for cash advances. This rate is usually higher than the interest rate for purchases. However, the total cost of paying an overdraft with your credit card is usually a lot less than the cost of paying an overdraft fee.

I Opted Into Debit Overdraft But The Bank/Credit Union Still Declined To Allow A Debit Purchase I Made. Can The Bank Do That?

Yes. Banks and credit union can decide whether to pay any particular item that would cause an overdraft.

How Many Overdrafts Can I Get In A Single Day?

Some banks and credit unions have their own maximum per day; check with your bank or credit union to see what its policies are.

I Overdrew My Account By Only One Penny Yet Was Charged The Full Overdraft Fee. What Can I Do About This?

Some banks and credit unions will let you overdraft your account by a small amount without a fee, so check with your bank or credit union to determine its policy. Try to avoid overdrafts even if your bank or credit union currently allows small overdrafts without a fee.

Can My Bank/Credit Union Deduct Bounced Check Fees From My Account?

Yes. Your bank or credit union can directly remove funds from your accounts to pay fees assessed on that account.

Does My Bank/Credit Union Have To Allow Overdrafts?

No. Your bank or credit union may set and change its own limit on how often and by how much it will let each customer overdraw his or her account.

The Bank Or Credit Union Raised The Fees On My Checking Account. Can The Bank Or Credit Union Do This?

Yes, but your bank or credit union must give you advance written notice 30 days before it increases the fees on your checking account.

Chapter 18

Protecting Yourself From Identity Theft

Identity Theft

Consumers increasingly rely on computers and the Internet—the "cyber" world—for everything from shopping and communicating to banking and bill-paying. But while the benefits of faster and more convenient cyber services for bank customers are clear, the risks posed by these services as well as the strategies for preventing or recovering from cyber-related crimes may not be as well-known by the average consumer and small business owner.

Common cyber-related crimes include identity theft, frauds, and scams. Identity theft involves a crime in which someone wrongfully obtains and uses another person's personal data to open fraudulent credit card accounts, charge existing credit card accounts, withdraw funds from deposit accounts, or obtain new loans. A victim's losses may include not only

About This Chapter: Text beginning with the heading "Identity Theft" is excerpted from "Cybersecurity Awareness Basics," Federal Deposit Insurance Corporation (FDIC), March 20, 2017; Text under the heading "Protect Your "Cyber Home" With A Solid Foundation" is excerpted from "Protect Your "Cyber Home" With A Solid Foundation," Federal Deposit Insurance Corporation (FDIC), March 7, 2016; Text under the heading "Using Social Networking Sites: Be Careful What You Share" is excerpted from "Using Social Networking Sites: Be Careful What You Share," Federal Deposit Insurance Corporation (FDIC), March 7, 2016; Text under the heading "Beware Of Phishing Scams: Don't Take The Bait" is excerpted from "Beware Of Phishing Scams: Don't Take The Bait," Federal Deposit Insurance Corporation (FDIC), March 2, 2016; Text beginning with the heading "Going Mobile: How To Be Safer When Using A Smartphone Or Tablet" is excerpted from "Going Mobile: How To Be Safer When Using A Smartphone Or Tablet," Federal Deposit Insurance Corporation (FDIC), March 3, 2016; Text under the heading "A Cybersecurity Checklist" is excerpted from "A Cybersecurity Checklist," Federal Deposit Insurance Corporation (FDIC), March 7, 2016; Text under the heading "Beware Of Malware: Think Before You Click!" is excerpted from "Beware Of Malware: Think Before You Click!" Federal Deposit Insurance Corporation (FDIC), March 8, 2016.

out-of-pocket financial losses but also substantial costs to restore credit history and to correct erroneous information in their credit reports.

In addition to identity theft, every year millions of people are victims of frauds and scams, which often start with an e-mail, text message, or phone message that appears to be from a legitimate, trusted organization. The message typically asks consumers to verify or update personal information. Similarly, criminals create bogus websites for such things as credit repair services in the hopes that consumers will enter personal information.

If you think you are a victim of a fraud or scam, contact your state, local, or federal consumer protection agency. Also, a local law enforcement officer may be able to provide advice and assistance. By promptly reporting fraud, you improve your chances of recovering what you have lost and you help law enforcement. The agency you contact first may take action directly or refer you to another agency better positioned to protect you.

Violations of federal laws should be reported to the federal agency responsible for enforcement. Consumer complaints are used to document patterns of abuse, allowing the agency to take action against a company.

People who have no intention of delivering what is sold, who misrepresent items, send counterfeit goods or otherwise try to trick you out of your money are committing fraud. If you suspect fraud, there are some additional steps to take.

- Contact the Federal Trade Commission (FTC). The FTC enters Internet, telemarketing, identity theft and other fraud-related complaints into Consumer Sentinel, a secure, online database available to hundreds of civil and criminal law enforcement agencies in the United States and abroad.

- If the fraud involved mail or an interstate delivery service, contact the U.S. Postal Inspection Service (USPIS). It is illegal to use the mail to misrepresent or steal money.

How To Avoid Identity Theft

The best protection against identity theft is to carefully protect your personal information, for example:

- Do not share personal information over the phone, through the mail, or over the internet unless you initiated the contact or know the person you are dealing with;

- Be suspicious if someone contacts you unexpectedly online and asks for your personal information. It doesn't matter how legitimate the e-mail or website may look. Only open e-mails that look like they are from people or organizations you know, and even then, be cautious if they look questionable. Be especially wary of fraudulent e-mails or websites that have typos or other obvious mistakes;

- Don't give out valuable personal information in response to unsolicited requests. Social Security numbers, financial account information and your driver's license number are some of the details that should be kept confidential;

- Shred old receipts, account statements, and unused credit card offers;

- Choose personal identification numbers (PIN) and passwords that would be difficult to guess and avoid using easily identifiable information such as your mother's maiden name, birth dates, the last four digits of your social security number, or phone numbers;

- Pay attention to billing cycles and account statements and contact your bank if you don't receive a monthly bill or statement since identity thieves often divert account documentation;

- Review account statements thoroughly to ensure all transactions are authorized;

- Guard your mail from theft, promptly remove incoming mail, and do not leave bill payment envelopes in your mailbox with the flag up for pick up by mail carrier;

- Obtain your free credit report annually and review your credit history to ensure it is accurate;

- Use an updated security program to protect your computer; and

- Be careful about where and how you conduct financial transactions, for example, don't use an unsecured Wi-Fi network because someone might be able to access the information you are transmitting or viewing.

How To Avoid Frauds And Scams

There are numerous scams presented daily to consumers so you must always exercise caution when it comes to your personal and financial information. The following tips may help prevent you from becoming a fraud victim.

- Be aware of incoming e-mail or text messages that ask you to click on a link because the link may install malware that allows thieves to spy on your computer and gain access to your information;

- Be suspicious of any e-mail or phone requests to update or verify your personal information because a legitimate organization would not solicit updates in an unsecured manner for information it already has;

- Confirm a message is legitimate by contacting the sender (it is best to look up the sender's contact information yourself instead of using contact information in the message);

- Assume any offer that seems too good to be true, is probably a fraud;

- Be on guard against fraudulent checks, cashier's checks, money orders, or electronic fund transfers sent to you with requests for you to wire back part of the money;

- Be wary of unsolicited offers that require you to act fast;

- Check your security settings on social network sites. Make sure they block out people who you don't want seeing your page;

- Research any "apps" before downloading and don't assume an "app" is legitimate just because it resembles the name of your bank or other company you are familiar with;

- Be leery of any offers that pressure you to send funds quickly by wire transfer or involve another party who insists on secrecy; and

- Beware of Disaster-Related Financial Scams. Con artists take advantage of people after catastrophic events by claiming to be from legitimate charitable organizations when, in fact, they are attempting to steal money or valuable personal information.

Protect Your "Cyber Home" With A Solid Foundation

Simple Steps To Secure Your Computers And Mobile Devices For Internet Banking And Shopping

Your home has locks on the doors and windows to protect your family and prevent thieves from stealing cash, electronics, jewelry, and other physical possessions. But do you have deterrents to prevent the loss or theft of your electronic assets, including bank account and other information in your personal computers, at home and when banking or shopping remotely online?

"Think about all of the access points to and from your computer—such as Internet connections, e-mail accounts, and wireless networks," said Michael Benardo, manager of the Federal Deposit Insurance Corporation's (FDIC) Cyber Fraud and Financial Crimes Section. "These always need to be protected. Otherwise, it's like leaving your front door wide open while you are away so that anyone could come in and take what they please."

Consider these strategies.

For Banking By Computer Or Mobile Device

Take extra precautions for logging into bank **and other financial accounts.** These measures include using "strong" user IDs and passwords by choosing combinations of upper- and lower-case letters, numbers, and symbols that are hard for a hacker to guess. Don't use your birthdate, address or other words or numbers that can be easy for con artists to find out or guess. Don't use the same password for different accounts because a criminal who obtains one password can then log in to your other accounts. Keep your user IDs and passwords secret, and change them regularly. Make sure to log out of financial accounts when you complete your transactions or walk away from the computer.

Consider using a separate computer solely for online banking or shopping. A growing number of people are purchasing basic PCs and using them only for banking online and not Web browsing, e-mailing, social networking, playing games, or other activities that are more susceptible to malicious software—known generally as "malware"—that can access computers and steal information. As an alternative, you can use an old PC for this limited purpose, but uninstall any software no longer needed and scan the entire PC to check for malicious software before proceeding.

Take precautions if you provide financial account information to third parties online. For example, some people use online "account aggregation" services that, from one website, can provide a convenient way to pay bills, monitor balances in deposits and investment accounts, and even keep track of your frequent flyer miles. While these websites may be beneficial, they can also present potential issues related to the security of the account information you have shared with them. If you want to use their services, thoroughly research the company behind the website, including making sure that you're dealing with a legitimate entity and not a fraudulent site. Also ask what protections the website offers if it experiences a data breach or loss of data.

Periodically check your bank accounts for signs of fraud. If you bank online, check your deposit accounts and lines of credit at regular intervals to spot and report errors or fraudulent transactions, just as you would review a paper statement. Online banking makes it easier and faster to monitor your accounts. This is important, because the sooner you can detect a problem with a transaction, the easier it should be to fix.

Federal laws generally limit your liability for unauthorized use of your debit, credit, and prepaid cards, especially if you report the problem to your financial institution within specified time periods, which vary depending on the circumstances. A good rule of thumb is to check your accounts online once or twice a week. Also, many banks make it easier for customers to keep track of their accounts by offering e-mail or text message alerts when balances fall below a certain level or when there is a transaction over a certain amount.

Basic Security Tips

Keep your software up to date. Software manufacturers continually update their products to fix vulnerabilities or security weaknesses when they find them. "All of your software should be checked and updated as generally recommended by the manufacturer or when flaws are found," explained Kathryn Weatherby, a fraud examination specialist for the FDIC. "This advice goes for everything from your operating system to your word processing software, Internet browsers, spreadsheet software, and even your digital photography applications. A vulnerability in one piece of software, no matter how insignificant it may seem, can be exploited by a hacker and used as a pathway into your whole computer."

Some software manufacturers may issue "patches" that you need to install to update a program. Others may simply provide you with a completely new version of the software. "Before installing any update you receive, make sure it is legitimate, especially if it is e-mailed to you," said Benardo. "Check the software manufacturer's website or contact the company directly to verify the update's validity. Criminals have been known to imitate software vendors providing a security update when, in fact, they are distributing malware. Once you confirm that an update is legitimate, install it as soon as possible to correct whatever security flaw might exist."

Install anti-virus software that prevents, detects, and removes malicious programs. Crooks and computer hackers are always developing new malware that can access computers and steal information, such as account passwords or credit or debit card numbers. These programs also may be able to destroy data from the infected computer's hard drive.

Malware can enter your computer in a variety of ways, perhaps as an attachment to an e-mail, a downloaded file from an infected website, or from a contaminated thumb drive or disk. Fight back by installing anti-virus software that periodically runs in the background of your computer to search for and remove malware. Also be sure to set the software to update automatically so that it can protect you from the latest malware.

Use a firewall program to prevent unauthorized access to your PC. A firewall is a combination of hardware and software that establishes a barrier between your personal computer and an external network, such as the Internet, and then monitors and controls incoming and outgoing network traffic. In simple terms, a firewall acts as a gatekeeper that helps screen out hackers, malware, and other intruders who try to access your computer from the Internet.

Only use security products from reputable companies. Some anti-virus software and firewalls can be purchased, while others are available free. Either way, it's a good idea to check out these products by reading reviews from computer and consumer publications. Look for products that have high ratings for detecting problems and for providing tech support if your computer becomes infected. Other ways to select the right protection products for your computer are to consult with the manufacturer of your computer or operating system, or to ask someone you know who is a computer expert.

Take advantage of Internet safety features. When you are banking online, shopping on the Internet or filling out an application that requests sensitive personal information such as credit card, debit card, and bank account numbers, make sure you are doing business with reputable companies. You also can have greater confidence in a website that encrypts (scrambles) the information as it travels to and from your computer. Look for a padlock symbol on the page and a Web address that starts with "https://." The "s" stands for "secure."

Also, current versions of most popular Internet browsers and search engines often will indicate if you are visiting a suspicious website or a page that cannot be verified as trusted. It's best not to continue on to pages with these kinds of warnings. Review your Internet browser's user instructions and explore the "tools" and "help" tabs to learn more about the security settings and alerts offered.

Be careful where and how you connect to the Internet. A public computer, such as at an Internet café or a hotel business center, may not have up-to-date security software and could be infected with malware. Similarly, if you are using a portable computer (such as a laptop or mobile device) for online banking or shopping, avoid connecting it to a wireless (Wi-Fi) network at a public "hotspot" such as a coffee shop, hotel or airport. Wi-Fi in public areas can be used by criminals to intercept your device's signals and as a collection point for personal information.

The bottom line, especially for sensitive matters such as online banking and activities that involve personal information, is to consider only accessing the Internet using your own computer with a secure, trusted connection, and to only connect laptops and mobile devices to trusted networks.

Using Social Networking Sites: Be Careful What You Share

A lot of people use social media sites—such as Facebook, LinkedIn, Twitter, Google+, and Instagram—to stay in touch with family and friends, meet new people and interact with businesses like their bank. However, identity thieves can use social media sites in hopes of learning enough information about individuals to be able to figure out passwords, access financial accounts or commit identity theft.

Identity thieves create fake profiles on social networks pretending to be financial institutions and other businesses, and then lure unsuspecting visitors into providing Social Security numbers, bank account numbers, and other valuable personal information. Identity thieves also have created fraudulent profiles and then sent elaborate communications to persuade "friends" to send money or divulge personal information. "They might claim to work at the same organization, to have attended the same school, or share similar interests and hobbies," said Susan Boenau, manager of the FDIC's Consumer Affairs Section. "They know that communicating a false sense of trust can be easy on social media."

"Valuable pieces of information to someone seeking to steal your identity include, for example, a mother's maiden name, date or place of birth, high school mascot or pet's name," explained Amber Holmes, a financial crimes information specialist with the FDIC. "Fraud artists use social networking sites to gather this kind of information because it can help them guess passwords to online accounts or answers to 'challenge questions' that banks and other businesses frequently use for a second level of authentication beyond a password. Someone who has your password and can successfully answer challenge questions may be able to access your accounts, transfer money, or even reset passwords to something they know and you don't."

What safety measures can you take with your social media accounts?

Check your security settings on social network sites. Make sure they block out people who you don't want seeing your page. If you have doubts about your security settings, avoid including information such as your birthday or the year you graduated college. Otherwise, though, experts say it is OK to provide that kind of information on your social media pages.

Take precautions when communicating with your bank. If you want to communicate with your bank on social media, keep in mind that your posts could become public, even though you can protect your posts to some extent through your account settings. You should not include any personal, confidential or account information in your posts. "Also, reputable social media sites will not ask you for your Social Security, credit card or debit card numbers, or your bank account passwords," said FDIC Counsel Richard Schwartz.

Before posting information such as photos and comments, you should look for a link that says "privacy" or "policies" to find out what can be shared by the bank or the bank's social media site with other parties, including companies that want to send you marketing e-mails. Read what the policies say about whether and how the bank will keep personal information secure. Find out what options you may have to limit the sharing of your information.

It is a good rule of thumb to avoid posting personal information on any part of a bank's social media site. "That type of information is often requested by banks for their security 'challenge questions' that are used to control access to accounts," advised Schwartz. "A criminal could use that information to log in to your account."

Be cautious about giving third-party programs or apps, such as sites for games or quizzes, the ability to use information from your social networking pages. "Some of these third parties may use information from your page to help you connect with others or build your network—for example, to pair you with strangers wanting to play the same game," Boenau said. "But they could also be selling your information to marketing sites and others, possibly even to people who might use your information to commit a fraud."

Periodically search to see if someone has created a fake account using your name or personal information on social networking sites. Checking common search engines for your name and keywords or phrases (such as your address and job title) may turn up evidence that someone is using your information in a dishonest way.

Beware Of Phishing Scams: Don't Take The Bait

Identity thieves like to go "phishing"—pronounced "fishing"—on the Internet for consumers' personal financial information using fake e-mails and websites to trick people into providing Social Security numbers, bank account numbers, and other valuable details.

Typically, the most common phishing e-mails pretend to be from a bank, a retail store or government agency to lure you into divulging personal financial information, and often use a variety of tricks to make the e-mail look legitimate. They might include a graphic copied from a bank's website or a link that looks like it goes to a bank's site, but actually leads to a fake site.

Also beware of "pharming." In this version of online identity theft, a hacker hijacks Internet traffic so when you type in the address of a legitimate website you're taken to a fake site. If you enter personal information at the phony site, it is harvested and used to commit fraud or sold to other identity thieves.

Here are some tips to avoid becoming a victim of a phishing or pharming scam.

Be suspicious if someone contacts you unexpectedly online and asks for your personal information. It doesn't matter how legitimate the e-mail or website may look. Only open e-mails that look like they are from people or organizations you know, and even then, be cautious if they look questionable.

For example, scam artists may hack into someone's e-mail account and send out fake e-mails to friends and relatives, perhaps claiming that the real account owner is stranded abroad and might need your credit card information to return home.

Be especially wary of e-mails or websites that have typos or other obvious mistakes. "Because some requests come from people who primarily speak another language, they often contain poor grammar or spelling," said Amber Holmes, a financial crimes information specialist with the FDIC.

Remember that no financial institution will e-mail you and ask you to put sensitive information such as account numbers and PINs in your response. In fact, most institutions publicize that they will never ask for customer personal information over the phone or in an e-mail because they already have it.

Assume that a request for information from a bank where you've never opened an account is probably a scam. Don't follow the link and enter your personal information.

Verify the validity of a suspicious-looking e-mail or a pop-up box before providing personal information. Criminals can create e-mails stating that "you're a fraud victim" or a pop-up box with another urgent-sounding message to trick people into providing information or installing malware (malicious software). If you want to check something out, independently contact the supposed source (perhaps a bank or organization) by using an e-mail address or telephone number that you know is valid.

Going Mobile: How To Be Safer When Using A Smartphone Or Tablet

Everywhere you look, people are using smartphones and tablets as portable, hand-held computers. "Unfortunately, cybercriminals are also interested in using or accessing these devices to steal information or commit other crimes," said Michael Benardo, manager of the FDIC's Cyber Fraud and Financial Crimes Section. "That makes it essential for users of mobile devices to take measures to secure them, just as they would a desktop computer."

Here are some basic steps you can take to secure your mobile devices.

Avoid apps that may contain malware. Buy or download from well-known app stores, such as those established by your phone manufacturer or cellular service provider. Consult your financial institution's website to confirm where to download its official app for mobile banking.

Keep your device's operating system and apps updated. Consider opting for automatic updates because doing so will ensure that you have the latest fixes for any security weaknesses the manufacturer discovers. "Cybercriminals try to take advantage of known flaws, so keeping your software up to date will help reduce your vulnerability to foul play," said Robert Brown, a senior ombudsman specialist at the FDIC.

Consider using mobile security software and apps to protect your device. For example, anti-malware software for smartphones and tablets can be purchased from a reputable vendor.

Use a password or other security feature to restrict access in case your device is lost or stolen. Activate the "time out" or "auto lock" feature that secures your mobile device when it is left unused for a certain number of minutes. Set that security feature to start after a relatively brief period of inactivity. Doing so reduces the likelihood that a thief will be able to use your phone or tablet.

Back up data on your smartphone or tablet. This is good to do in case your device is lost, stolen or just stops working one day. Data can easily be backed up to a computer or to a back-up service, which may be offered by your mobile carrier.

Have the ability to remotely remove data from your device if it is lost or stolen. A "remote wipe" protects data from prying eyes. If the device has been backed up, the information can be restored on a replacement device or the original (if you get it back). A number of reputable apps can enable remote wiping.

A Cybersecurity Checklist

Reminders about 10 simple things bank customers can do to help protect their computers and their money from online criminals.

1. **Have computer security programs running and regularly updated to look for the latest threats.** Install anti-virus software to protect against malware (malicious software) that can steal information such as account numbers and passwords, and use a firewall to prevent unauthorized access to your computer.

2. **Be smart about where and how you connect to the Internet for banking or other communications involving sensitive personal information.** Public Wi-Fi networks and computers at places such as libraries or hotel business centers can be risky if they don't have up-to-date security software.

3. **Get to know standard Internet safety features.** For example, when banking or shopping online, look for a padlock symbol on a page (that means it is secure) and

"https://" at the beginning of the Web address (signifying that the website is authentic and encrypts data during transmission).

4. **Ignore unsolicited e-mails asking you to open an attachment or click on a link if you're not sure it's who truly sent it and why.** Cybercriminals are good at creating fake e-mails that look legitimate, but can install malware. Your best bet is to either ignore unsolicited requests to open attachments or files or to independently verify that the supposed source actually sent the e-mail to you by making contact using a published e-mail address or telephone number.

5. **Be suspicious if someone contacts you unexpectedly online and asks for your personal information.** A safe strategy is to ignore unsolicited requests for information, no matter how legitimate they appear, especially if they ask for information such as a Social Security number, bank account numbers and passwords.

6. **Use the most secure process you can when logging into financial accounts.** Create "strong" passwords that are hard to guess, change them regularly, and try not to use the same passwords or PINs (personal identification numbers) for several accounts.

7. **Be discreet when using social networking sites.** Criminals comb those sites looking for information such as someone's place of birth, mother's maiden name or a pet's name, in case those details can help them guess or reset passwords for online accounts.

8. **Be careful when using smartphones and tablets.** Don't leave your mobile device unattended and use a device password or other method to control access if it's stolen or lost.

9. **Parents and caregivers should include children in their cybersecurity planning.** Talk with your child about being safe online, including the risks of sharing personal information with people they don't know, and make sure the devices they use to connect to the Internet have up-to-date security.

10. **Small business owners should have policies and training for their employees on topics similar to those provided in this checklist for customers, plus other issues that are specific to the business.** For example, consider requiring more information beyond a password to gain access to your business's network, and additional safety measures, such as requiring confirmation calls with your financial institution before certain electronic transfers are authorized.

Beware Of Malware: Think Before You Click!

Malicious software—or "malware" for short—is a broad class of software built with malicious intent. "You may have heard of malware being referred to as a 'computer bug' or 'virus' because most malware is designed to spread like a contagious illness, infecting other computers it comes into contact with," said Michael Benardo, manager of the FDIC's Cyber Fraud and Financial Crimes Section. "And if you don't protect your computer, it could become infected by malware that steals your personal financial information, spies on you by capturing your keystrokes, or even destroys data."

Law enforcement agencies and security experts have seen an increase in a certain kind of malware known as "ransomware," which restricts someone's access to a computer or a smartphone—literally holding the device hostage—until a ransom is paid. While businesses have been targeted more than consumers to date, many home computer users have been victims of ransomware. For more information, see an alert issued by the U.S. Department of Homeland Security (DHS).

The most common way malware spreads is when someone clicks on an e-mail attachment—anything from a document to a photo, video or audio file. Criminals also might try to get you to download malware by including a link in the wording of an e-mail or in a social media post that directs you somewhere else, often to an infected file or Web page on the Internet. The link might be part of a story that sounds very provocative, such as one with a headline that says, "How to Get Rich" or "You Have to See This!"

Malware also can spread across a network of linked computers, be downloaded from an infected website, or be passed around on a contaminated portable storage device, such as a thumb drive or flash drive.

Here are reminders plus additional tips on how to generally keep malware off your computer.

Don't immediately open e-mail attachments or click on links in unsolicited or suspicious-looking e-mails. Think before you click! Cybercriminals are good at creating fake e-mails that look legitimate but can install malware. Either ignore unsolicited requests to open attachments or files or independently verify that the supposed source did send the e-mail to you (by using a published e-mail address or telephone number). "Even if the attachment is from someone you know, consider if you really need to open the attachment, especially if the e-mail looks suspicious," added Benardo.

Install good anti-virus software that periodically runs to search for and remove malware. Make sure to set the software to update automatically and scan for the latest malware.

121

Be diligent about using spam (junk mail) filters provided by your e-mail provider. These services help block mass e-mails that might contain malware from reaching your e-mail inbox.

Don't visit untrusted websites and don't believe everything you read. Criminals might create fake websites and pop-ups with enticing messages intended to draw you in and download malware. "Anyone can publish information online, so before accepting a statement as fact or taking action, verify that the source is reliable," warned Amber Holmes, a financial crimes information specialist with the FDIC. "And please, don't click on a link to learn more. If something sounds too good to be true, then most likely it's fraudulent or harmful."

Be careful if anyone—even a well-intentioned friend or family member—gives you a disk or thumb drive to insert in your computer. It could have hidden malware on it. "Don't access a disk or thumb drive without first scanning it with your security software," said Holmes. "If you are still unsure, don't take a chance."

Part Three
Establishing And Using Credit

Chapter 19

What You Need To Know About Credit

Your Credit History

What Is A Credit History?

Sometimes, people talk about your credit. What they mean is your credit history. Your credit history describes how you use money:

- How many credit cards do you have?

- How many loans do you have?

- Do you pay your bills on time?

If you have a credit card or a loan from a bank, you have a credit history. Companies collect information about your loans and credit cards.

Companies also collect information about how you pay your bills. They put this information in one place: your credit report.

What Is A Credit Report?

Your credit report is a summary of your credit history. It lists:

- your name, address, and Social Security number

- your credit cards

- your loans

___

About This Chapter: This chapter includes text excerpted from "Credit, Loans And Debt," Consumer.gov, Federal Trade Commission (FTC), October 1, 2012.

- how much money you owe
- if you pay your bills on time or late

Why Do I Have A Credit Report?

Businesses want to know about you before they lend you money. Would you want to lend money to someone who pays bills on time? Or to someone who always pays late?

Businesses look at your credit report to learn about you. They decide if they want to lend you money, or give you a credit card. Sometimes, employers look at your credit report when you apply for a job. Cell phone companies and insurance companies look at your credit report, too.

Who Makes My Credit Report?

A company called a credit reporting company collects your information. There are three big credit reporting companies:

- TransUnion
- Equifax
- Experian

These companies write and keep a report about you.

Can I See My Credit Report?

You can get a free copy of your credit report every year. That means one copy from each of the three companies that writes your reports.

The law says you can get your free credit reports if you:

- call Annual Credit Report at 877-322-8228 or
- go to AnnualCreditReport.com

Free Credit Report

The Fair Credit Reporting Act (FCRA) requires each of the nationwide credit reporting companies—Equifax, Experian, and TransUnion—to provide you with a free copy of your credit report, at your request, once every 12 months. The FCRA promotes the accuracy and privacy of information in the files of the nation's credit reporting companies.

(Source: "Free Credit Reports," Federal Trade Commission (FTC).)

Someone might say you can get a free report at another website. They probably are not telling the truth.

What Is A Credit Score?

A credit score is a number. It is based on your credit history. But it does not come with your free credit report unless you pay for it.

A high credit score means you have good credit. A low credit score means you have bad credit. Different companies have different scores. Low scores are around 300. High scores are around 700–850.

Do I Need To Get My Credit Score?

It is very important to know what is in your credit report. But a credit score is a number that matches your credit history. If you know your history is good, your score will be good. You can get your credit report for free.

It costs money to find out your credit score. Sometimes a company might say the score is free. But if you look closely, you might find that you signed up for a service that checks your credit for you. Those services charge you every month.

Before you pay any money, ask yourself if you need to see your credit score. It might be interesting. But is it worth paying money for?

What If I Do Not Have Credit?

You might not have a credit history if:

- you have not had a credit card
- you have not gotten a loan from a bank or credit union

Without a credit history, it can be harder to get a job, an apartment, or even a credit card. It sounds crazy: You need credit to get credit.

How Do I Get Credit?

Do you want to build your credit history? You will need to pay bills that are included in a credit report.

- Sometimes, utility companies put information into a credit report. Do you have utility bills in your name? That can help build credit.
- Many credit cards put information into credit reports.

- Sometimes, you can get a store credit card that can help build credit.

- A secured credit card also can help you build your credit.

Why Is My Credit Report Important?

Businesses look at your credit report when you apply for:

- loans from a bank

- credit cards

- jobs

- insurance

If you apply for one of these, the business wants to know if you pay your bills. The business also wants to know if you owe money to someone else. The business uses the information in your credit report to decide whether to give you a loan, a credit card, a job, or insurance.

Why Should I Get My Credit Report?

An important reason to get your credit report is to find problems or mistakes and fix them:

- You might find somebody's information in your report by mistake.

- You might find information about you from a long time ago.

- You might find accounts that are not yours. That might mean someone stole your identity.

You want to know what is in your report. The information in your report will help decide whether you get a loan, a credit card, a job or insurance.

If the information is wrong, you can try to fix it. If the information is right—but not so good—you can try to improve your credit history.

Where Do I Get My Free Credit Report?

You can get your free credit report from Annual Credit Report. That is the only free place to get your report. You can get it online: AnnualCreditReport.com, or by phone: 877-322-8228.

You get one free report from each credit reporting company every year. That means you get three reports each year.

What Should I Do When I Get My Credit Report?

Your credit report has a lot of information. Check to see if the information is correct. Is it your name and address? Do you recognize the accounts listed?

If there is wrong information in your report, try to fix it. You can write to the credit reporting company. Ask them to change the information that is wrong. You might need to send proof that the information is wrong—for example, a copy of a bill that shows the correct information. The credit reporting company must check it out and write back to you.

How Do I Improve My Credit?

Look at your free credit report. The report will tell you how to improve your credit history. Only you can improve your credit. No one else can fix information in your credit report that is not good, but is correct.

It takes time to improve your credit history. Here are some ways to help rebuild your credit.

- Pay your bills by the date they are due. This is the most important thing you can do.
- Lower the amount you owe, especially on your credit cards. Owing a lot of money hurts your credit history.
- Do not get new credit cards if you do not need them. A lot of new credit hurts your credit history.
- Do not close older credit cards. Having credit for a longer time helps your rating.

After six to nine months of this, check your credit report again. You can use one of your free reports from Annual Credit Report.

Using Credit

How Do I Use Credit?

When you use credit, it usually means using a credit card. It also might mean that you get a loan. A loan is another way to use credit.

Using credit means you borrow money to buy something.

- You borrow money (with your credit card or loan).
- You buy the thing you want.
- You pay back that loan later with interest.

What Is Interest?

Interest is what you pay for using someone else's money. You repay money to whoever gave you the credit card or loan.

Credit cards and loans have different interest rates. Look for the "APR." APR means annual percentage rate. It is how much interest you pay during a whole year.

A lower interest rate means you pay less money. A higher interest rate means you pay more money. For example, a loan with a 2 percent interest rate costs less than a loan with an 18 percent interest rate.

When Can I Use Credit?

Many people use a credit card to buy everyday things. You might use a credit card to pay for:

- Gas

- Groceries

- Services, like a haircut

Loans usually are for more expensive things. You might get a loan for:

- Furniture

- Education

- A car or home

How Can I Get Credit?

If you do not have credit, the best place to start is with a credit card.

Compare several credit cards. Apply for the one that gives you the best deal. Look for:

- a low annual fee

- a low APR, or annual percentage rate

- lower fees:

  - if a payment is late

  - if you go over your credit limit

- a long grace period. This is the time between when you spend money and when the card charges you interest. Look for one that is at least 25 days long

If you cannot get a regular credit card, try to get a secured credit card. Apply only for cards that report your history to the three credit reporting companies.

Look for a secured card with:

- no application fee

- a low APR, or annual percentage rate

- lower annual fees

- no processing fees

- higher interest rates on the money you deposit

How Can I Improve My Credit?

You can use credit to build and improve your credit history.

- Use your credit card a few times a month.

- Buy things you can pay for that month.

- Pay the whole credit card bill every month. Do not leave a balance on your card.

- Pay your bill by the date it is due. Paying even one day late will cost you money.

People who do this start to see a better credit history. But it takes time.

Tip. If you are new to credit, consider getting a product designed to help you establish and build credit. Financial institutions have developed an array of products and services, such as secured credit cards and credit builder loans, tailored to helping consumers new to credit to establish and build credit.

(Source: "How Do I Get And Keep A Good Credit Score?" Consumer Financial Protection Bureau (CFPB).)

Chapter 20

Borrowing Basics

Need Cash Fast? Ask Your Bank

If you need a small loan fast, where can you turn? "Start with your bank," says Jonathan Miller, Deputy Director in the Federal Deposit Insurance Corporation's (FDIC) Division of Depositor and Consumer Protection (DCP). "Too many people go to companies such as car title lenders, payday loan stores, and pawnshops, because they don't know that the vast majority of banks offer small-dollar loans at better rates and terms than what nonbanks provide." That's among the key messages from two new studies by the FDIC, both based on surveys conducted in 2011.

One survey revealed that about one in five households that use car-title lenders and other alternative providers for credit did so because they mistakenly thought banks only made large loans, like mortgage loans or auto loans, and not small loans. "The survey showed that many consumers also think they won't qualify for loans made by banks, and that may not always be true," added Susan Burhouse, an FDIC Senior Consumer Researcher.

The other found that about eight out of 10 banks do, in fact, offer small, unsecured personal loans. Those institutions offered loans under $2,500 with repayment terms of 90 days or longer, annual percentage rates (APRs) at or below 36 percent, and loan approvals in less than 24 hours." Results from both surveys suggest that consumers who want a small loan should find

About This Chapter: Text under the heading "Need Cash Fast? Ask Your Bank" is excerpted from "Need Cash Fast? Ask Your Bank," Federal Deposit Insurance Corporation (FDIC), June 14, 2014; Text under the heading "How To Get Your Best Deal On A Loan Or Credit Card? Plan Ahead" is excerpted from "How To Get Your Best Deal On A Loan Or Credit Card? Plan Ahead," Federal Deposit Insurance Corporation (FDIC), December 16, 2015; Text under the heading "Your Mortgage: Tips For Finding, Managing A Home Loan" is excerpted from "Your Mortgage: Tips For Finding, Managing A Home Loan," Federal Deposit Insurance Corporation (FDIC), June 13, 2014.

out if their bank or another financial institution nearby can offer that product and on better terms than those of nonbank loans," said Sherrie Rhine, a Senior Economist with the FDIC.

In addition, in 2008 the FDIC began a two-year pilot project to review affordable and responsible small-dollar loan programs in financial institutions. The FDIC pilot demonstrated that banks can feasibly offer reasonably priced loans as an alternative to high-cost credit products, such as payday loans or overdrafts.

"Most banks offer an option to borrow small amounts of money on reasonable terms," said DCP Director Mark Pearce. "Consumers should explore options at their bank before going to alternative lenders that may offer small loans that are easy to get into but can be costly and hard to escape from because the loans need to be repaid in full in a short time—typically a couple of weeks—or be rolled over into a new loan with additional fees."

How To Get Your Best Deal On A Loan Or Credit Card? Plan Ahead

Many consumers think they cannot influence whether a loan or credit card application will be approved or what interest rate they'll get. But the reality is that prospective borrowers can take certain steps before filling out an application that may increase their chances of getting an approval, with a favorable interest rate and attractive account terms.

Consider simple ways to improve your credit scores. Paying your bills and loans on time and owing as little as possible on your credit card(s) compared to the credit limits are two of the most important things you can do to boost your scores and get a better deal on a lending product.

Also think twice before closing older credit card accounts or lines of credit. "Don't immediately believe that you have to close an old account because of its age or because you're no longer using it," said Susan Boenau, Chief of the FDIC's Consumer Affairs Section. "Lenders making credit decisions like to see an established history of credit use, and the length of your credit history is figured into your credit score. So in general, the longer you can show you've been using credit the better." Striking the right balance is key, so when in doubt, a reputable credit counseling service can help.

Check your credit reports for accuracy. A credit report is a compilation of how you have been paying your credit card bills, loans, and selected other debts. By law, you are entitled to at least one free copy of your report from each of the nationwide credit bureaus every 12 months. To order your free credit report from the three major credit bureaus (Experian, Equifax, and TransUnion), visit www.AnnualCreditReport.com or call toll-free 877-322-8228.

It's important to go through your reports carefully to identify errors, such as loan or credit card accounts in your name that you did not authorize (and are likely to be fraudulent) or incorrect payment histories or account balances. Some mistakes can significantly lower your credit scores, which lenders often use in deciding on loan applications and interest rates.

"It's best to order copies of your credit report from each of the three main credit bureaus because an error that appears on one report might not appear on another," said Heather St. Germain, a Senior Consumer Affairs Specialist at the FDIC. "That way, if the bank you eventually apply to only uses one of your three reports, and it's one with an error, you'll have an opportunity to get that corrected before you apply."

If you do find an error on your free annual credit report from a credit bureau, contact the company to dispute the information. Once a credit bureau receives your complaint, it has 45 days to finish its investigation. Generally, consumers can file disputes with the credit bureau online, by phone or through the mail. A credit counseling service can help here, too. You may also contact the creditor directly because it can provide updated or corrected information to the credit bureau at your request.

Sometimes consumers have difficulty ensuring that erroneous information is corrected or removed from their credit reports. If you've tried to resolve the issue on your own without success, you can turn to the appropriate federal regulator for help.

If the problem is with a bank and you're not sure which federal regulator to contact (remember that the FDIC is not the primary regulator for all of the institutions it insures), you can call the FDIC toll-free at 877-ASK-FDIC (877-275-3342) or use an online directory of insured banks. (For help with a problem involving a credit bureau or a nonbank creditor (such as a finance company or a retail store), you can submit a complaint to the Consumer Financial Protection Bureau.

Shop around. Before submitting an application, it's important to get the best deal you can by researching the terms and conditions of different loans and credit cards offered by your bank and a few competitors. Think about the type of loan you need (for example, a fixed– or an adjustable–rate loan) and be realistic about what you can afford. Know the fees that may be assessed and what would trigger them.

Keep in mind that a loan or credit card may seem like a good deal on the surface, but a closer look at the fine print may reveal that it is not the best option for you. One of the most important things to remember: Be clear on whether an attractive interest rate being advertised is locked in or if it's an introductory offer that may increase in the future.

135

Also be aware that when you apply for a loan or a credit card a record of that "inquiry" will show up on your credit report. "Because too many inquires may hurt your credit score, it's best to only submit applications for credit products that you think will meet your needs," said St. Germain.

The Equal Credit Opportunity Act [ECOA]

The Equal Credit Opportunity Act [ECOA], 15 U.S.C. 1691 et seq. prohibits creditors from discriminating against credit applicants on the basis of race, color, religion, national origin, sex, marital status, age, because an applicant receives income from a public assistance program, or because an applicant has in good faith exercised any right under the Consumer Credit Protection Act.

(Source: "The Equal Credit Opportunity Act," U.S. Department of Justice (DOJ).)

Your Mortgage: Tips For Finding, Managing A Home Loan

Buying a home is one of the most significant decisions a consumer will ever make. Given what has occurred in the housing market during the past few years, consumers need to be well-informed when considering and managing a mortgage. "It's important to thoroughly think through all the aspects of a mortgage, even if you have not yet applied for one," said Jonathan Miller, Deputy Director in the FDIC's Division of Depositor and Consumer Protection.

These tips may help you navigate the process, from preparing to be a homeowner to making your final payment.

Considering A Home Purchase

Think about what you can afford to spend on a mortgage and other living expenses. Based on your savings and your budget, ask yourself how much you can devote to monthly loan payments as well as related costs such as real estate taxes, condo or homeowners association fees, insurance (which may include mortgage insurance if you make a down payment of less than 20 percent), and home maintenance. The answers will help you determine whether to buy a home, how much to pay, and what type of mortgage will meet your needs.

Also make sure that after you make your home payments you will have a cushion of savings and income for other purposes. "It's important to keep in mind other financial goals and obligations you may have, such as saving for retirement or a child's education," said Glenn Gimble, an FDIC Senior Policy Analyst.

Order a free copy of your credit report before you apply for a mortgage. Review the report carefully to verify its accuracy and dispute any errors. Errors in your credit report may affect your credit score, and higher credit scores can mean lower interest rates. To order a free copy of your credit report from each of the three major credit bureaus every 12 months, and to purchase your credit score, visit www.AnnualCreditReport.com or call toll-free 877-322-8228.

If you have questions about your readiness for a mortgage, consider speaking with a reputable housing counselor. "A good housing counselor can help potential borrowers prepare for homeownership," said FDIC Policy Analyst Matt Homer.

Looking For A Mortgage

Stick to your budget. "Borrow only what you can comfortably afford to pay," said Elizabeth Khalil, an FDIC Senior Policy Analyst. "Even if you are approved for a higher loan amount, consider borrowing less. You'll save money in interest payments, plus you can avoid overextending yourself."

Make sure your mortgage loan originator is registered with the government.

Shop for a mortgage that meets your needs, and don't be afraid to negotiate. "Lenders are required by law to provide important information to help you understand mortgage-related offers and compare multiple options," noted Luke Brown, an Associate Director in the FDIC's Division of Depositor and Consumer Protection (DCP). "We urge you to review these documents carefully and ask any questions that you have."

It's especially important to remember that nearly all of the terms of a mortgage, such as the interest rate and fees, are negotiable and lenders may not initially offer you the best package.

As you shop around, compare multiple options and scenarios and consider the following:

- Fees can vary widely from lender to lender. In addition, you may be able to purchase "points" to reduce your interest rate. Points have to be paid at the loan closing ("settlement").

- With interest rates currently at low levels, consider a fixed-rate loan even if an adjustable-rate mortgage (ARM) offers a slightly lower rate at first. If you are considering an ARM, ask the lender how high the rate may rise. Lenders also may offer variations that start with low payments and increase to much higher ones, with names such as interest-only loans, hybrid mortgages and balloon payment loans. These loans can carry significant risks for borrowers if they can't make the new, higher payments.

137

- The annual percentage rate (APR) represents the overall cost of the loan as a yearly rate and incorporates the interest rate as well as other costs, such as upfront points. "The APR is the fully-loaded price tag that conveys the total cost of a loan," says FDIC Senior Policy Analyst Kathleen Keest. "But keep in mind that if you are considering an adjustable-rate mortgage, the APR may not be as useful since it can change over time."

Review all loan documents carefully. Within three days of applying for a mortgage, your lender must provide you a "Good Faith Estimate" of costs and additional disclosures of key loan terms. Also, before you go to sign the loan documents at settlement, the lender must provide the actual fees, which you can compare to what you received in the Good Faith Estimate.

When loan documents are provided at settlement, review them to be sure that the terms accurately reflect the agreement you made with your lender. Only then should you sign.

Managing Your Mortgage

Establish a system for making your payments on time. Good choices may be automatic payments from your bank account or online bill paying.

Build a rainy-day fund. You may be able to rely on that to make mortgage payments if you fall on tough times.

If possible, consider paying off your mortgage faster. Doing so will reduce future interest costs and save you money. Consider adding extra money to each mortgage payment to reduce principal.

Carefully review all correspondence from your lender or servicer. If your loan is sold to a new servicer, for example, your new servicer will notify you where to send your mortgage payment.

Keep up with insurance payments and respond quickly to any notices regarding a lapse of coverage. If you fail to obtain required insurance or your policy expires, lenders may take out "force-placed" insurance on your behalf and pass along the cost, which is generally very high. But you can still obtain your own less-costly insurance policy so that the bank can cancel its force-placed policy.

If you have questions or concerns about home insurance and you need some guidance, consider starting with your state or local consumer affairs office or your state's insurance department.

Always be on guard against mortgage-related scams. Fraud artists typically make false promises to erase a bad credit history or rescue a home from foreclosure. But these claims often prove too good to be true. Look at these offers with a critical eye, and don't hesitate to seek assistance before committing to anything. Here, too, consider contacting your state or local consumer affairs department.

If you're struggling to make mortgage payments, immediately contact your loan servicer, perhaps with the help of a housing counselor, to discuss your options to stay in your home and avoid foreclosure.

Chapter 21

Credit Reports And Credit Scores

People sometimes confuse the words *debt* and *credit* because they are both connected to borrowing money. *Credit* is your ability to borrow money if you want a loan or mortgage. Debt is the money you owe when you take on a loan.

When you use your credit and have loans to pay, your track record in making your payments becomes part of your *credit report*. A credit report is a consumer report that looks at some of your bill paying history, public record information, and a record of your applications for credit. Your credit reports show information about how you have used credit, such as how much credit you have, how much of your available credit you are using, whether you have made your payments on time, and whether anyone has sent a delinquent (late) debt you owe to a debt collector.

Credit scores are calculated using the information in your credit report, and many lenders use them to decide how much money they can lend you and how much interest to charge.

Why Do Credit Reports And Scores Matter?

Some people say credit reports and scores don't matter to them, because they never plan to get a loan. But many different people and businesses use reports and scores to make decisions about you.

- A bank or credit card will use them to decide whether to give you a loan or offer you a credit card.

About This Chapter: This chapter includes text excerpted from "Your Money, Your Goals: A Financial Empowerment Toolkit For Community Volunteers," Consumer Financial Protection Bureau (CFPB), April 2015.

- A credit card company may use them to decide what interest rate you will pay on your future charges if you are approved.

- A landlord may use your reports or scores to determine whether to rent an apartment to you.

- In many states, an insurance company may use your reports or scores to determine whether to give you insurance coverage and the rates you will pay for coverage.

- Other service providers, like cell phone and utilities companies, may use them to screen you for deposit levels and cost of service.

- A potential employer may use your reports to determine whether you will get a job or a security clearance for a job. (**Note:** According to the credit reporting agencies, credit scores are not used by employers. Instead, a special version of the credit report is used by employers. Some states do not allow employers to use these reports in their hiring decisions unless credit history is relevant to the job's duties.)

- An existing employer may use your reports to determine whether you will get or keep a security clearance.

Having a positive credit history and good credit scores can open doors for you. Not having a positive credit history or good credit scores can create obstacles for you and end up costing you more money in terms of the price you will pay for loans, credit cards, and other services.

That's why it's important to pay bills on time and pay attention to what's in your credit report. The score is calculated based on the information in the report—so at least once a year, take the time to make sure the information in your report is accurate.

What Is In A Credit Report?

Companies collect information about consumers from many sources, some of which are called information furnishers. Credit reporting agencies organize this information into reports and sell these reports to businesses so they can make decisions about you. The biggest nationwide credit reporting agencies or credit bureaus that make credit reports include Equifax, Experian, and TransUnion. Each of these companies is likely to have a file on you. Your files at all three are likely to be *similar,* but there may be differences.

A credit report contains five sections. These sections include:

- **Header/identifying information**—This includes your name and current address, as well as other information that can be used to distinguish or trace your identity, either by itself, like your Social Security number, or when combined with other personal information, including date and place of birth. This information may not be complete—all of the jobs you have held, for example, may not be listed. But what is listed should be accurate. A credit report does not include some personal information such as race or ethnicity.

- **Public record information**—This section includes public record data of a financial nature, including consumer bankruptcies, judgments, and state and federal tax liens. Records of arrests and convictions generally do not appear on your credit file, but other types of consumer reporting agencies, such as employment background screening agencies, often include them. Other public records that usually do not appear in credit reports are marriage records, adoptions, and records of civil suits that have not resulted in judgments.

- **Collection agency account information**—This section will show if you have or have had any accounts with a collection agency and the status of those accounts.

- **Credit account information**—This section may include accounts you have now or that you had before with creditors. This may include:

  - The company name

  - Account number

  - Date opened

  - Last activity

  - Type of account and status

  - Date closed if the account is no longer open

  - Credit limit

  - Items as of date (any amount currently owed and whether you are current or late

  - Whether you have a past due amount and the number of payments that were 30, 60, and 90 days late.

  - Whether the account was charged off

  - The date information was reported to the credit bureau.

- **Some accounts may not be listed,** especially older accounts or those you have closed. So there may be inconsistencies across credit files and credit reporting agencies in the contents of this section. It is important to make sure what is listed, however, does or did belong to you.

- **Inquiries made to your account**—Companies look at your credit report when you apply for credit, when they review your account, or when they offer you a special promotional rate. When you apply for credit and a lender reviews your credit report, it is listed as an "inquiry" on your report. You will see promotional inquiries, periodic reviews of your credit history by one of your creditors, and your requests for a copy of your report when you obtain your own report, but these aren't listed as an "inquiry" when your report is provided to others.

- Consumer reporting agencies collect this information and sell it to other businesses, which use it to make decisions about you. How do they use this information to make decisions? Businesses that use this information believe that how you have handled credit in the past is a good predictor of how you will handle it in the future. If you have struggled with managing your credit in the past (especially the recent past), they believe you are likely to struggle again.

Negative Information

In general, negative information can be reported to those who request your credit report for only a specified period of time—seven years for most items. A bankruptcy can stay on your credit report for 10 years, and certain other court records can be reported on your credit report for longer than seven years. For civil suits and judgments, as well as arrest records, the information can be reported on your credit report for seven years or for the duration allowed by the statute of limitations, whichever is longer. For criminal convictions, there's no time limit. There is no legal limit to the length of time that positive information can stay on your credit report.

Negative Information In A Credit Report

Negative information in a credit report can include public records—tax liens, judgments, bankruptcies—that provide insight into your financial status and obligations. Bankruptcies can be kept on your report for up to 10 years, and unpaid tax liens for 15 years.

(Source: "Credit Reports And Scores" USA.gov.)

Even though consumer reporting agency cannot include information that is beyond the limits provided in the Fair Credit Reporting Act (FCRA) in most consumer credit reports, they may continue to keep the information in your file. Why? Because there is no time limit in terms of reporting information (positive or negative) when you are:

- Applying for credit of $150,000 or more

- Applying for life insurance with a face value of $150,000 or more

- Applying for a job with an annual salary of $75,000 or more

Disputing Errors On Credit Reports

If you find something wrong on your credit report, you should dispute it. You may contact both the credit reporting agency (most often TransUnion, Equifax, or Experian) and the company that provided the incorrect information (the information furnisher).

You will need to explain what you think is wrong and why. If you have evidence (a receipt for payment, copy of a canceled check, etc.) you can include a copy of this and a copy of your credit report with the incorrect information highlighted.

If you submit your dispute in writing rather than online, never send original documents—only send copies. You may want to send this information with your letter using certified mail *return receipt requested*. This will give you notification of when the credit reporting agency and information furnisher receive your dispute letter. The credit reporting agency generally has 30–45 days to respond to your request from the time it receives it. You can also submit a complaint to the Consumer Financial Protection Bureau (CFPB).

What Are Credit Scores?

Credit scores sum up key pieces of your credit history in a number at a moment in time—like a photograph. Companies that make credit scores each use their own complicated mathematical formulas to do this. The information used in this formula comes from your credit reports—such as information on the number and type of loans and other forms of credit you have used and are currently using, whether you're making your payments on time, and whether you're 30 days or more late (delinquent) on any of these accounts. The formulas are created by looking at how other people whose credit file looks like yours have paid their bills over time.

Credit scores provide a standardized way for businesses that offer credit to understand the risk that you may have difficulty paying back a loan. The current common credit scoring formulas are designed to predict whether someone is likely to fall behind on loan payments for 90 days or more. For these scores, the higher the number, the less risky you are predicted to be.

These scores can make it easier for businesses to make decisions about whether to offer you credit and how much interest they will charge. Without scores, they would have to take more time to read and interpret both your credit application and your credit report.

There are multiple companies that calculate and sell credit scores. Credit scores vary because different score companies use the information stored by the three large credit bureaus in different ways. Scores produced by different companies may also vary because they don't always share the same score range. Sometimes the three large credit bureaus store slightly different information used to calculate the score, which can also contribute to differences.

As a result, you have more than one credit score. Each company generates its own scores, and they may differ from each other, sometimes significantly. And, each company that creates credit scores generates different scores for different kinds of users—they may sell educational scores to consumers, but provide different scores to lenders. This can make deciding which credit score to purchase, if any, confusing for consumers.

How Are Scores Calculated?

FICO scores (calculated using formulas made by Fair Isaac Corporation) are the most commonly used scores. These scores range from 300–850. A FICO score above 700 is considered good by most businesses, and the scores considered the best are 750 and higher.

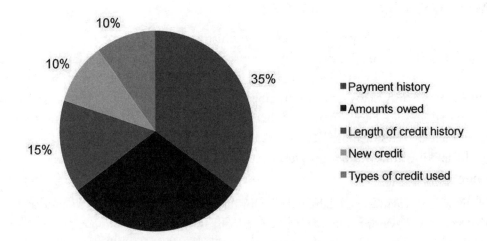

Figure 21.1. What Goes Into FICO Scores?

The actual way that FICO scores (and other scores) are calculated is considered a trade secret. But FICO makes some information available to the public on what goes into its scores.

Payment history tracks whether you are paying your bills on time and as agreed. This is the biggest factor in your FICO Scores. Paying bills late, not paying bills at all, and having bills that go to collections will cause your scores to drop. The impact on a score from a single late or missed payment decreases over time. Paying your bills on time can help increase your score, and debts that go to collections and to judgment will cause it to fall.

Amounts owed include the amount you are paying down on loan balances as agreed. It also includes your credit utilization rate. Your credit utilization rate is how much of your available credit you are using. As your revolving balance relative to the credit limit increases, your score will drop.

Length of credit history is the next factor that impacts your scores. Your score increases the longer you have a credit history. The more established credit accounts you have, the "thicker" your credit file will be. This is a credit record with strong evidence of how you use credit and your payment behavior. If you have just one or only a few credit accounts, you will have a "thin file."

New credit is tracked by measuring your inquiries for credit. If you have too many inquiries, the model interprets this to mean you have a high demand for credit, which may be an indicator of risk, and your scores may drop. When you are shopping for credit, however, you can compare offers for a home, car, or student loan. FICO and most other models give you a short window of time—generally 30 days—when multiple inquiries for the same type of product will be considered as only one inquiry. And your score is not affected at all when companies "prescreen" you for credit or when you check your credit report yourself (such as at annualcreditreport.com).

Finally, **types of credit used** are considered. Your FICO scores increase if you have both credit cards (revolving credit) and loans (installment credit such as a mortgage or car loan) in good standing. Generally, it is considered a positive to have a mortgage, an auto loan, and not too many credit cards.

Scores provided by VantageScore, another score provider, range from 300–850. Scores calculated with its earlier models ranged from 501–990. Like the FICO Scores, the actual method used to calculate VantageScore credit scores is secret. But VantageScore provides information to the public like the graphic below, which explains how your credit history, credit usage, and other actions can influence the scores it calculates.

Credit Utilization Rate

If you want to maintain your credit score, many experts advise keeping your use of revolving credit low in relation to your credit limit.

That's because credit scoring formulas penalize you for using too much of the credit you have available to you. This means your credit score may drop if you use more than a certain percentage of the revolving credit you have available to you.

For example, you may have a high percentage of your credit limit charged on a card, and you want to qualify for better rates on new credit. In this case, you may want to lower the amount you are revolving from month to month by paying down your credit card before you apply for new credit.

The easiest way to understand credit utilization is through an example:

If someone had a credit card with a $5,000 credit limit, and she has charged $3,500 on this card, her credit utilization rate is calculated as follows:

$3,500 (amount charged to credit card) divided by $5,000 (credit limit) = .7 or 70 percent

If she sets a goal of lowering her revolving utilization of this card to 25 percent or less, her revolving balance should be no more than:

$5,000 (the credit limit) multiplied by .25 (25%) = $1,250

Does this mean that only the unpaid balance is counted toward the credit utilization rate? The answer is no. If at any time during the month your total charges are higher than the limit the credit scoring model is based on, you run the risk of lowering your credit score.

Chapter 22

Your Access To Free Credit Reports

The Fair Credit Reporting Act (FCRA) requires each of the nationwide credit reporting companies—Equifax, Experian, and TransUnion—to provide you with a free copy of your credit report, at your request, once every 12 months. The FCRA promotes the accuracy and privacy of information in the files of the nation's credit reporting companies. The Federal Trade Commission (FTC), the nation's consumer protection agency, enforces the FCRA with respect to credit reporting companies.

A credit report includes information on where you live, how you pay your bills, and whether you've been sued or have filed for bankruptcy. Nationwide credit reporting companies sell the information in your report to creditors, insurers, employers, and other businesses that use it to evaluate your applications for credit, insurance, employment, or renting a home.

Here are the details about your rights under the FCRA, which established the free annual credit report program.

Q: How do I order my free report?

A: The three nationwide credit reporting companies have set up a central website, a toll-free telephone number, and a mailing address through which you can order your free annual report. You may order your reports from each of the three nationwide credit reporting companies at the same time, or you can order your report from each of the companies one at a time. The law allows you to order one free copy of your report from each of the nationwide credit reporting companies every 12 months.

About This Chapter: This chapter includes text excerpted from "Free Credit Reports," Federal Trade Commission (FTC), March 2013.

Request Your Free Credit Report

Online: Visit AnnualCreditReport.com

By Phone: Call 877-322-8228. Deaf and hard of hearing consumers can access the TTY service by calling 711 and referring the Relay Operator to 800-821-7232.

By Mail: Complete the Annual Credit Report Request Form and mail it to:

Annual Credit Report Request Service

P.O. Box 105281

Atlanta, GA 30348-5281

(Source: "Credit Reports And Scores" USA.gov.)

A Warning About "Imposter" Websites

Only one website is authorized to fill orders for the free annual credit report you are entitled to under law—annualcreditreport.com. Other websites that claim to offer "free credit reports," "free credit scores," or "free credit monitoring" are not part of the legally mandated free annual credit report program. In some cases, the "free" product comes with strings attached. For example, some sites sign you up for a supposedly "free" service that converts to one you have to pay for after a trial period. If you don't cancel during the trial period, you may be unwittingly agreeing to let the company start charging fees to your credit card.

Some "imposter" sites use terms like "free report" in their names; others have (uniform resource locators) URLs that purposely misspell annualcreditreport.com in the hope that you will mistype the name of the official site. Some of these "imposter" sites direct you to other sites that try to sell you something or collect your personal information.

Annualcreditreport.com and the nationwide credit reporting companies will not send you an e-mail asking for your personal information. If you get an e-mail, see a pop-up ad, or get a phone call from someone claiming to be from annualcreditreport.com or any of the three nationwide credit reporting companies, do not reply or click on any link in the message. It's probably a scam. Forward any such e-mail to the FTC at spam@uce.gov.

Q: What information do I need to provide to get my free report?

A: You need to provide your name, address, Social Security number, and date of birth. If you have moved in the last two years, you may have to provide your previous address. To maintain the security of your file, each nationwide credit reporting company may ask you for some information that only you would know, like the amount of your monthly mortgage payment. Each company may ask you for different information because the information each has in your file may come from different sources.

Q: Why do I want a copy of my credit report?

A: Your credit report has information that affects whether you can get a loan—and how much you will have to pay to borrow money. You want a copy of your credit report to:

- make sure the information is accurate, complete, and up-to-date before you apply for a loan for a major purchase like a house or car, buy insurance, or apply for a job.

- help guard against identity theft. That's when someone uses your personal information—like your name, your Social Security number, or your credit card number—to commit fraud. Identity thieves may use your information to open a new credit card account in your name. Then, when they don't pay the bills, the delinquent account is reported on your credit report. Inaccurate information like that could affect your ability to get credit, insurance, or even a job.

Q: How long does it take to get my report after I order it?

A: If you request your report online at annualcreditreport.com, you should be able to access it immediately. If you order your report by calling toll-free 877-322-8228, your report will be processed and mailed to you within 15 days. If you order your report by mail using the Annual Credit Report Request Form, your request will be processed and mailed to you within 15 days of receipt.

Whether you order your report online, by phone, or by mail, it may take longer to receive your report if the nationwide credit reporting company needs more information to verify your identity.

Q: Are there any other situations where I might be eligible for a free report?

A: Under federal law, you're entitled to a free report if a company takes adverse action against you, such as denying your application for credit, insurance, or employment, and you ask for your report within 60 days of receiving notice of the action. The notice will give you the name, address, and phone number of the credit reporting company. You're also entitled to one free report a year if you're unemployed and plan to look for a job within 60 days; if you're on welfare; or if your report is inaccurate because of fraud, including identity theft. Otherwise, a credit reporting company may charge you a reasonable amount for another copy of your report within a 12-month period.

To buy a copy of your report, contact:

- Equifax: 800-685-1111; equifax.com

- Experian: 888-397-3742; experian.com

- TransUnion: 800-916-8800; transunion.com

Q: Should I order a report from each of the three nationwide credit reporting companies?

A: It's up to you. Because nationwide credit reporting companies get their information from different sources, the information in your report from one company may not reflect all, or the same, information in your reports from the other two companies. That's not to say that the information in any of your reports is necessarily inaccurate; it just may be different.

Q: Should I order my reports from all three of the nationwide credit reporting companies at the same time?

A: You may order one, two, or all three reports at the same time, or you may stagger your requests. It's your choice. Some financial advisors say staggering your requests during a 12-month period may be a good way to keep an eye on the accuracy and completeness of the information in your reports.

Q: What if I find errors—either inaccuracies or incomplete information—in my credit report?

A: Under the FCRA, both the credit reporting company and the information provider (that is, the person, company, or organization that provides information about you to a consumer reporting company) are responsible for correcting inaccurate or incomplete information in your report. To take full advantage of your rights under this law, contact the credit reporting company and the information provider.

- Tell the credit reporting company, in writing, what information you think is inaccurate.

   Credit reporting companies must investigate the items in question—usually within 30 days—unless they consider your dispute frivolous. They also must forward all the relevant data you provide about the inaccuracy to the organization that provided the information. After the information provider receives notice of a dispute from the credit reporting company, it must investigate, review the relevant information, and report the results back to the credit reporting company. If the information provider finds the disputed information is inaccurate, it must notify all three nationwide credit reporting companies so they can correct the information in your file.

When the investigation is complete, the credit reporting company must give you the written results and a free copy of your report if the dispute results in a change. (This free report does not count as your annual free report.) If an item is changed or deleted, the credit reporting company cannot put the disputed information back in your file unless the information provider verifies that it is accurate and complete. The credit reporting company also must send you written notice that includes the name, address, and phone number of the information provider.

- Tell the creditor or other information provider in writing that you dispute an item. Many providers specify an address for disputes. If the provider reports the item to a credit reporting company, it must include a notice of your dispute. And if you are correct— that is, if the information is found to be inaccurate—the information provider may not report it again.

Q: What can I do if the credit reporting company or information provider won't correct the information I dispute?

A: If an investigation doesn't resolve your dispute with the credit reporting company, you can ask that a statement of the dispute be included in your file and in future reports. You also can ask the credit reporting company to provide your statement to anyone who received a copy of your report in the recent past. You can expect to pay a fee for this service.

If you tell the information provider that you dispute an item, a notice of your dispute must be included anytime the information provider reports the item to a credit reporting company.

Q: Can anyone else get a copy of my credit report?

A: The FCRA specifies who can access your credit report. Creditors, insurers, employers, and other businesses that use the information in your report to evaluate your applications for credit, insurance, employment, or renting a home are among those that have a legal right to access your report.

Q: Can my employer get my credit report?

A: Your employer can get a copy of your credit report only if you agree. A credit reporting company may not provide information about you to your employer, or to a prospective employer, without your written consent.

For More Information

The FTC works for the consumer to prevent fraudulent, deceptive, and unfair business practices in the marketplace and to provide information to help consumers spot, stop, and avoid them. To file a complaint, visit ftc.gov/complaint or call 877-FTC-HELP (877-382-4357). The FTC enters Internet, telemarketing, identity theft, and other fraud-related complaints into Consumer Sentinel, a secure online database available to hundreds of civil and criminal law enforcement agencies in the United States and abroad.

Report Scams

If you believe you've responded to a scam, file a complaint with:

- the FTC
- your state Attorney General

Chapter 23

Loan Basics

There are many types of loans, such as student loans, vehicle loans, and business loans. Consumer protections may vary by loan type. .

Business Loans

Business loans are not subject to most federal consumer protection laws and regulations. However, the Federal Deposit Insurance Corporation (FDIC), along with other federal and state financial regulatory agencies, issued a statement on prudent lending to small businesses titled, "Meeting the Credit Needs of Creditworthy Small Business Borrowers." The FDIC also reviews industry practices regarding the accessibility of credit and to ensure the availability of financing to creditworthy small business borrowers. If you have a question or issue concerning a business loan involving an FDIC-supervised institution, please contact the FDIC by submitting the Business Assistance Form.

Consumer Protections Available

Certain types of loans are covered by consumer protection laws and regulations but others are not. For example, commercial and agricultural loan transactions are not subject to most federal consumer protection laws and regulations. Generally, consumer protection laws cover

About This Chapter: Text in this chapter begins with excerpts from "Consumer Protection Topics—Loans," Federal Deposit Insurance Corporation (FDIC), March 3, 2017; Text under the heading "Student Loans" is excerpted from "Consumer Protection Topics—Student Loans," Federal Deposit Insurance Corporation (FDIC), March 3, 2017.

loans established primarily for personal, family, or household purposes. Some common consumer protections include:

- Lenders must show you the cost of credit as a dollar amount and an annual percentage rate (APR) and disclose terms in a meaningful and uniform manner.

- Debt collectors may not use abusive, unfair, or deceptive practices to collect money from you.

- Your lender, servicer, or debt collector must provide accurate information to credit reporting agencies. Credit reporting agencies must also report accurate information you. Once a year, you may request a free copy of your credit report from each agency by telephone, mail, or at annualcreditreport.com.

- Your lender may not discriminate in any aspect of a credit transaction based on race, religion, national origin, sex, marital status, age, if you receive public assistance, or if you exercise your rights under the Consumer Credit Protection Act (CCPA). (This protection also applies to business loans.)

Student Loans

Going to school can be expensive. Many students and their families use federal or private student loans to help pay for education after high school.

Federal student loans come from the U.S. Department of Education (ED). These include:

- Direct Subsidized Loans—made to eligible students who demonstrate a financial need to help cover the costs of school;

- Direct Unsubsidized Loans—made to eligible students regardless of their financial need;

- Direct PLUS Loans—made to graduate and professional students as well as parents of dependent undergraduate students to assist with paying for costs not covered by other financial aid;

- Direct Consolidation Loans—allow students to combine all of their eligible federal student loans into one loan with one loan servicer; and,

- Perkins Loans—made by schools to students with exceptional financial need.

These loans offer important benefits. For example, if you have a Direct Subsidized Loan, the federal government will pay the interest on the loan while you are in school. In addition, the interest rates on federal loans typically are fixed, meaning you will not be surprised by a potential increase in your loan's interest rate. Federal loans also allow you to make payments based on your income, defer payments under certain circumstances (such as if you go back to school), and may be forgiven after ten years if you pursue a career in public service.

Private student loans are made by a lender, such as a bank, credit union, or other financial institution. Generally, the lender will consider several factors when reviewing your application for private student loans, including your credit history and whether you have a co-signor. Private loans offer variable interest rates, so the interest rate may rise during the life of the loan. These loans also often have fewer options to reduce or postpone payments and less flexible payment options.

Consumer Protections Available

Many consumer protection laws apply to student loans. Some of these include:

- Lenders must show you the cost of credit as a dollar amount and an annual percentage rate (APR) and also disclose terms in a meaningful and uniform manner.

- Debt collectors may not use abusive, unfair, or deceptive practices to collect money from you.

- Your lender, servicer, or debt collector must provide accurate information to credit reporting agencies. Credit reporting agencies must also report accurate information to you. Once per year, you may request a free copy of your credit report from each agency by telephone, mail, or at annualcreditreport.com.

- Your lender may not discriminate in any aspect of a credit transaction based on race, religion, national origin, sex, marital status, age, whether you receive public assistance, or whether you exercise your rights under the Consumer Credit Protection Act.

- Schools must allow you to choose how you want to receive any financial aid, which may include federal student loans, that is over and above tuition and fees paid directly to the school. (These amounts are called credit balances and are generally used to pay for living expenses.) If a school delivers funds to you electronically using a debit or prepaid card, it must limit the fees you can be charged for balance inquiries and automated teller machine (ATM) access.

Tips

If you are in school or plan to be in school:

- Complete the *Free Application for Federal Student Aid* (FAFSA®). Visit fafsa.gov to find the deadline for applying and to complete your application. You must complete the FAFSA® to qualify for federal and state grants, loans, and work-study.

- Calculate how much you need to borrow and determine what your monthly payment will be. Your anticipated costs (tuition, textbooks, housing, food, transportation) minus your education savings, family contributions, income from work-study or a job, scholarships, and/or grants will help determine how much you may need. Even if you are approved for a larger loan, limit what you borrow in order to limit your future monthly payment.

- Keep track of the total amount you have borrowed and consider reducing it. For example, if your loan accrues interest while you are in school, you may be able to make interest payments while you are still enrolled. This can reduce how much you pay overall. You could also repay some of the principal (the amount borrowed) before the repayment period officially begins.

If you are out of school:

- Visit the U.S. Department of Education's (ED) National Student Loan Data System (NSLDS) to determine what type of federal loans you hold, how much you owe, and what entity services your loans.

- See if you are eligible to make reduced payments based on your income. The ED offers a Repayment Estimator that can help you to determine if you are eligible, as well as complete information on income-driven repayment plans.

- Determine if you qualify for loan forgiveness, cancellation or discharge. You may be eligible for forgiveness after a number of payments if you are a teacher, if you work in certain public service professions, or if your school closes while you are enrolled. Visit the U.S. Department of Education's (ED) Loan Forgiveness page for more information.

- Make your loan payments on time. Student loans are typically reported to credit bureaus, so paying on time can help build a good credit history, and paying late can harm your credit history. To help you stay on schedule, consider having your payments automatically deducted from your bank account or arranging for e-mail or text message reminders.

- Look into refinancing opportunities. You may be able to obtain a lower interest rate and even consolidate multiple loans of the same type into one loan. However, be aware that if you refinance a federal loan into either a private loan or into a different kind of federal loan, you may lose important benefits (such as loan forgiveness for entering public service).

Chapter 24

Subsidized And Unsubsidized Loans

Since college is so expensive, most students can only afford it by borrowing money in the form of loans. Low-interest student loans are available from the U.S. government to help eligible students cover the costs associated with higher education. As of 2016, more than 44 million Americans had student loan debt totaling nearly $1.3 trillion. About 40 percent of these loans were used to pay for graduate or professional degrees.

> **Did You Know...**
> The average 2016 college graduate had $37,172 in student loan debt, an increase of 6 percent from the previous year, and faced at least a decade of loan payments averaging $350 per month.

The U.S. Department of Education (ED) offers two main types of loans through its Federal Student Aid program: subsidized loans and unsubsidized loans. A subsidy is a form of monetary or financial support. In a subsidized loan, the U.S. government contributes money to reduce the interest cost for student borrowers who demonstrate financial need. Although unsubsidized loans are available regardless of students' financial circumstances, borrowers are responsible for paying back the full amount of the loan, plus interest, without financial support from the federal government.

All first-time borrowers in the federal government's student loan program are required to undergo entrance counseling before they can receive their money. Since taking out a loan is a serious, long-term financial commitment, entrance counseling provides borrowers with

About This Chapter: "Subsidized And Unsubsidized Loans And Entrance Counseling," © 2017 Omnigraphics.

important information about their legal rights and responsibilities, repayment options, and the consequences of failing to repay their loans.

Comparing Subsidized And Unsubsidized Loans

Federal Direct Subsidized Loans, sometimes called Stafford Loans, are intended for low-income undergraduate students. They are not available to graduate students. Since subsidized loans are a form of need-based aid, you must qualify by submitting the *Free Application for Federal Student Aid* (FAFSA®) and demonstrating financial need. Your school's financial aid office determines the amount you are eligible to receive based on your FAFSA®, but the total cannot exceed your calculated financial need.

Subsidized loans have lower annual limits than unsubsidized loans. As of 2016, the limits were $3,500 for first-year college students, $4,500 for second-year students, and $5,500 for third-year students and beyond, with a cumulative limit per student of $23,000. In addition, subsidized loans issued after July 1, 2013, have a time limit—known as the maximum eligibility period—of 150 percent of the published length of your academic program. The time limit is 3 years for a 2-year associate's degree program, for instance, and 6 years for a 4-year bachelor's degree program. You are no longer eligible to receive federally subsidized loans once the maximum eligibility period expires, although the time limit may be extended if you change to a longer academic program.

The main benefit of federally subsidized loans is that the government pays the interest on the loan under the following circumstances:

- while you are enrolled at least half-time at a four-year college or university, community college, or trade, career, or technical school;

- during periods of deferment or forbearance, when you are eligible to pause or postpone making loan payments because you go back to school, serve in the military or Peace Corps, or suffer a serious illness or financial hardship; and

- during a six-month grace period following your graduation.

Federal Direct Unsubsidized Loans do not offer any government subsidies to help cover interest costs. Instead, borrowers are responsible for paying the interest, which begins to accrue as soon as you receive your loan funds. Interest accumulates while you are in school, during the six-month grace period after graduation, and even if you receive a deferment.

Unsubsidized loans are not based on financial need, however, so it is easier to qualify. They are available to graduate as well as undergraduate students, and the annual loan limits are higher than subsidized loans. As of 2016, the limits were $5,500 for first-year undergraduate students and $9,500 for first-year graduate students. The limits increase for each additional year of schooling, with a cap of $31,000 per student. There is no maximum eligibility period for unsubsidized loans.

Subsidized and unsubsidized loans carry the same interest rates and similar fees. For the 2016–2017 academic year, the interest rate for both subsidized and unsubsidized undergraduate student loans was 3.76 percent, while the interest rate for unsubsidized graduate student loans was 5.31 percent. Both types of loans charged fees of slightly more than 1 percent of the loan amount. However, the fact that the government pays the interest on subsidized loans during your college years, the six-month grace period, and any deferments means that you should always repay unsubsidized loans first.

Entrance Counseling

All first-time recipients of federal student loans, whether subsidized or unsubsidized, are required to complete entrance counseling. This process must be completed before your school can disburse any of your loan funds. Depending on the school, you may attend an entrance counseling meeting in person at the financial aid office, pick up a packet of written materials to review at home, or get the information through an interactive, online program.

Taking out a loan is a significant, long-term financial obligation. Entrance counseling is intended to help you understand how the loan process works, the terms and conditions of your loan, and your legal rights and responsibilities as a borrower. The program also provides information about other financial resources that may be available to help pay for your education, as well as tips on budgeting and managing your college costs.

One of the most important topics discussed in entrance counseling is your obligation to repay your loans. Federal student loans must be repaid even if you do not finish your degree, are unhappy with the education you received, or cannot find a job in your field after graduation. Although your loan payments may be reduced or temporarily deferred if you encounter financial hardship or meet other requirements, federal student loan debts are not erased if you file for bankruptcy. There are only a few circumstances in which your student loan debts may be discharged or canceled, such as if you die or become permanently disabled.

In most cases, you are required to begin repaying your student loan six months after you graduate, leave school, or drop below half-time enrollment. Your loan servicer will contact you during this period to provide repayment instructions. Payments are usually due monthly for a period of 10–25 years, although there is no penalty for paying off the loan in advance.

Failure to repay a federal loan can have serious consequences, including collection charges, litigation, or seizure of a portion of your wages, Social Security payments, or income tax refunds. The negative credit reports associated with defaulting on a student loan can affect your ability to qualify for credit cards, car loans, or a mortgage. Therefore, it is important to understand the types of loans available and the terms and conditions associated with them in order to make smart choices about taking on debt to pay for college.

References

1. "Entrance Counseling," Federal Student Aid, U.S. Department of Education, 2017.

2. "Entrance Counseling For Federal Student Loans," Edvisor, 2017.

3. Sisolak, Paul. "What's The Difference Between Subsidized And Unsubsidized Student Loans?" Student Loan Hero, March 3, 2016.

4. "Subsidized And Unsubsidized Loans," Federal Student Aid, U.S. Department of Education, 2017.

Chapter 25

Beware Of Predatory Lending Practices

What Is Predatory Lending?

Predatory lending practices, broadly defined, are the fraudulent, deceptive, and unfair tactics some people use to dupe us into mortgage loans that we can't afford. Burdened with high mortgage debts, the victims of predatory lending can't spare the money to keep their houses in good repair. They strain just to keep up their mortgage payments. Often, the strain is too much. They succumb to foreclosure. Their houses have been taken or stolen from them.

Rundown and vacant houses, the inevitable result of predatory lending wreak havoc on neighborhoods. Property values fall. People move away. Once sturdy neighborhoods start to crack, then crumble. Something that has been so important for so many people lays in ruins. Everyone who lived in a neighborhood destroyed by predatory lending becomes a victim.

The United States Attorney's Office (USAO) has made combating predatory lending a priority. The Office is taking a comprehensive approach to addressing the problem of predatory lending through education, prosecution, and remediation.

Education. An educated consumer is the predatory lending syndicate's worst customer. Educated consumers know what loans are right for them and where to find them.

Prosecution. The Office has prosecuted and will continue to prosecute the worst predatory lenders. The Office can use your help. Pay attention to what is going on in your community. If something looks suspicious, check it out. Report it.

About This Chapter: Text beginning with the heading "What Is Predatory Lending?" is excerpted from "Predatory Lending," U.S. Department of Justice (DOJ), April 16, 2015; Text under the heading "Payday Loans And Cash Advances" is excerpted from "Credit, Loans And Debt," Consumer.gov, Federal Trade Commission (FTC), October 1, 2012.

Fair Lending Laws

Fair lending laws contain provisions to address predatory lending practices. Some examples follow:

- **Collateral or equity "stripping":** The practice of making loans that rely on the liquidation value of the borrower's home or other collateral rather than the borrower's ability to repay.

- **Inadequate disclosure:** The practice of failing to fully disclose or explain the true costs and risks of loan transactions.

- **Risky loan terms and structures:** The practice of making loans with terms or structures that make it more difficult or impossible for borrowers to reduce their indebtedness.

- **Padding or packing:** The practice of charging customers unearned, concealed, or unwarranted fees.

- **Flipping:** The practice of encouraging customers to frequently refinance mortgage loans solely for the purpose of earning loan-related fees.

- **Single-premium credit insurance:** The requirement to obtain life, disability, or unemployment insurance for which the consumer does not receive a net tangible financial benefit.

(Source: "Consumer Protection—Fair Lending," Office of Comptroller of the Currency (OCC), U.S. Department of the Treasury (USDT).)

Tips To Protect Your Home

Get help! There are scores of housing and credit counselors who can help you decide whether a loan is right for you.

Know your credit rating. Get your credit report. If you have credit trouble, fix it.

Trust your instincts. If it sounds too good, it probably isn't true. Many predatory lenders are slick salesmen. They know how to talk. They don't always tell you the whole truth. If a deal doesn't sound right to you, then don't do it.

Ask questions; demand answers. Predatory lenders will try to fool you by making your loan confusing. If you don't understand anything, ask. Demand an answer.

Read everything. Get all the loan documents before closing. Don't sign anything until you have read it. If there is something incorrect, fix it. If you're confused about something, ask.

Don't fall for a "bait and switch." If what you read in your loan papers is not what you wanted, expected, or agreed to, don't sign. Be prepared to walk out.

Learn about your loan. There are many organizations that produce publications that can be helpful.

Shop around. There are lots of people who may be willing to give you a loan. Most of them are honest, responsible people. Find them. Call as many banks as you can. Look in your newspaper's real estate section for advertisements. Go to the library and search the internet; try "mortgage," "mortgage rate," and "mortgage companies."

Take your time. A predatory lender will try to rush you so you can't ask questions. Take all the time you need to understand what your deal is.

Say "No." Don't let someone talk you into something you really don't want or need. Also, it's okay to change your mind.

Never let a contractor get a loan for you. If you are doing home improvements, a contractor may tell you that he can get a loan for you. **Don't let him.** Find the loan yourself; it will be cheaper.

Don't make final payment to a contractor until all the work is done. Some contractors may ask you to sign over checks to them or to sign so-called "completion certificates" before they finish the work on your house. Don't. Make sure you're happy with the work on your house before you give any money to a contractor.

Avoid prepayment penalties. If possible, don't take a loan that penalizes you for refinancing. You may get stuck in a loan that you can't get out of.

Don't lie. No matter what anyone else may tell you, it's not okay to lie on a form, even a little. If you get a loan based on false documents, you may be getting in over your head. You won't be able to afford the loan.

Report wrongdoing. If you learn that someone did something illegal, report it.

Red Flags

Aggressive solicitations. Whose idea was it to get this loan? Did someone sell it to you? Be wary of anyone who came to you trying to sell you a loan. If you need a loan, shop around for it yourself.

Loan flipping. Loan flipping is pressuring you to refinance your loan over and over. Before you refinance, make sure a new loan makes you better off. For instance, do not refinance a low-interest loan into one with a higher interest rate. See a housing counselor.

High fees. Look at your Good Faith Estimate of Costs and your settlement sheet. Do you know what each fee is for? If not, ask. If your total fees are more than 5 percent of your loan, that's probably too much.

Property taxes. If you don't save enough money to pay your tax bill, a predatory lender will try to lend you money for your taxes. You may want to have your taxes "escrowed." That means that you will put aside some money each month for your taxes.

Balloon Payments. A balloon payment is one very large payment you make at the end of the loan. Predatory lenders like balloon payments because they can tell you that your monthly payment is low. The problem is that you may not be able to make the payment and will need to refinance. You'll need a new loan with new fees and costs.

Consolidating debt. It's not always a good idea to pay off your credit cards with a mortgage loan. If you can't pay your credit cards, it's almost impossible for someone to take your house. If you consolidate, however, your house is collateral. Consolidating means you risk losing your house to pay your credit cards.

Payday Loans And Cash Advances

What Is A Payday Loan Or Cash Advance Loan?

A payday loan or a cash advance loan is a loan for a short time. You pay a fee to borrow the money, even if it is for a week or two.

A payday loan or cash advance loan can be very expensive. Before you get one of these loans, consider other ways to borrow.

What Are Some Other Ways To Borrow Money?

You might be able to borrow money from:

- family or friends

- a bank or credit union

- your credit card

You might ask for more time to pay your bills. You can talk to a credit counselor to get help.

What If I'm In The Military?

If you are in the military, the law protects you and your dependents. The law limits the interest rate on payday loans. The law also tells lenders to give you information about your rights and the cost of the loan. The military also offers financial help and help managing your money.

How Does A Payday Loan Or Cash Advance Loan Work?

• You give the lender a check for the amount of money you want to borrow plus a fee.

• The lender keeps your check and gives you cash less the fee they charge.

• On your next payday, you have to pay the lender in cash. You owe the amount you borrowed plus the fee.

How Much Do These Loans Cost?

A payday loan or cash advance loan can cost a lot. Even if you only borrow money for a week or two until you get your paycheck.

For Example

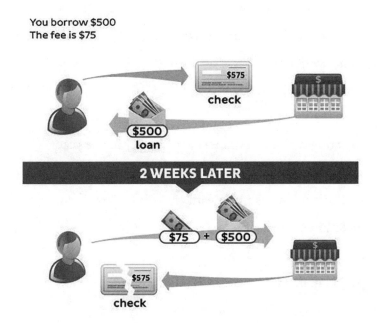

Figure 25.1. How A Payday Loan Works

• You borrow $500. The fee is $75

• You give the lender a check for $575.

• The lender keeps your check and gives you $500 in cash.

• After two weeks, you give the lender $575 in cash and you get your check back.

- The bottom line: You paid $75 to borrow $500 for two weeks.

How Do I Compare Costs?

Most loans have an annual percentage rate. The annual percentage rate is also called APR. The APR is how much it costs you to borrow money for one year. The APR on payday loans and cash advances is very high.

When you get a payday loan or cash advance loan, the lender must tell you the APR and the cost of the loan in dollars.

What Is An APR?

The annual percentage rate, or APR, is based on:

- the amount of money you borrow
- the monthly finance charge or interest rate
- how much you pay in fees
- how long you borrow the money

For Example

- You need to borrow $500. You will repay the money in one year.
- You compare the costs of borrowing that money:
- The bank or credit union has a loan with an APR of 7.5 percent
- You will pay $21 in interest
- A credit card has an APR of 20 percent
- You will pay $56 in interest
- A payday lender has an APR of 390 percent
- You will pay $1,518 in interest

What Happens If I Can't Pay The Lender The Money I Owe?

If you cannot pay the lender the money you owe, you borrow the money for two more weeks. This is called a "rollover," or "rolling over" the loan. To rollover the loan, you pay another fee. If you roll over the loan a few times, you will pay a lot to borrow the money. It becomes harder to get back to where you started.

For Example

- You borrow $500. You pay a $75 fee to get the money. But in two weeks you cannot repay the loan.

- You pay another $75 to rollover the loan. But in two more weeks, you still cannot repay the loan.

- Every two weeks, you pay another $75 fee. You might pay the lender more in fees than you first borrowed. But you would still owe the original $500.

Payday loans or cash advance loans are loans made for a short time, often two weeks. These loans can be very expensive.

What Should I Do Before I Get A Payday Loan Or A Cash Advance Loan?

Before you get one of these loans, consider other ways to borrow money:

- Can I get a loan from a bank or credit union?
- Can I get more time to pay my bills by talking with creditors or a credit counselor?
- Do I have any money saved that I can use?
- Can I borrow money from family or friends?
- Can I use a credit card instead?

How Do I Choose Which Way To Borrow Money?

Compare the costs, if you have more than one choice. For each choice, find out:

- what is the APR?
- what are the fees?
- how soon must I repay the money?
- what happens if I cannot repay?

Write the answers to these questions. Decide which choice is best for you.

I Decided To Get A Payday Loan. What Should I Do?

- ask the lender to tell you how much it will cost in dollars
- ask the lender to tell you the APR
- borrow only what you can pay back with your next paycheck

Service Members What To Do

If you are in the military, the law protects you and your dependents. The APR on payday loans cannot be more than 36 percent. The lender must give you documents that explain the cost of the loan and your rights.

Should I Get A Payday Loan Or Cash Advance Loan?

Even with these protections for service members, payday loans can be very expensive. Before you get a payday loan, consider these choices:

- Get financial help from military aid societies like:

  - Army Emergency Relief 703-428-0000

  - Navy and Marine Corps Relief Society 703-696-4904

  - Air Force Aid Society 800-769-8951

  - Coast Guard Mutual Assistance 800-881-2462

- Borrow money from family or friends

- Ask your employer if you can get an advance on your paycheck

- Talk to a credit counselor about getting more time to pay your bills

Where Can I Get More Information About Borrowing Money?

For more information about other ways to borrow money or to get help managing your finances:

- Call the Department of Defense at 800-342-9647. This line is staffed 24 hours a day, 7 days a week.

- Go to militaryonesource.com.

Chapter 26

Installment Loans

What Is An Installment Loan?

An installment loan is a loan that is repaid in equal monthly payments or installments for a specific period of time, usually several years.

Types Of Installment Loans

There are two types of installment loans:

- Secured loans

- Unsecured loans

Secured Installment Loans

A secured installment loan is one where the borrower offers collateral for the loan. The borrower gives up the collateral to the lender if the loan is not paid back as agreed.

Collateral

Collateral is security you provide a lender. Giving the lender collateral means that you promise an asset you own, such as your car, to the lender in case you cannot repay the loan.

Generally, if the collateral is not enough to repay your loan, you are still responsible for:

- The remaining balance.

- Any fees and interest associated with the loan.

About This Chapter: This chapter includes text excerpted from "Module 7: Paying For College And Cars," Federal Deposit Insurance Corporation (FDIC), March 28, 2009.

Unsecured Installment Loans

Unsecured installment loans can be used for a variety of personal expenses such as education or medical expenses. Unsecured loans are sometimes called personal or signature loans. An unsecured loan is a loan that is not secured by collateral.

- There is no collateral requirement for an unsecured loan. The terms of the loan might range from 1–5 years.

- Since credit cards have become popular, the use of unsecured consumer installment loans has declined. However, some financial institutions still offer unsecured installment loans.

Benefits of Unsecured Loans

Some benefits of unsecured installment loans include:

- Fast approval time.

- Interest rates might be lower than credit card rates.

Loan Approval

The Four Cs Of Loan Decision Making

Lenders generally review the Four Cs to decide whether to make a loan to you. The Four Cs are capacity, capital, character, and collateral.

- Capacity refers to your present and future ability to meet your payment obligations. This includes whether you have enough income to pay your bills and other debts.

- Capital refers to the value of your assets and your net worth.

- Character refers to how you have paid bills or debts in the past. Your credit report is one tool lenders use to consider your willingness to repay your debts.

- Collateral refers to property or assets offered to secure the loan

Chapter 27

Vehicle Financing

Before You Buy Or Lease A Car

Determine How Much You Can Afford

Before you finance or lease a car, look at your financial situation to make sure you have enough income to cover your monthly living expenses.

Should you take on a new monthly payment? Finance or lease a car only when you can afford to take on a new payment. Saving for a down payment or trading in a car can reduce the amount you need to finance or lease, which then lowers your financing or leasing costs.

Do you have a trade-in? In some cases, your trade-in will take care of the down payment on your new car. But if you still owe money on your car, trading it in might not help much. If you owe more than the car is worth, that's called negative equity, which can affect the financing of your new car or the lease agreement. And consider paying down the debt before you buy or lease another car. If you do use the car for a trade-in, ask how the negative equity affects your new financing or lease agreement. For example, it may increase the length of your financing agreement or the amount of your monthly payment.

Get A Copy Of Your Credit Report

It's a good idea to check your credit report and credit score when you are considering financing or leasing a car, and before you make any major purchase. You can get a free copy of your report from each of the three nationwide reporting agencies every 12 months. To order,

About This Chapter: This chapter includes text excerpted from "Financing Or Leasing A Car," Federal Deposit Insurance Corporation (FDIC), August 2017.

visit www.AnnualCreditReport.com, call 877-322-8228, or complete the Annual Credit Report Request form and mail it to Annual Credit Report Request Service, P.O. Box 105281, Atlanta, GA 30348-5281.

If you want a copy of your credit report, but have already gotten your free copy, you can buy your report for a small fee. Contact any of the three nationwide credit reporting agencies:

- Equifax Credit Information Services: 800-685-1111

- Experian: 888-397-3742

- TransUnion Corporation: 800-916-8800

Usually, you will get your credit score after you apply for financing or a lease. You also may find a free copy of your credit score on your credit statements.

What About A Co-Signer?

If you don't have a credit history—or a strong credit history—a creditor may require that you have a co-signer on the finance contract or lease agreement. Co-signers assume equal responsibility for the contract. The account payment history will appear on your credit report and the co-signer's—which means late payments will hurt both of your credit. If you can't pay what you owe, your co-signer will have to. Make sure that both you and the co-signer know the terms of the contract and can afford to take on the payments.

Should I Use Financing To Buy A Car?

Know Your Financing Options

You have two financing options: direct lending or dealership financing.

Direct Lending

You might borrow money directly from a bank, finance company, or credit union. In your loan, you agree to pay the amount financed, plus a finance charge, over a period of time. Once you're ready to buy a car from a dealer, you use this loan to pay for the car.

If you chose to finance your car this way, you can:

- **Comparison shop.** You get to shop around and ask several lenders about their credit terms even before you decide to buy a specific car.

- **Get your credit terms in advance.** By getting preapproval for financing before you shop for a car, you can know the terms in advance, including the annual percentage rate

(APR), length of term, and maximum amount. Take this information to the dealer to improve your ability to negotiate.

Dealership Financing

You might apply for financing through the dealership. You and a dealer enter into a contract where you buy a car and also agree to pay, over a period of time, the amount financed plus a finance charge. The dealer typically sells the contract to a bank, finance company or credit union that services the account and collects your payments.

Dealership financing may offer you:

- **Convenience.** Dealers offer cars and financing in one place and may have extended hours, like evenings and weekends.

- **Multiple financing options.** The dealer's relationships with a variety of banks and finance companies may mean it can offer you a range of financing choices.

- **Special programs.** Dealers sometimes offer manufacturer-sponsored, low-rate or incentive programs to buyers. The programs may be limited to certain cars or may have special requirements, like a larger down payment or shorter contract length (36 or 48 months). These programs might require a strong credit rating; check to see if you qualify.

Shop For The Best Financing Deal

Before you finance a car, shop around and compare the financing terms offered by more than one creditor. You are shopping for two products: the financing and the car. Negotiate the terms and consider several offers. Comparison shop to find both the car and the finance terms that best suit your needs.

Take the time to know and understand the terms, conditions, and costs to finance a car before you sign a contract. Know that the total amount you will pay will depend on several factors, including:

- the price you negotiate for the car

- the APR, which may be negotiable, and

- the length of the credit contract

Many creditors now offer longer-term credit, such as 72 or 84 months to pay. These contracts can reduce your monthly payments, but they may have high rates. And you'll be paying for longer. Cars lose value quickly once you drive off the lot. So, with longer-term financing, you could end up owing more than the car is worth.

If you sign a contract, get a copy of the signed papers before you leave the dealer or other creditor. Make sure you understand whether the deal is final before you leave in your new car.

Sample Comparison

Consider the total costs of financing the car, not just the monthly payment. It is important to compare different payment plans for both the monthly payment and total of payments required, for example, for a 48-month/4-year and a 60-month/5-year credit purchase. In general, longer contract lengths mean lower monthly payments, higher total finance charges, and higher overall costs. Be sure you will have enough income available to make the monthly payment throughout the life of the finance contract. You also will need to account for the cost of insurance, which may vary depending on the type of car you buy, and other factors.

Table 27.1. Sample Comparison Of Finance Charges

Term	4 Years–48 Months	5 Years–60 Months
Purchase Price	$34,000	$34,000
Taxes, Title, and Required Fees	$2,200	$2,200
Down Payment (20%)	$7,240	$7,240
Amount Financed	$28,960	$28,960
Contract Rate (APR)	4.00%	4.00%
Finance Charge	$2,480	$3,080
Monthly Payment Amount	$655	$534
Total of Payments	$31,440	$32,040

Note: All dollars have been rounded. The numbers in this sample are for example purposes only. Actual finance terms will depend on many factors, including your credit rating.

Your Own Comparison

Table 27.2. Shopping For The Best Financing Deal Worksheet

	Creditor 1	Creditor 2	Creditor 3
Negotiated Price of Car	$_____	$_____	$_____
Down Payment	$_____	$_____	$_____
Trade-In Allowance (If trading in your car, this may involve negative equity)	$_____	$_____	$_____

Table 27.2. Continued

	Creditor 1	Creditor 2	Creditor 3
Extended Service Contract (Optional)*	$_____	$_____	$_____
Credit Insurance(Optional)*	$_____	$_____	$_____
Guaranteed Auto Protection (Optional)*	$_____	$_____	$_____
Other Optional* Products	$_____	$_____	$_____
Amount Financed	$_____	$_____	$_____
Annual Percentage Rate (APR)	_____%	_____%	_____%
Finance Charge	$_____	$_____	$_____
Length of Contract in Months	_____	_____	_____
Number of Payments	$_____	$_____	$_____
Monthly Payment Amount	$_____	$_____	$_____

*Note: You are not required to buy items that are optional. If you do not want these items, tell the dealer and do not sign for them. Be sure they are not included in the monthly payments or elsewhere on a contract that you sign.

If You Apply For Dealer Financing

Most dealerships have a Finance and Insurance (F&I) Department that will tell you about its available financing options. The F&I Department manager will ask you to complete a credit application, which may include your:

- name

- Social Security number (SSN)

- date of birth

- current and previous address(es) and length of stay

- current and previous employer(s) and length of employment

- occupation

- sources of income

- total gross monthly income

- financial information on current credit accounts, including debt obligations

Most dealerships will get a copy of your credit report, which has information about your current and past credit, your payment record, and data from public records (like a bankruptcy filing from court documents). It may also include your credit score.

Make sure to ask the dealer about:

- **Manufacturer incentives.** Your dealer may offer manufacturer incentives, such as reduced finance rates or cash back on certain makes or models. Make sure you ask your dealer if the model you are interested in has any special financing offers. Generally, these discounted rates are not negotiable and may be limited by your credit history.

- **Rebates, discounts or special prices.** Ask if you qualify for any available rebates, discounts or offers, as they can reduce your price and, therefore, the amount you finance or that is part of your lease. Dealers who promote rebates, discounts or special prices must clearly explain what is required to qualify for these incentives. Look closely to see if there are restrictions on these special offers. For example, these offers may involve being a recent college graduate or a member of the military, or they may apply only to specific cars. Don't assume that the rebates have already been included in the price or terms you are offered.

- **Your APR.** When no special financing offers are available, you usually can negotiate the APR and the terms for payment with the dealership, just as you would negotiate the price of the car. The APR that you negotiate with the dealer usually includes an amount that compensates the dealer for handling the financing. The APR will vary depending on your credit rating. Negotiation can take place before or after the dealership accepts and processes your credit application. Try to negotiate the lowest APR with the dealer, just as you would negotiate the best price for the car.

Ask questions about the terms of the contract before you sign. For example, are the terms final and fully approved before you sign the contract and leave the dealership with the car? If the dealer says they are still working on the approval, the deal is not yet final. Consider waiting to sign the contract and keeping your current car until the financing has been fully approved. Or check other financing sources before you sign the financing and before you leave your car at the dealership. Also, if you are a military service member, find out if the credit contract lets you move your car out of the country. Some credit contracts may not.

Should I Lease A Car?

When you lease a car, you have the right to use it for an agreed number of months and miles.

How is leasing different than buying? The monthly payments on a lease usually are lower than monthly finance payments if you bought the same car. You are paying to drive the car, not buy it. That means you're paying for the car's expected depreciation during the lease period, plus a rent charge, taxes, and fees. But at the end of a lease, you must return the car unless the lease agreement lets you buy it.

To figure out if leasing fits your situation:

- Consider the beginning, middle, and end of lease costs

- Consider how long you may want to keep the car

- Compare different lease offers and terms, including mileage limits

Think about how much you drive. The mileage limit in most standard leases is typically 15,000 or fewer per year. You can negotiate a higher mileage limit, but that normally increases the monthly payment, because the car depreciates more during the life of the lease. If you go beyond the mileage limit in the lease agreement, you probably will have to pay an additional charge when you return the car.

Consider all of the lease terms. When you lease, you are responsible for excess wear and damage and any missing equipment. You also must service the car according to the manufacturer's recommendations and maintain insurance that meets the leasing company's standards. If you end the lease early, you often have to pay an early termination charge that could be substantial.

Might you move during the lease period? Some leases may not let you move the car out of state or out of the country. Find out the rules for the deal you are considering.

TIP: Some dealerships, known as "lease here pay here" dealerships, lease older used vehicles. These dealerships lease to consumers with poor or no credit that often need quick access to a vehicle. Common features of a lease may be weekly or bi-weekly payments, high rent charges, and no repair or maintenance coverage. If the vehicle breaks down, you may be responsible for repairs. Before leasing any vehicle, determine if you will be able to afford the payments into the future and if this is the right deal for you. You should also ask if the vehicle will be equipped with a starter interrupt device that will shut down the ignition if you miss a lease payment.

(Source: "What Should I Know About The Differences Between Leasing And Buying A Vehicle?" Consumer Financial Protection Bureau (CFPB).)

After Signing

Be sure you have a copy of the credit contract or lease agreement, with all signatures and terms filled in, before you leave the dealership. Do not agree to get the papers later because the documents may get misplaced or lost.

If you financed the car, understand:

- **The creditor has a lien on the car's title** (and in some cases holds the actual title) until you have paid the contract in full.

- **Make your payments on time.** Late or missed payments can have serious consequences: late fees, repossession, and negative entries on your credit report can make it harder to get credit in the future. Some dealers may place tracking devices on a car, which might help them locate the car to repossess it if you miss payments or pay late. Find out if the dealer expects to place the device on your car as part of the sale, what it will be used for, and what to do if the device sets off an alarm.

Were you called back to the dealership because the financing was not final or did not go through? Carefully review any changes or new documents you're asked to sign. Consider whether you want to proceed. **You do not have to continue with the financing.** If you don't want the new deal being offered, tell the dealer you want to cancel or unwind the deal and you want your down payment back. If you do unwind the deal, be sure the application and contract documents have been canceled. If you agree to a new deal, be sure you have a copy of all the documents.

Having Financial Problems?

If you will be late with a payment, contact your creditor right away. Many creditors work with people they believe will be able to pay soon, even if slightly late. You can ask for a delay in your payment or a revised schedule of payments. Sometimes, the creditor might agree to change your original contract. If they do, get it in writing to avoid questions later.

If you are late with your car payments or, in some states, if you do not have the required auto insurance, your car could be repossessed. The creditor may repossess the car or may sell the car and apply the proceeds from the sale to the outstanding balance on your credit agreement. If the car is sold for less than what you owe, you may be responsible for the difference.

In some states, the law allows the creditor to repossess your car without going to court.

Chapter 28

Financing Your Education After High School

What Is Federal Student Aid?

It's money from the federal government—specifically, the U.S. Department of Education (ED)—that helps you pay for college or career school, or graduate school expenses. More than $150 billion in federal student aid is available through grants, work-study, and loans every year.

Who Gets Federal Student Aid?

Every student who meets certain eligibility requirements can get some type of federal student aid, regardless of age or family income. The most basic eligibility requirements are that you must

- demonstrate financial need (for most programs);

- be a U.S. citizen or an eligible noncitizen;

- have a valid Social Security number (SSN);

- register (if you haven't already) with Selective Service if you're a male between the ages of 18 and 25;

- maintain satisfactory academic progress in college or career school; and

- show you're qualified to obtain a college or career school education by

---

About This Chapter: This chapter includes text excerpted "Federal Student Loans Funding Your Education—Federal Student Aid," Federal Student Aid, U.S. Department of Education (ED), December 16, 2017.

- having a high school diploma or General Educational Development (GED) certificate or

- completing a high school education in a homeschool setting approved under state law.

How Do I Apply For Federal Student Aid?

To apply for federal student aid, you need to complete the *Free Application for Federal Student Aid* (FAFSA®) at www.fafsa.gov. Completing and submitting the FAFSA® is free and quick, and it gives you access to the largest source of financial aid to pay for college or career school.

When Do I Complete The FAFSA®?

If you plan to attend school in the fall, you should apply for aid by completing the FAFSA® as soon as possible after January 1 of the year you plan on attending. A few things to remember:

- The deadline for submitting the FAFSA®.

- You need to apply as soon as you can! Schools and states often use FAFSA® information to award nonfederal aid. Their deadlines are usually early in the year. Check with the schools you're interested in to find out about their deadlines. Find state deadlines at www.fafsa.gov.

- You must reapply for federal student aid every year.

- If you change schools, your aid doesn't automatically transfer with you. Check with your new school to find out what you need to do to continue receiving financial aid.

Your FAFSA® helps you apply for federal, state, and school financial aid!

If you're not ready to apply for federal student aid, but you'd like to estimate your aid, visit StudentAid.gov/fafsa/estimate to try *FAFSA4caster*, an early eligibility estimator.

What Information Do I Report On The FAFSA®?

The FAFSA® asks for information about you (your name, Social Security number, date of birth, address, etc.) and about your financial situation. A series of questions will also determine whether you must provide information about your parents. Whether you must report that information or not depends on whether you're a "dependent" or an "independent" student.

Where Does My FAFSA® Information Go Once I Submit It?

Your information is shared with the schools you list on the FAFSA®.

- The financial aid office at a school to which you applied uses your FAFSA® information to determine how much federal student aid you may receive at that school.

- If the school has its own funds to use for financial aid, it might use your FAFSA® information to determine your eligibility for that aid. (The school might also have other forms it wants you to fill out to apply for aid there, so check with the school's financial aid office to be sure.)

Your FAFSA® information also goes to state higher education agencies where your chosen schools are located. Many states have financial aid funds that they give out based on FAFSA® information.

I Completed The FAFSA®... Now What?

After you apply, you'll receive a Student Aid Report (SAR), which is a summary of the FAFSA® data you submitted. You'll get your SAR within three days to three weeks after you submit your FAFSA®, depending on the method of delivery you selected. Be sure to look over your SAR to make sure you didn't make any mistakes on your FAFSA®. The SAR won't tell you how much financial aid you'll get; it's a summary of the information being sent to the schools you listed on your FAFSA®. If you don't need to make any changes to the information listed on your SAR, just keep it for your records. To find out how to correct mistakes, or update your FAFSA®, visit StudentAid.gov/fafsa/next-steps/accept-aid. Next, expect to receive an award letter from the schools at which you were accepted.

What's An Award Letter?

If you applied for admission to a school and have been accepted (although not all schools require students to be accepted before telling them of their eligibility for aid), and you listed that school on your FAFSA®, the school will calculate your aid and send you an electronic or paper "award letter" telling you how much aid you're eligible to receive at that school. The timing of the award letter varies from school to school and could be as early as springtime (awarding for the fall) or as late as immediately before you start school. It depends on when you apply and how the school prefers to schedule awarding of aid.

How Much Will I Get?

When a school's financial aid office sends you an award letter, the letter will list the types of aid and amounts (from all sources) the school will offer you. How much aid you receive depends on

- cost of attendance (for each school);

- Expected Family Contribution (number used to calculate how much financial aid you're eligible to receive based on the information in your FAFSA®);

- year in school; and

- enrollment status (that is, full-time, half-time, etc.).

You can compare aid offers from the schools to which you applied and see which school is the most affordable once financial aid is taken into account. Keep in mind that the financial aid office at the school will determine how much financial aid you're eligible to receive. Contact the school's financial aid office if you have any questions about your award letter or the aid being offered to you.

Should I Accept All The Aid I'm Offered?

You don't have to. When your school financial aid office sends you an award letter, they'll tell you how to indicate which financial aid you want to accept. A good approach is to start by accepting the financial aid funds you don't have to pay back, such as grants. Look carefully at your options and make sure you accept only what you need, especially when it comes to loans, which you'll have to pay back.

How Will I Receive My Aid?

In most cases, your federal student aid will be applied directly to your school account. The financial aid staff at your school will explain exactly how and when your aid will be paid out. They will also let you know whether you need to meet any other requirements. If you're getting federal student loans for the first time, you must complete entrance counseling and sign a master promissory note before you receive your loan money.

Types Of Federal Student Aid

There are three categories of federal student aid: grants, work-study, and loans.

Table 28.1. Federal Student Aid Programs 2017–18

Program And Type Of Aid	Program Information	Annual Award Amount (Subject To Change)
Federal Pell Grant Grant: does not have to be repaid	For undergraduates with exceptional financial need who have not earned bachelor's or professional degrees.	Amounts can change annually. For 2017–18 (July 1, 2017 to June 30, 2018), the award amount is up to $5,920.
Federal Supplemental Educational Opportunity Grant (FSEOG) Grant: does not have to be repaid	For undergraduates with exceptional financial need.	Up to $4,000.
Teacher Education Assistance for College and Higher Education (TEACH) Grant Grant: does not have to be repaid unless student fails to carry out service obligation	For undergraduate, postbaccalaureate, and graduate students who are completing or plan to complete coursework needed to begin a career in teaching. As a condition for receiving this grant, student must sign a TEACH Grant Agreement to Serve in which the student agrees to perform four years of qualifying teaching service and meet other requirements.	Up to $4,000.
Iraq and Afghanistan Service Grant Grant: does not have to be repaid	For students who are not Pell-eligible due only to having less financial need than is required to receive Pell funds; whose parent or guardian died as a result of military service in Iraq or Afghanistan after the events of 9/11.	The grant award can be equal to the maximum Federal Pell Grant amount (see above), but cannot exceed your cost of attending school.
Federal Work-Study Work-Study: money is earned; does not have to be repaid	For undergraduate and graduate students; part-time jobs can be on campus or off campus. Money is earned while attending school.	No annual minimum or maximum amounts.

Table 28.1. Continued

Program And Type Of Aid	Program Information	Annual Award Amount (Subject To Change)
Direct Subsidized Loan Loan: must be repaid with interest	For undergraduate students who have financial need; U.S. Department of Education (ED) generally pays interest while the student is in school and during certain other periods; student must be at least half-time. Interest rate is 3.76 percent for loans first disbursed on or after July 1, 2016 and before July 1, 2017, and fixed for the life of the loan.	Up to $5,500 depending on grade level and dependency status.
Direct Unsubsidized Loan Loan: must be repaid with interest	For undergraduate and graduate or professional students; borrower is responsible for all interest; student must be at least half-time; financial need is not required. Interest rate is 3.76 percent (undergraduate) and 5.31 percent (graduate or professional) for loans first disbursed on or after July 1, 2016 and before July 1, 2017, and fixed for the life of the loan.	Up to $20,500 (less any subsidized amounts received for same period), depending on grade level and dependency status.
Direct PLUS Loan Loan: must be repaid with interest	For parents of dependent undergraduate students and for graduate or professional students; borrower is responsible for all interest; student must be enrolled at least half-time; financial need is not required; borrower must not have an adverse credit history. Interest rate is 6.31 percent for loans first disbursed on or after July 1, 2016 and before July 1, 2017, and fixed for the life of loan.	Maximum amount is cost of attendance minus any other financial aid received.

Table 28.1. Continued

Program And Type Of Aid	Program Information	Annual Award Amount (Subject To Change)
Federal Perkins Loan Loan: must be repaid with interest	For undergraduate and graduate students with exceptional financial need. Eligibility depends on the student's financial need and availability of funds at the school. For questions on Perkins Loan eligibility, students must contact the school's financial aid office. Interest rate is 5 percent and fixed for the life of the loan.	Undergraduate students: up to $5,500; graduate and professional students: up to $8,000.

(Source: "2017–18 Federal Student Aid At A Glance," Federal Student Aid, U.S. Department of Education (ED).)

Do I Have To Repay My Loans?

Student loans, unlike grants and work-study, are borrowed money that must be repaid, with interest, just like car loans and home mortgages. You cannot have these loans canceled because you didn't like the education you received, didn't get a job in your field of study, or are having financial difficulty. So think about the amount you'll have to repay before you take out a loan. Student loans aren't easily written off in bankruptcy.

You don't have to wait until you graduate to start repaying your loans.

You can use repayment estimator to estimate your federal student loan payments under each repayment plan. Visit StudentAid.gov/repayment-estimator to use the tool.

Steps To Remember When Applying For Financial Aid

Keep track of what you need to do when applying for federal student aid. Remember that free help is available any time during the application process.

1. Get free information and help from your school counselor, the financial aid office at the school you plan to attend, or the U.S. Department of Education (ED) at StudentAid.gov or 800-4-FED-AID (800-433-3243). You should never have to pay for help!

2. Apply online at www.fafsa.gov. You must complete the FAFSA® between January 1 and June 30 (no exceptions to either date!). Apply as soon as possible after January 1 to meet school and state aid deadlines.

3. Within a few days of receiving your FAFSA®, the ED will send you your Student Aid Report (SAR)—based on the information in your FAFSA®—by e-mail with a link to your electronic SAR. Whether you receive your SAR online or on paper depends on whether you provide an e-mail address on your FAFSA®. Review your SAR and, if necessary, make changes or corrections following the instructions in it. Your SAR has to be correct to ensure that you receive your aid.

4. Be sure to respond to any correspondence your school sends you.

5. Review award letters from schools to compare types and amounts of aid being offered. Each school will tell you how much aid you can get there. Contact the school's financial aid office if you have any questions about the aid being offered.

Chapter 29

Educational Loans

You won't be surprised to hear that a college education is expensive. According to the College Board, the average annual cost for tuition, books, and other fees for the 2016-17 school year was $33,480 at private colleges, and at public universities the average was $9,650 for state residents and $24,930 for nonresidents. Those might seem like overwhelming numbers, but the fact is that most students and their families don't rely just on savings and income to pay for college. A good portion of the money likely comes from scholarships, grants, and loans.

Students loans are funded by either the U.S. government or private sources, and in either case the interest rate could be lower than other types of loans, which can make them a relative bargain. However, student loans still mean borrowing money, and as with credit cards or other kinds of debt, it's always best to owe as little as possible. In total, Americans owed about $1.3 trillion in student-loan debt in 2017. That comes to an average of about $37,000 per student and an average monthly payment of $351. So, the first order of business is to try and keep the amount you borrow to a minimum.

> Pay attention to interest rates, since they drive up the total cost of the loan. For example, if the interest rate increases by one percentage point, that will result in about a 5 percent increase in your monthly payment on a ten-year fixed-interest loan.

About This Chapter: "Educational Loans," © 2017 Omnigraphics.

Minimizing Student Loans

The best way to reduce the amount borrowed is for parents to plan ahead and begin saving for their children's education early, and then for the children to add to the savings as they get older. But whether that saving has begun or not, there are some other ways to minimize the amount of student loans, including:

- **Work part time.** By working at a part-time job during high-school, you can sock away some money to help pay college expenses when the time comes. And if you work while attending college, you can help pay for some costs through income, rather than loans.

- **Choose a different school.** Ivy-League schools, private colleges, and out-of-state universities are the most expensive routes to a higher education. If money is tight, consider a state university in your own state, or think about attending a community college for a year or two before transferring to a four-year institution.

- **Apply for scholarships and grants.** Funds are available from a wide variety of public and private sources, including federal, state, and local governments, fraternal organizations, companies, and the colleges themselves. With a little research, you might find that you qualify for some of this support.

- **Reduce spending.** With a little careful budget management you should be able to hold down spending and lessen the amount you need to borrow. For example, look for used books or inexpensive eBooks when they're available, opt for a less expensive meal plan and make some food at home, and hold down entertainment expenses by taking advantage of the many forms of free entertainment on campus.

Advantages Of Student Loans

Despite trying to minimize loan amounts, most students are going to need to borrow some money for their education. Luckily, student loans offer a number of advantages over other types of borrowing, such as:

- **Easier approval.** Unlike car loans and mortgages, you can get some kinds of student loans without a credit history.

- **No co-signer.** Even students with little or no credit history can often get student loans without the need for a parent or other person to co-sign the loan.

- **Lower interest rates.** Student loans generally come with lower fees than other types of loans, because they're considered lower risk by lenders, and some are backed by the government.

- **Deferred payments.** With some kinds of students loans, you don't need to begin making payments until you're out of school. And if you become unemployed at some point, you may be able to stop making payments until you find another job.

Types Of Student Loans

There are two broad categories of education loans available to college students, federal loans, and private loans. But, as might be expected, the federal student loans are more complicated to get and come in several different flavors, although they do offer many unique benefits. Here's a brief overview of the types of federal student loans available:

- **Unsubsidized Federal Stafford Loans.** Probably the most common type of student loan, these feature a guaranteed low interest rate over the life of the loan, are not need-based, and are not subject to credit approval. Interest accrues while you're in college, and repayment begins when you graduate, drop below half-time, or leave college.

- **Subsidized Federal Stafford Loans.** Another common loan type, these are similar to the unsubsidized variety, except they are based on need. They're "subsidized" in that interest doesn't accrue while you're in school, have more flexible payment plans, and the repayment period doesn't begin until six months after you graduate, or when you drop below half-time or leave college.

- **Perkins Federal Loans.** Perkins loans are intended for students with the most severe financial need, so they're more difficult to get than Stafford loans. They carry a lower interest rate, and the interest is paid by the government while the student is attending school. There are also no origination fees with these loans, and there's a longer grace period after graduation before repayment begins.

- **PLUS Loans.** PLUS in this case stands for Parent Loan for Undergraduate Student, and these loans allow families to borrow money to pay for any college costs that are not covered by other financial aid. There are some need-based criteria attached to PLUS loans, as well as additional fees, and repayment must begin as soon as funds are dispersed, although there is the option of requesting a deferment.

- **Private Loans.** These are loans made by institutions like banks, credit unions, and loan agencies. Private loans are not overseen by the government, so they're similar to money borrowed to buy cars or other items. Rates vary widely, based on both the type of lender and the borrower's credit rating, but they're likely to be higher than federal loans, and most often they require a co-signer.

Selecting The Best Student Loan

In a nutshell, the cheapest loan is the best loan. But it's important to do your homework so you can make informed decisions about what educational funding will be best for you. In practice, most students and families use a combination of sources to pay for college, and the best place to start is with scholarships and grants, which provide free money. Then, savings and income should be used whenever possible. And, finally, you should investigate the various types of student loans.

Generally speaking, the best loan terms can be obtained in this order:

- **Perkins Loans.** The terms are very good, but they're based on extreme need and therefore hard to get.

- **Subsidized Federal Stafford Loans.** These come with good terms and are easier to get than a Perkins loan, but they're still need-based.

- **Unsubsidized Federal Stafford Loans.** These have decent terms, but not as good as the first two. The biggest issue is that interest accrues while you're in college. On the other hand, they're not based on need.

- **PLUS Loans.** These have a need-based component, carry additional fees, and repayment starts immediately, so they rank lower on the list. But their intention is to fill gaps left by other sources of funding.

- **Private Loans.** Obviously, these carry the most disadvantages in that the interest is highest, it accrues while you're in college, a co-signer will likely be required for a student, and repayment starts immediately. Nevertheless, they're the third-most common way for students and families to borrow at least some of the money for a college education.

If all else fails, there are some alternative loan sources that you might consider, although they do come with downsides.

- Loans from family members: may put family relationships at risk
- Home equity loans: puts home ownership at risk
- Unsecured loans (also called signature loans): require excellent credit scores
- Loans from friends or acquaintances: may put personal relationships at risk
- Credit cards: likely have very high interest rates

How To Get A Student Loan

The first step in applying for an education loan is to contact the financial-aid office of the college you're planning to attend for information on the types of aid available, including scholarships and grants. The next step is to complete a *Free Application for Federal Student Aid* (FAFSA®), which is required for federal loans. This form gathers information on your finances in order to determine what need-based loans you may qualify for. Based on the FAFSA®, the college will send you a financial-aid offer, which might include federal loans, and will let you know the process for accepting a loan. Finally, in the case of federal loans, you will be required to complete entrance counseling to make sure you understand the terms and obligations of the loan, and you will need to sign a Master Promissory Note (MPN) agreeing to the terms.

If you don't qualify for scholarships, grants, and federal loans, or if they're not enough to cover your total annual education costs, you may need to take out a private loan. The advantage is that they're easier to get, assuming you have good credit or have a co-signer with good credit. But it will require a lot of research to be sure you're getting the best possible terms. It's probably best to start with a bank or credit union with which you or your co-signer are already doing business. Then investigate other banks and credit unions and, finally, credit agencies, which will often have the least attractive terms.

You can get an estimate of your eligibility for federal financial aid by using *FAFSA4caster*, which can be found at studentaid.ed.gov/sa/fafsa/estimate. This tool can be used by students and parents to receive early estimates, create scenarios based on future earnings, and establish college funding strategies.

References

1. "Borrow For College," Edvisors.com, n.d.

2. Pritchard, Justin. "An Overview Of Private Student Loans," TheBalance.com, January 11, 2017.

3. Shin, Laura. "Understanding Student Loans 101," Learnvest.com, June 1, 2012.

4. "Student Loans 101," MyCollegeOptions.com, n.d.

5. "Student Loans 101: A Guide For College Graduates," SmartMoneyForLife.com, July 21, 2015.

6. "Trends In Higher Education," CollegeBoard.org, 2017

Chapter 30

Private Education Loans

More than two-thirds of college students must borrow money to help cover the costs of their education. The vast majority of student loans (91% as of 2014) come from lending programs funded by the U.S. government. Federal education loans are a good option for students and their families because they offer low, fixed interest rates and generous borrower protections. You are allowed to defer or postpone repaying your loan under certain circumstances, for instance, and you can apply to adjust the amount of your payments based on your income. But federal loan programs place annual and cumulative limits on how much you can borrow, so some students must seek additional financing in the form of private education loans.

Private or alternative education loans are funded by private, commercial lenders, such as banks, credit unions, credit card companies, and online lenders. Some of the most prominent companies that offer private student loans include Citizens Bank, College Ave, Common Bond, Discover, Navient, PNC Bank, Sallie Mae, SoFi, and Wells Fargo. Private student loan programs vary widely in terms of the interest rates, fees, loan limits, loan terms, and repayment options they offer. Since commercial lenders are in business to make a profit, however, private student loans are usually more expensive for borrowers than federal student loans.

Apply For Federal Student Loans First

College financial aid officers recommend considering private student loans only after you have exhausted all other options for covering the costs of your education, including savings, scholarships, grants, work-study income, and federal student loans. Before applying for private loans, you should fill out and submit the *Free Application for Federal Student Aid* (FAFSA®).

About This Chapter: "Private Education Loans," © 2017 Omnigraphics.

Both the federal and state governments use FAFSA® information to determine whether you qualify for government assistance based on financial need. Even if you are not eligible for need-based financial aid, you can still qualify for unsubsidized federal student loans, which are not based on financial need.

The amount you can borrow in federal student loans depends on your cost to attend college, how much other financial aid you receive, your year in school, and whether you are considered a dependent of your parents. If you borrow the maximum amount and still cannot meet your college expenses, then you may have to take out private student loans. Private loans are also the only option available to graduates of medical school or law school who need funds to cover the cost of obtaining professional qualifications, such as taking the bar exam or finding a medical residency. Federal student loans are not available for these purposes.

Factors To Consider With Private Loans

If you decide that you need to take out a private education loan, it is important to compare the interest rates, fees, borrower protections, repayment plans, and customer service offered by various lenders. Here are some important factors to consider:

- **Your credit history and co-signers**

  Keep in mind that the final cost of the loan and the amount you are able to borrow will be based on your credit history. Private lenders prefer borrowers who have good credit, a solid employment history, and enough cash or assets on hand to make loan payments in an emergency. As a result, many college students can only obtain private loans if a parent or guardian co-signs the loan agreement.

- **Interest rates**

  The interest rates on private student loans may be fixed or variable. Fixed interest rates remain the same for the entire life of the loan. Variable rates, on the other hand, carry some risk because they can increase or decrease depending on general economic conditions. Some lenders offer low, introductory interest rates while you are in school that increase once you graduate. Others offer discounted interest rates following a certain number of on-time payments.

- **Fees**

  The fees charged by lenders can add to the cost of the loan. Experts point out that every 3- to 4-percent increase in loan fees is roughly equivalent to paying a 1-percent higher interest rate. Most lenders reserve the most favorable interest rates and lowest fees for customers with excellent credit histories, and only about 20 percent of borrowers qualify. If you have poor credit, you should expect to pay up to 6 percent higher interest rates and 9 percent higher fees than lenders advertise for their best customers.

- **Borrower protections**

  Private education loan packages can include various options for borrowers. Some lenders offer options for you to defer payments while you are enrolled in school, during a six-month grace period after you graduate, or later if you experience financial hardship. Other lenders offer flexible repayment plans that are based on your income. In most cases, however, adding these sorts of options will increase the cost of the loan.

Did You Know...

According to the Institute for College Access and Success, 47 percent of private student loan borrowers failed to maximize their use of safer, more affordable federal student loans before applying for private loans during the 2011–2012 academic year.

Many colleges will provide students with a list of preferred lenders for private education loans. Although schools are not allowed to recommend a specific lender, these lists usually only include lenders that offer fair loan terms and good customer service. Research each lender option, compare the features of various loans carefully, and only borrow what you need and can manage to repay.

References

1. "Nine Best Private Student Loan Options In 2017," NerdWallet, 2017.

2. "Private Education Loan Checklist," Office of Financial Aid, Brown University, November 2015.

3. "Private Education Loans," FinAid, 2017.

Chapter 31

Planning For Independence

Thinking About Moving Out

Imagine that you have just finished school and you have your first full-time job in retail, as an associate at your favorite clothing store. You make $1,500 per month (about $9.40/hr), and take home about $1,200. You also get a monthly bonus of $400 if you meet your sales goals. You have about $600 in savings from your old part-time pizza job. Do you think you have enough to move out of your parents' house and get your own apartment, or even buy your own home? You think you might be ready to move out and get your own space. This chapter will talk about how to figure out if you are financially ready to do that, and go over some things you might need to know.

Renting Your Own Space

How much do you think it costs to move into a house or apartment?

Costs To Move In

When you want to rent an apartment, landlords will typically ask for additional money, called a deposit, to assure that you will take care of their property and pay your rent on time. They will probably also ask you to sign a lease. This lease protects both of you by clearly stating the arrangement between you.

A **lease** is a legal document. It states that the landlord agrees to provide a space for you to live, and that it is in "livable" condition (free of bugs and mechanical defects). A lease also

About This Chapter: This chapter includes text excerpted from "Module 8: A Roof Over Your Head," Federal Deposit Insurance Corporation (FDIC), March 28, 2009.

states that you agree to pay a certain amount for a set period of time for the apartment. The lease lists your responsibilities as a renter, such as keeping the apartment in good condition. You have certain rights as a renter; see the U.S. Department of Housing and Urban Development (HUD) site.

The costs of securing a rental property usually include:

- Security deposit.

- Payment of the first month's rent.

- Fees, including credit report fees and pet fees or deposits.

- Costs of connecting utilities (electric, phone, water) which may be required by the utility companies.

Security Deposit

A security deposit is money you put on deposit with the landlord when you sign the lease. It is held in an account by the landlord during the term of your lease. You may instead be asked to pay the deposit once your application is approved to reserve the unit, as it lets the landlord know that you are serious about moving in.

The deposit guarantees to the landlord that you will stay for the length of your lease term and not move out early or without notice. Some landlords may allow you to break your lease and walk away by paying a substantial fee. For example, if your rent is $600 per month and there are three months left on your lease when you move out, you may be legally obligated to pay the landlord $1,800. If your security deposit were $600, the landlord might take you to court to obtain the remaining $1,200. These details should be discussed with the landlord and written in the lease before you sign it.

The security deposit is also used when you move out to help pay for any damages to the property other than normal wear and tear. If there are no damages, the money is returned to you. The amount of a security deposit can vary, but it is usually equal to at least one month's rent. It may be based, in part, on your credit history.

Upfront Payments

Landlords usually require you to pay your first month's rent along with your security deposit when you sign a lease. They probably will also require you to pay for the remaining days in a month if you move in before the first of the month.

Additional Fees

Nonrefundable move-in fees are common in some areas. These cover the cost of preparing the apartment for your move-in. Some landlords may charge nonrefundable application or credit report fees to assess your eligibility to rent the apartment. These fees may be negotiable and restricted by law in some cities or states.

Utility Connection Fees

Utility companies (water, gas, electric, telephone, cable, etc.) usually charge a connection fee to begin service. Sometimes you have to pay the fees before your service is connected, and other times you can pay with your first bill. If a fee is charged, it can be anywhere from a few dollars to $60 or more. They may also ask for a security deposit in addition to connection fees. This is based on your credit and utility payment history, if you have one.

Paying For Your Space

Your income must cover your expenses for each month. The continuing costs of renting an apartment are:

- Rent and other fees (storage, pet fees, parking, etc.).
- Utilities.
- Renter's insurance (usually optional).
- The possibility of rent increases.

Rent And Fees

Some properties have fees in addition to the rent. Are you going to have a cat or dog? Many landlords charge extra fees and a deposit for pets, possibly including an upfront fee, and extra rent on top of that. You might also need storage or a parking space that can cost extra in some neighborhoods. A good rule of thumb is that no more than 30 percent of your gross income should be spent on rent. That means that if your gross income is $1,500, you should spend no more than $450 on rent. Then you have the remainder of your income for other expenses.

Utilities

You paid to have your utilities connected, but you still have to pay for the service every month. Depending on your apartment, your utilities may be included. Ask before you rent; you might save some money! And watch out: utility bills can vary with the seasons, and they can be very expensive. Many companies have a budget plan so that you pay the same amount throughout the year.

Renters Insurance

Renters insurance protects you against the loss or destruction of your possessions in the event your property is stolen or damaged, such as through a fire or burglary. It also covers your living expenses if you are unable to live in your apartment because of a fire or other covered peril. Renters insurance also provides liability protection if, for example, someone is injured at your home while visiting. Other types of coverage like earthquake or flood insurance may be available at an additional cost. Renters insurance is usually optional, although some landlords may require you to obtain coverage when you move in.

Rent Increases

The cost of everything rises; even your rent. Your landlord is not allowed to raise the rent during the term of your lease. For example, if you sign a 1-year lease, your rent payment will be the same for that year. But at the end of your lease, the landlord may raise your rent. Some communities may have rent-control laws that govern these rent increases; others do not. Be prepared. Look for an apartment that charges less than what your income allows. That way, if you stay after your lease expires, you will have some financial room to cover rent increases.

Sharing Space: Roommates

In order to keep the costs affordable, many young people share an apartment with one or more roommates. In exchange for sharing common areas like a living room, bathroom, and kitchen, you also share all the costs of renting.

Buying A Home

A mortgage is a loan, provided by a financial institution to buy a house or condo. Homes can be expensive, and are often not affordable for a person just starting off in life who has yet to accumulate savings and build a credit history. Mortgages are large sums of money. Mortgage payments are made over long periods of time, usually 15–30 years. There are many different types of loans that will meet the needs of people in different situations.

Costs Of A Mortgage

Mortgages are not free; in addition to paying them back, you have to pay additional money to obtain one. The costs involved in buying a home include: Buying a Home

- **Closing costs:** Closing costs are fees associated with buying and settling, or finalizing, your loan. They can include property taxes, broker and attorney fees, inspection fees, title insurance, and many other items.

- **Taxes and insurance:** You will probably have to pay some taxes upfront. The locality (usually county and state) where you live will charge taxes on the property, which are generally paid upfront at first and then either monthly with your mortgage payment or separately by you once or twice a year. They can amount to several thousand dollars per year, depending on the value of your house and the state where you live. You also need homeowner's insurance, in case your house catches on fire, the basement floods in a storm, or a window breaks due to your next door neighbor's son's baseball. You may also obtain other insurance, such as flood or earthquake insurance.

- **Interest over the course of the loan:** Interest is money that the bank charges you to borrow money. A portion of every mortgage payment goes toward interest.

The Mortgage Payment

What Makes Up A Mortgage Payment?

A mortgage payment is more than just paying back the amount you owe on a home loan. The two parts of the mortgage that pay back the loan are the principal and the interest.

1. Principal is the amount applied to the outstanding balance of the loan. This part is the loan itself.

2. Interest is the amount that the lender, or financial institution, charges for borrowing money.

Escrow

Taxes and homeowner's insurance are paid using a system called escrow. An escrow is a special bank account held by a financial institution for the purpose of paying taxes and insurance. When the bank calculates your mortgage payment, they include 1/12th of your taxes and 1/12th of your homeowners insurance. When you pay your mortgage, the lender takes this part of the payment and deposits it into the escrow account. Then the financial institution pays the taxes on your behalf to the government and pays your insurance premiums.

In some cases, private mortgage insurance is required to protect the lender if the buyer does not pay the loan. Although this is paid with the mortgage, it is also deposited into the escrow account and paid to the mortgage insurance company.

You can pay taxes and insurance separately. But then you have to remember to save the money each month to pay at the end of the year when the taxes and insurance are due. If you don't, you could have some large bills, maybe several thousand dollars, which you owe but can't pay. Paying separately keeps your mortgage low, but you have to be disciplined enough to save.

Renting Versus Buying

There are many advantages and disadvantages of renting and owning a home.

Advantages Of Renting

When you rent:

- Property maintenance is the responsibility of the landlord.

- You are only under a rental contract for one year or less.

- You do not have other costs associated with owning a home, such as property taxes or homeowner's insurance.

Renter's insurance can be obtained from the same companies as homeowner's insurance. Renter's insurance is generally cheaper than homeowner's insurance.

Disadvantages Of Renting

When you rent:

- You are not the owner of your home.

- Your rent might increase.

- You might not be able to renew your rental contract and then you will have to find a new place to live.

- You are essentially paying your landlord's mortgage.

- You will not obtain a federal tax deduction for your rent payments, while mortgage interest is tax deductible

As a homeowner, you can enjoy several benefits of ownership:

- You can build equity. Equity refers to the value of the home minus the debt you owe on it. As you pay down the loan and your home value increases, you build up equity.

- One of the benefits of equity is that you can borrow against it for many purposes, usually at a relatively low interest rate. But, remember you could lose your home if you don't pay back the loan.

- Homes have traditionally increased in value over time; so many people consider a home to be an investment.

- Once your mortgage is paid in full, the home is yours.

- Home ownership may reduce the amount of income tax you owe, since mortgage interest and property taxes are deductible.

Costs Of Owning A Home

When you own a home, property maintenance and upkeep are your responsibility. You are also responsible for the additional costs of:

- Homeowner's insurance.

- Real estate taxes.

- Mortgage interest.

- Homeowner's/condominium association fees, in some cases. These fees pay for maintenance of the common areas and the exterior of the buildings and grounds.

- Maintenance or repair expenses.

When you own a home, it is not as easy to move as it is when you rent. You will typically have to sell or rent your home before you can afford to buy or rent another one.

It is also important to understand that you can lose your home, and your investment in it, if you do not make timely mortgage payments.

Part Four
Credit Cards

Chapter 32

Basic Facts About Credit Cards

Find out your rights when it comes to credit cards and how to choose the right one.

Choose A Credit Card

When applying for credit cards, it's important to shop around. There are several credit cards with various features, but there is no one single best card. When you're trying to find the credit card that best suits your needs, consider these factors:

- **Annual Percentage Rate (APR)**—The APR is a measure of the cost of credit, expressed as a yearly interest rate. If the interest rate is variable, you should ask how it is determined and when it can change.

- **Periodic Rate**—This is the interest rate used to determine the finance charge on your balance each billing period.

- **Annual Fee**—While some credit cards have no annual fee, others expect you to pay an amount each year for being a cardholder.

- **Rewards Programs**—Can you earn points for flights, hotel stays, and gift certificates to your favorite retailers? Use online tools to find the card that offers the best rewards for you.

- **Grace Period**—This is the number of days you have to pay your bill in full before finance charges start. Without this period, you may have to pay interest from the date you use your card or when the purchase is posted to your account.

About This Chapter: This chapter includes text excerpted from "Credit Cards," USA.gov, August 30, 2016.

- **Finance Charges**—Most lenders calculate finance charges using an average daily account balance: the average of what you owed each day in the billing cycle. Look for offers that use an adjusted balance, which subtracts your monthly payment from your beginning balance. Avoid offers that use the previous balance in calculating what you owe; this method has the highest finance charge. Also, find out if there is a minimum finance charge.

- **Other Fees**—Are there fees if you get a cash advance, make a late payment, or go over your credit limit? Some credit card companies also charge a monthly fee. Be careful: sometimes companies may also try to upsell by offering other services such as credit protection, insurance, or debt coverage.

- **Terms and Conditions**—Read the agreement before you apply for the card to make sure that you agree with the requirements, such as mandatory arbitration or repossession clauses.

- **Security Features**—Does the card allow you to switch it on or off, receive fraud alerts, or text messages immediately after purchases?

- **Chip and Personal Identification Number (PIN)**—Does the card issuer offer chip and PIN security features that use an embedded strip instead of a magnetic strip? You may need this card type if you travel internationally.

The Fair Credit and Charge Card Disclosure Act (FCCCDA) requires credit and charge card issuers to include this information on credit applications.

Credit Card Laws

Credit card regulation protects you from unfair practices, gives you the right to dispute charges on your credit card, and allows you to file a complaint with your credit card company.

Credit Cardholders Rights

Often called the Credit Cardholders Bill of Rights, the Credit CARD Act protects you in two ways:

- **Fairness**—By prohibiting certain practices that are unfair or abusive, such as hiking up the rate on an existing balance, or allowing you to go over limit and then imposing an overlimit fee.

- **Transparency**—Making the rates and fees on credit cards more transparent, so that you can understand how much you are paying for your credit card.

Dispute A Credit Card Charge

Under the Fair Credit Billing Act (FCBA), you have the right to dispute charges on your credit card that you didn't make or are incorrect, or for goods or services you didn't receive. To dispute a charge, follow these guidelines:

- Send a letter to the creditor within 60 days of the postmark of the bill with the disputed charge.

- Include your name and account number, the date and amount of the disputed charge, and a complete explanation of why you are disputing the charge.

- To ensure it is received, send your letter by certified mail with a return receipt requested.

- The creditor or card issuer must acknowledge your letter in writing within 30 days of receiving it and conduct an investigation within 90 days. You do not have to pay the amount in dispute during the investigation.

- **If there was an error,** the creditor must credit your account and remove any fees.

- **If the bill is correct,** you must be told in writing what you owe and why. You must pay it along with any related finance charges.

- If you do not agree with the creditor's decision, file an appeal with the Consumer Financial Protection Bureau (CFPB).

File A Complaint

To complain about a credit card company, call the number on the back of your card or contact the CFPB. If you fail to resolve the issue, ask for the name, address, and phone number of the card company's regulatory agency.

Credit Card Protections

Did you know that your credit card may offer you other protections that are not typically advertised?

When using your credit card for travel purchases, your credit card issuer may offer you travel insurance in certain situations:

- Your trip is delayed.

- You have to cancel your trip because you or a family member becomes ill.

- Your luggage gets lost during travel.

If you rent a car, you may be offered auto insurance coverage as part of the rental. Some credit card networks even offer return assistance programs that extend the window for returning unused merchandise. Keep in mind: the rules vary between cards and the issuers.

Security Tips

If you use a credit card, charge card, or debit card, take the following precautions:

- Never lend it to anyone.

- Never sign a blank charge slip. Draw lines through blank spaces on charge slips above the total so the amount can't be changed.

- Never put your account number on the outside of an envelope or on a postcard.

- Always be cautious about disclosing your account number on the telephone unless you know the person you're dealing with represents a reputable company.

- Carry only the cards you expect to use to minimize the damage of a potential loss or theft.

- Always report lost or stolen credit cards, charge cards, and debit cards to the card issuers as soon as possible. Follow up with a letter that includes your account number, when you noticed the card was missing, and when you first reported the loss.

(Source: "Paying Down Credit Card Debt," Federal Trade Commission (FTC).)

Credit Card Resources

Credit card resources can help you learn important tips and security information, find your card agreement, and file a complaint.

Credit Card Tips

To find tips on using and getting the most from your credit card, refer to these resources:

- Get information from the Federal Trade Commission (FTC) about how to use a credit card. Topics include refunds, errors, disputes, unauthorized charges, and security.

- The Federal Reserve Board explains how to get the most from your credit card. This includes how to avoid unnecessary fees and keep track of changes in the terms of your account.

Chip And PIN Technology

Some card issuers have introduced chip and PIN security features on cards that contain an embedded strip rather than a magnetic strip and are protected by a personal identification number (PIN). Chip cards are based on a global card payment standard called EMV (Europay, MasterCard, and Visa), currently used in more than 80 countries around the world.

Beginning on October 1, 2015, merchants and businesses in the United States will be required to add in-store technology and processing systems so that you can make a purchase using a chip card. You may already need this type of card if you travel internationally since magnetic strip credit cards are not accepted in some countries.

Credit Card Sample Agreement

A credit card agreement covers the structure, features, terms, and conditions of a credit card.

File A Complaint

For problems with your credit card company, call the number on the back of your card or try to resolve it with the Consumer Financial Protection Bureau (CFPB).

- Submit a complaint to the CFPB about problems with managing your credit card account, billing disputes, changes to your APR, fees, unauthorized transactions, and many other issues. If you fail to resolve the problem, ask for the name, address, and phone number of the card company's regulatory agency.

Chapter 33

Important Differences Between Debit And Credit Cards

Many consumers use debit, credit, and prepaid cards, often interchangeably, to purchase goods and services. However, these three types of cards are quite different.

Each card works differently. If you use a credit card, you are borrowing money that you must pay back, in addition to interest, if you do not pay the balance in full by the due date. But, if you use a debit card, which is issued by your bank and linked to your checking or savings account, the money taken from the account is yours and you will never incur interest charges.

> Debit cards look like credit cards. But they do not work the same way. Credit cards use money that you borrow. Debit cards use money that is already in your checking account.
>
> *(Source: "Using Debit Cards," Federal Trade Commission (FTC).)*

With prepaid cards, you are spending the money deposited onto them, and they usually aren't linked to your checking or savings account. Prepaid products include "general-purpose reloadable" cards, which display a network brand such as American Express, Discover, MasterCard, or Visa; gift cards for purchases at stores; and payroll cards for employer deposits of salary or government benefit payments. Be aware of the possibility of unanticipated fees and, with certain types of these cards, the potential for limited consumer protections against unauthorized transactions.

About This Chapter: This chapter includes text excerpted from "Debit, Credit And Prepaid Cards: There Are Differences," Federal Deposit Insurance Corporation (FDIC), May 1, 2017.

Watch for fees. You may be charged an overdraft fee if you use a debit card for a purchase but there aren't enough funds in the account and you have given your bank written permission to charge you for allowing the transaction to go through. "You can always revoke that authorization if you don't want to risk paying these fees, and future debit card transactions will be declined if you don't have the funds in your account," explained Federal Deposit Insurance Corporation (FDIC) Consumer Affairs Specialist Heather St. Germain.

Similarly, a credit card issuer may decline a transaction that puts you over your credit limit unless you have explicitly agreed to pay a fee to permit over-the-limit transactions.

How Is A Debit Card Different From A Credit Card?

For example, with debit cards:

- You can get a debit card from the bank when you open a checking account
- Money comes out of your checking account when you pay with a debit card
- You don't pay extra money in interest when you pay with a debit card
- You can use a debit card at an automated teller machine (ATM) to get money from your checking account
- You do not build a credit history using a debit card

With credit cards:

- You apply for a credit card at a bank or store
- You get a bill once a month for everything you buy with a credit card
- You might pay extra money in interest if you don't pay all of your credit card bill every month
- You can use a credit card as a safer way to pay for things online
- You can build a credit history using a credit card if you pay the whole bill every month when it is due

(Source: "Using Debit Cards," Federal Trade Commission (FTC).)

Prepaid cards are sometimes marketed with celebrity endorsements and promotional offers. "While some prepaid card offers seem attractive, remember that you may have to pay various fees on the card," said Susan Boenau, Chief of the FDIC's Consumer Affairs Section. "These costs may include monthly fees, charges for loading funds onto the card, and fees for each transaction."

As an alternative to a traditional checking account or prepaid card, consumers who don't plan to write checks but do want to bank electronically may want to consider opening a "checkless" transaction account that allows you to pay bills and make purchases online or with a debit card.

Your liability for an unauthorized transaction varies depending on the type of card. Federal law limits your losses to a maximum of $50 if a credit card is lost or stolen. For a debit card, your maximum liability under federal law is $50 if you notify your bank within two business days after learning of the loss or theft of your card. But, if you notify your bank after those first two days, under the law you could lose much more.

Chapter 34

Choosing And Using Credit Cards

Credit cards can offer numerous benefits to consumers, including a convenient way to pay for purchases, the ability to build a credit history, and the potential for rewards. But to make the most of your credit cards, it helps to be an informed consumer. First, remember that any purchase you make with your credit card is a loan that must be repaid. And as with any loan, it's important to select the right product for you and to use it wisely.

To help you maximize the benefits and avoid the potential pitfalls, here are some tips for choosing and using credit cards.

Pay Your Bills On Time, Every Time

"On time" means the payment gets to the company by the day the bill is due. Mail your bills a few days before they're due.

Think about signing up for text alerts to make sure you don't pay late or miss a payment. Or, consider automatic payments from your bank to help make sure your bills get paid on time. Keep track of automatic payments so you know you have enough money in your account to cover them.

(Source: "How To Rebuild Your Credit," Consumer Financial Protection Bureau (CFPB).)

About This Chapter: This chapter includes text excerpted from "Be In Charge Of Your Credit Cards: Our Latest Tips For Choosing And Using Them," Federal Deposit Insurance Corporation (FDIC), August 16, 2016.

Choosing A Credit Card

Maximize your ability to get a good credit card by ensuring that your credit report is accurate. Correcting inaccuracies may help you improve your credit history and credit score, which card issuers will consider when deciding whether to offer you a card and how they will determine your interest rate and credit limit. You also can find out if an identity thief has opened credit cards or other accounts in your name.

By federal law, you are entitled to one free copy of your credit report every 12 months from each of the three major nationwide consumer reporting agencies (also called "credit bureaus")—Equifax, Experian, and TransUnion. Each company issues its own report, and because some lenders do not furnish information to all three of them, it's useful to request your report from each one in order to get a comprehensive view of your credit history. Go to www.AnnualCreditReport.com or call toll-free 877-322-8228 to order free credit reports or for more information.

If you find errors, each reporting agency provides ways to ask for an investigation and a correction. In addition, you can request a correction directly from the entity that supplied the incorrect information.

"Your credit reports play a large role in what credit you will qualify for, so it's important that they be accurate," said Jonathan Miller, Deputy Director for Policy and Research in the Federal Deposit Insurance Corporation's (FDIC) Division of Depositor and Consumer Protection (DCP). "If you find any mistakes on a report, you have both a need and a right to have them corrected. And, be wary of companies that promise to 'fix' your credit report. If there is negative information that is legitimate, there is no way to remove it, although it will expire from your report after a period of time."

Determine what type of card best meets your needs. First, think about how you will use the card. In particular, do you expect to pay your card balance in full each month or carry a balance from month to month?

If you don't pay your card balance in full each month, the best card for you will likely be one with a low Annual Percentage Rate (APR). But if you do plan to pay in full each month, you might instead focus on whether there is an annual fee, rewards or other features, such as a waiver of foreign transaction fees (helpful for international trips or purchases).

Shop around and compare product terms and conditions. Although you may receive credit card offers, don't assume these are the best deals for you. If you decide you need to apply for a card, compare multiple products from several lenders. Various websites can help you compare product offerings from different institutions, but be aware that some sites list only companies that pay to advertise there.

What factors should you consider? Federal law requires creditors to disclose important rate and fee information to you before you apply. "This enables you to make apples-to-apples comparisons for the most important factors," pointed out Elizabeth Khalil, an FDIC Senior Policy Analyst.

Here is additional guidance on how to compare key terms and conditions:

- **Annual percentage rate (APR):** The APR represents the annual cost of the credit. In general, there are three types of APRs that might be applicable to your card: those for purchases, for balance transfers from another card, and for cash advances. Also pay attention to introductory rates. Some credit offers, such as balance transfers, come with special low interest rates that will increase after the promotional period.

- **Fees:** These can include annual fees, balance transfer fees, and cash advance fees (in addition to any interest you might pay), foreign transaction fees, and penalties for late payments or returned payments. Determine if fees can change over time, as many cards will waive an annual fee for the first year but will charge it in later years.

- **Rewards:** These programs can be complicated, with specific eligibility rules. Know what you need to do to qualify for rewards, which might include meeting spending requirements, and how much you would have to spend to accumulate enough points or miles to get what you want. Also understand what you need to do to maintain your reward points, since they can sometimes expire if an account is closed or considered inactive.

Do your homework before signing up for promotional offers or additional products. Some credit cards come with promotions that are enticing but may cost you more money in the long run. For instance, some credit cards marketed by retail stores offer "no interest" on balances for a certain period of time, such as the first 12 months after purchase. But if you don't pay off the entire purchase balance by the end of the timeframe that was disclosed, you may be charged all of the interest that accrued since the date of purchase. "With any deferred interest offer, it's important to pay the balance in full before the promotional period ends," said Matt Homer, a Policy Analyst at the FDIC. "If you can't do that, a better fit might be a credit card with a low APR that doesn't expire after the promotional period."

Additionally, credit card companies might offer other credit-related products, such as credit protection (to pay, suspend or cancel part or all of your outstanding balance in the event of a specific hardship) and identity theft protection (to monitor your credit reports for signs that a crook attempted to use your name to commit fraud). "Make sure you fully understand how these products work and how much they cost by reading the fine print and asking questions before you sign up," advised Homer. "Also evaluate whether the price you will pay justifies the value you will get from the product."

For example, he said, as an alternative to paying for identity theft protection, you can look for warning signs of fraud by monitoring your free annual credit reports, especially if you space out the requests for a different company's report approximately every four months.

Using A Credit Card

Carefully review your card statements for billing errors and other problems, and report them quickly. The FDIC's Consumer Response Center reports that billing disputes and error resolution problems and processes are the most common types of complaints it received in 2012 and 2013 related to credit cards. And, according to the Consumer Financial Protection Bureau (CFPB), many consumers are confused and frustrated by the process of challenging inaccuracies on their monthly statements.

If you notice a billing error, such as an unauthorized charge on your statement, contact the card issuer as soon as possible.

Checking your account periodically also can help you monitor your spending. "You may want to sign up for alerts on your mobile phone or through e-mail that inform you when your credit card has hit a specific balance amount or you are close to your credit limit. Other alerts can remind you about an upcoming bill," Homer added.

Review all communications from your lender. Keep a copy of your cardholder agreement and look at all other mailings from your lender because they may include notices about adjustments to the important terms of your card. For example, a credit card issuer must typically provide customers a 45-day advance notice of an interest rate increase.

Pay on time to limit late fees and protect your credit history. If you miss a payment, you'll likely be charged a late fee, which can sometimes be up to $35 or more. Late payments are also reported to the major consumer reporting agencies, which can harm your credit history.

Pay as much as you can to avoid or minimize fees and interest charges. While it may sound like a bargain to pay the minimum amount due, the long-term costs can be staggering. You will generally be charged interest on the unpaid portion of your balance at the beginning of a new billing cycle and your credit card issuer may start charging you interest from the time of purchase. If you can't pay the full amount, paying even slightly more than the minimum amount due can reduce your interest costs.

If you add an "authorized user" to the account, set rules and monitor transactions. Adding an authorized user can be a way to jointly manage your finances (for your convenience) or to help someone else (such as a relative under 21 years old) establish a credit history. But remember that you will be liable for any charges the authorized user makes with the card, so it's best to have a mutual understanding about your expectations as the account owner. Also consider asking your card issuer to place a spending limit on the card assigned to the authorized user. And, of course, be sure to regularly monitor the account and take appropriate action, if necessary.

Protect your card from fraud. Never provide your credit card numbers—including the account number and expiration date on the front and the security code on the front and/or back—in response to an unsolicited phone call, e-mail or other communication. When using your credit card online, make sure you're dealing with a legitimate company.

Also, take precautions at the checkout counter and gas pump, watching for card reading devices that look suspicious, such as a plastic sleeve inside a card slot or other possible signs of tampering.

If you have lost your card or are the victim of identity theft, contact your credit card company as soon as possible. Write down the contact number printed on the back of your card and keep it somewhere else that you can quickly access.

Recent security breaches at a few major retailers have some consumers concerned about using their credit cards. Federal law protects consumers from unauthorized activity, and card issuers often will waive any liability for fraudulent purchases that are reported promptly.

To try to resolve a complaint, first contact your card issuer. Before calling, think through and summarize what the problem is and what you'd like done about it. This will help you remember the key points of the issue. In case the financial institution doesn't agree to your solution, think about other alternatives you might propose or accept.

"If you're having trouble resolving a complaint with the credit card issuer you can consider taking your concerns to the institution's federal regulator," pointed out DCP Director Mark Pearce. "Doing so not only can assist a consumer with a legitimate complaint, but it also provides the regulator with important information on consumer concerns and trends in general."

The FDIC and other banking regulators can't settle contract disputes between a bank and a consumer, but they often can assist consumers in other ways, such as helping people understand confusing information, contacting the issuer and initiating a formal review process, and/or taking supervisory actions if the institution is in violation of a law or regulation.

Chapter 35

Using Credit Wisely

The responsible use of credit can have a major impact on a student's future. Obviously, you need to have an established, healthy credit history if you plan to buy a car or home and make other large purchases, but the way you handle credit can also have other significant implications. For example, landlords review credit history before they'll rent you an apartment, and many employers check your credit record as part of the hiring process. The smart thing to do is to begin building a positive credit history now, taking small steps to demonstrate your ability to handle money effectively. A good record of repayment will not only make it easier to get the credit you need in the future but will also result in lower interest rates when you do borrow money.

Don't Apply For Too Much Credit In A Short Time

Your credit score may go down if you apply for or open a lot of new accounts in a short time.

This includes getting a new card so you can transfer balances, or opening a new store card account so you can get a discount.

(Source: "How To Rebuild Your Credit," Consumer Financial Protection Bureau (CFPB).)

Credit Score

When someone checks your credit history, what they're looking at is your credit score. This is a number, generally from 300–850, tallied by large credit reporting agencies (CRAs) using

---

About This Chapter: "Using Credit Wisely," © 2017 Omnigraphics.

information about past purchases and repayment that is obtained from various retailers and other creditors. The three largest CRAs are Equifax, Experian, and TransUnion, and prospective lenders use their scores as predictors of your likelihood to default on future credit.

There can be more than 30 factors that go into calculating a credit score, but these are generally grouped together into five major categories:

- **Credit history.** This is the most important factor and makes up 35 percent of your credit score. Unsurprisingly, lenders want to know that you regularly pay back money you owe.

- **Total indebtedness.** This makes up 30 percent of the score and is important because having a lot of debt can make it hard to pay it all back. The ratio of debt to available credit is also critical. Having a lot of available credit but only using a small amount is good; using up all or most of your available credit hurts your score.

- **Length of credit history.** Accounting for 15 percent of the total score, this includes both how long you have had a credit record and how long individual accounts have been open. A longer history gives potential lenders a better idea of how you handle credit.

- **Type of credit.** This generally makes up 10 percent of the score, although it is more important for individuals with a short credit history. A mix of different kinds of credit shows potential lenders that you can handle various types of indebtedness responsibly.

- **New credit.** This makes up another 10 percent of the total and includes newly opened accounts as well as "hard inquiries," which go on your record any time you apply for credit, whether you actually borrow money or not. (Soft inquiries, such as when you check your own credit record, have no impact on your score.) Lenders may see too much new credit—or applying for new credit—as an indication that you'll be adding more indebtedness in the near future.

Building A Credit Record

Students building a credit history will need to start small and take carefully measured steps to demonstrate fiscal responsibility. One of the first things to do is to check your current credit history, if you have one. There are several online sites that allow you to do this, including Freecreditreport.com, Annualcreditreport.com, and Creditkarma.com, as well as the three major CRAs. Here are some suggestions for next steps:

- **Open savings and checking accounts.** It's always good to have some savings in the bank, and the regular use of a checking account and debit card shows that you can budget and handle money responsibly.

- **Pay your monthly bills.** Regular payment of phone, electric, and cable bills is another indicator of prudent financial management.

- **Pay your student loans.** Most students need loans to help pay for college, and making payments on time shows that you take your responsibilities seriously.

- **Get a student credit card.** One of the best ways to begin building credit is to select a suitable card with a low credit limit, then use it regularly and make payments in full each month. To start with, you may need a joint card with a parent or other person with established credit.

Note that not all of these go directly into a credit score. For example, the use of a debit card won't have an impact on the total. But each of these steps provides an indication of financial responsibility and helps develop good money-management habits.

> Take advantage of technology. Most banks and credit-card issuers have mobile apps that make it easier to conduct transactions and keep track of spending. Many also offer text messages for low-balance alerts, overdrafts, and payment-due reminders.

Types Of Credit

There are a number of kinds of credit that are commonly available to students, and it's important to understand how they work. Unless you have an established credit history, it's likely that you'll need a co-signer or joint account holder, but as long as your name is on the account, you'll be building a positive credit history.

- **Credit cards.** These are cards, such as Visa, Mastercard, and Discover, issued by a bank or other financial institution that you can use to purchase goods or services. The card-issuer pays the merchant or service provider, then you pay back the money to the issuer. About one-third of college students have a credit card of some kind, because they're a convenient way to pay expenses and buy things on campus. But if you don't pay off the entire balance each month, a finance charge will be added, and this will continue to build until the balance is paid off. Look for a card with no annual fee and the lowest interest rate possible.

- **Retail cards.** Also called "store cards," these are usually issued by department stores for use at their retail locations or online. They have limited use, since they can only be used with one retailer, and for that reason they're not as common as they once were. (Most retailers now partner with a major credit-card issuer for a store-branded card that can be used anywhere.) But retail cards have the advantage of generally being easier to get than a major credit card, so they can be a good way to start building credit history.

- **Gasoline cards.** Another type of retail card, these are issued by gasoline companies for use at their own stations. Like store cards, they tend to be easier to get than major credit-card brands, and they're a good way for students with cars to keep track of fuel and maintenance expenses and build a good credit score.

- **Student loans.** Education loans most often come from government-backed sources. Some are based on need and some are open to anyone. Most of the time, repayment is deferred until you graduate or leave school, and interest may also not begin accruing until then. Other student loans come from private sources and work like any other credit instrument, such as a car loan. In either case, maintaining a regular schedule of repayment works to build a strong credit history.

Consider a secured credit card. This is a card that requires a cash deposit in the amount of the credit limit. So if you deposit $200, you can spend up to $200 with the card. They're easy to get, although some carry an annual fee, and most allow you (or your parents) to add funds to the account on a regular basis. And, unlike prepaid cards, secured cards help build your credit score.

Good Credit Practices

Many people get into trouble by not using credit wisely. Developing solid credit practices while avoiding some common pitfalls can help ensure that you build and maintain a good credit score and create financial health. Here are some tips:

- **Shop for credit.** Fees and interest rates vary widely, and they can really add up. Speak to several lenders and examine their websites carefully before signing anything.

- **Read the fine print.** Credit applications contain a lot of detail. Be sure you know if, for example, you're signing up for a low introductory interest rate that goes up after a period of time.

- **Don't borrow more than you can pay back.** It may seem strange, but lenders will often loan you more money than you can repay. Know your finances and live within your budget.

- **Use cash or a debit card when possible.** Credit cards are convenient, but they let you spend more than you have. Sticking to cash or debit cards limits you to the funds you have on hand.

- **Have only one credit card.** Credit-card offers are tempting, but with multiple cards you run the risk of overextending your debt, and applying for them negatively affects your credit score.

- **Avoid annual fees.** Some credit cards come with an annual fee, but so many of them don't that there's no need to pay for the privilege of having a card.

- **Avoid late fees.** If you don't make payments on time, you'll be assessed a late fee. This not only costs money, it also negatively affects your credit score and may result in a higher interest rate.

- **Pay your balance every month.** By paying off the amount you charge each month, you'll avoid accruing interest, which costs you money. (**Note:** There's a common myth that paying the balance each month has a negative impact on your credit score. This is false. It will help build your score.)

- **Don't get cash advances.** Read the fine print. Cash advances on credit cards almost always come with higher interest rates and possibly some additional fees.

- **Take advantage of points and other perks.** When shopping for a credit card, look for one that offers reward points, travel rewards, discounts, and other perks. These can save you money.

- **Check your monthly statements.** You want to be sure the lender's accounting is accurate and that there are no charges you didn't initiate. If you find a discrepancy, call the lender immediately.

- **Check your credit score at least annually.** Make sure it's accurate and there are no accounts listed that you didn't open. If something looks wrong, contact the lender and the CRA right away.

Keep in touch with your creditors. If you can't make a payment on time, for example, ask for an extension. There's usually not a problem doing this (once, anyway), and it might help you avoid a late fee. If payments are due at a bad time of month for you, ask for a revised due date.

References

1. "10 Tips For Using Credit Wisely," BusinessWire.com, April 7, 2015.

2. "Credit Basics: Using Credit Wisely," CapitolOne.com, 2017.

3. "How To Use Credit Cards Wisely," CollegeBoard.org, 2017.

4. Irby, LaToya. "Dos And Don'ts Of Using Credit Cards Wisely," TheBalance.com, June 26, 2016.

5. "Using Credit Wisely," Greenpath.com, n.d.

6. "Using Credit Wisely," HandsOnBanking.org, n.d.

Chapter 36

Avoiding Credit Card Pitfalls

Seven Ways To Avoid Pitfalls In Areas Such As Interest Rate And Fee Increases

As reported, Congress passed a new law for credit cards that helps protect consumers from most instances of sudden interest rate increases and other unfavorable changes in fees and account terms. Most of the rules implementing the law are in effect, and the remaining provisions will be effective. But here's something else to know—it's possible consumers could face account changes going forward, such as interest rate increases on future transactions and the imposition of new fees or penalties.

How can you avoid potential pitfalls in the new world of credit cards?

1. **Understand your right to cancel a credit card before certain significant account changes take effect.** Under the new law, card issuers now must generally tell customers about certain changes in account terms—in areas such as interest rate and fee increases—45 days in advance, up from 15 days in the past. In that same notice, they must inform consumers of their right to cancel the card before certain account changes take effect. These notices may come with your credit card bill or through a separate communication.

   "It's important to read everything from your card issuer, even what appears to be junk mail," said Kathleen Nagle, Federal Deposit Insurance Corporation (FDIC) Associate

About This Chapter: Text under the heading "Seven Ways To Avoid Pitfalls In Areas Such As Interest Rate And Fee Increases" is excerpted from "New Realities, New Directions For Credit Cardholders," Federal Deposit Insurance Corporation (FDIC), June 12, 2014; Text under the heading "Act Fast If You Can't Pay Your Credit Cards" is excerpted from "Act Fast If You Can't Pay Your Credit Cards," U.S. Government Publishing Office (GPO), 2012.

Director for Consumer Protection. "Be aware of when the new rate or fee will take effect, so you can have enough time to shop around for a new card, if necessary."

Consumers who notify their card company to cancel their card before fees are increased or certain other significant changes take effect will still be required to repay the outstanding balance, but they cannot be required to repay it immediately. However, the card company can increase the minimum monthly payment, subject to certain limitations.

Also note that there are exceptions to the 45-day notice requirement. For example, you will generally not receive advance notice of a rate increase on a card with a variable interest rate that will fluctuate based on an advertised index, such as the prime rate.

2. **Keep an eye on your credit limit.** Some people, even those with good credit histories, have recently seen their credit limits cut back. Reductions in credit lines can be harmful because your borrowing power will be diminished. Also remember that your credit score is based, in part, on what percentage of your credit limit you are using and how much you owe. Borrowers who carry large balances in proportion to their credit limit may see their credit scores fall. And a lower credit score can make it difficult or more expensive to get new credit in the future.

   How can you reduce the risk that your credit limit will be cut or your credit card account will be canceled? One factor that credit card companies consider is how you pay your bills. "It's important to show a steady, timely payment history," reported Evelyn Manley, a Senior Consumer Affairs Specialist at the FDIC. Paying all your credit-related bills by the due date—that includes your credit card bills as well as your car loan, mortgage, and other debts—shows that you're a responsible borrower.

   Also, pay as much of your credit card bill as you can each month. If possible, pay in full, but definitely try to pay more than the minimum balance due.

   What should you do if you've already had your credit limit cut? Put a renewed focus on lowering the amount of money you owe on your credit cards.

   Also, consumers who have difficulty making their minimum payments on time may benefit from speaking with a reputable credit counselor to get help or guidance at little or no cost.

3. **Decide how you want to handle transactions that would put you over your credit limit.** Under the new law, no fees may be imposed for making a purchase or other transaction that would put your account over the credit limit unless you explicitly

agree, in advance, that the credit card company can process these transactions for you and charge a fee.

"Even if you agree to over-the-limit fees, you have the right to change your mind down the road," said Luke W. Reynolds, Chief of the FDIC's Community Outreach Section. "You would simply instruct your card issuer to deny any transactions that would exceed your credit limit and would trigger a fee."

In either case, he said, "you still should monitor how much you've charged on your card so you don't exceed the credit limit."

4. **Be cautious with "no-interest" offers.** Many retailers, such as electronics or furniture stores, promote credit cards with "zero-percent interest" on purchases for a certain amount of time. These cards allow you to buy big-ticket items, perhaps a sofa or a stereo system, without paying interest for anywhere from six months to more than a year. While the chance to avoid interest payments sounds like a terrific deal, keep in mind that if you don't follow the rules for these offers, this "no-interest" special could end up being expensive.

The reason is, with many of these offers, you must pay off the entire purchase by the time the promotional period ends to take advantage of the zero-rate offer. If you don't, the lender will charge you interest from the date you bought the item. You would then have to pay interest—at the lender's standard rate—from the date of purchase. And if the annual percentage rate or APR on the retailer's card is higher than what you would pay on another card you have, the extra costs could really add up. The APR is the cost of credit expressed as a yearly rate, including interest and other charges.

5. **Keep only the credit cards you really need and then periodically use them all.** Some consumers have too many credit cards. Among the concerns: Those extra cards can lead some people to overspend. Also, having many cards with no existing balance or a very low balance can reduce your credit score because prospective lenders can conclude that you have the potential to use them and get into debt.

For the average person, two or three general-purpose cards are probably enough. Consider canceling and cutting up the rest. However, also remember that closing a credit card account can temporarily lower your credit score, especially if the canceled card was one you owned and used responsibly for many years.

With the credit cards you do keep, remember to avoid large balances on them in relation to the credit limit. And in the new environment, it also may be beneficial to periodically use all of your cards. Here's why. Even if you pay your card bill in full each month and never pay interest, using your card earns money for the card company because merchants pay a fee each time you use the card. So, consumers who regularly use their cards and repay their debt may be considered valued customers, even if they pay on time and don't pay interest. "Regular purchases promptly paid off may be enough to reduce the risk of a credit line reduction, inactivity fees, and other penalties," said Susan Boenau, Chief of the FDIC's Consumer Affairs Section.

6. **Do your research before paying high annual fees for a "rewards" card.** Rewards sound great in advertisements for credit cards, but the points formula can be complicated, the rules are subject to change, and the benefits may not be as generous as you think. You should always read the fine print and be realistic about your likely use of the card before you accept an expensive annual fee in return for rewards.

7. **Take additional precautions against interest rate increases.** "Although the law puts new limits on interest rate increases, you need to remain vigilant," Manley added. For example, while card companies cannot increase the interest rate on existing balances except in certain circumstances, they may raise rates on extensions of credit for new purchases as long as proper notice is provided.

"If you receive a notice that your interest rate is increasing," Manley said, "determine whether you have another way to make future purchases, such as by waiting until you have saved enough money for the purchase or by using a card with a lower interest rate."

Rate increases also may come in another form. For example, some fixed-rate cards may be converted to variable-rate cards after a notice has been sent to cardholders. This would result in variable rates being applied to new balances.

Also note that a credit card company can increase the rate on an existing balance if the consumer fails to send the minimum payment within 60 days of the due date. So, it's very important to avoid being more than 60 days late on a credit card. If you miss a due date, you can avoid a "penalty" interest rate on that existing balance by getting your payment in within 60 days. And if you're more than 60 days late and that does trigger a rate increase, get current on your credit card payments as soon as possible and then start consistently paying on time. Card issuers are required to reduce the penalty rate if they receive prompt payments for six months.

In general, what else can you do to get the best rates? Keep in mind that a credit score is built up over long periods, not just over one or two years, so make all your loan payments on time. Even if you have past blemishes, you can improve your credit score over time by managing your credit well. Be aware that if you can only afford to pay the minimum amount due, you probably won't get the best rates. But if you can pay more than the minimum each month—as much more as possible—that will work in your favor.

Also, carefully read the terms of a new credit card before using it. If the card has a high interest rate or fees, shop around for a better offer.

Act Fast If You Can't Pay Your Credit Cards

Call your credit card company if you believe you're unable to pay the minimum payment on your credit card. Many creditors may be willing to help if you're facing a financial emergency. You do not need to be behind on your payments to ask for help!

> **TIP!**
> Before signing up for credit counseling, ask if you will be charged, how much, and what services will be provided. Be sure your credit counselor takes the time to learn about your financial situation, and offers to help you learn how you can make it better.

Don't Ignore The Problem

That may only cause bigger problems, such as:

- Higher interest rates
- Higher minimum payments
- Losing your charging privileges
- Late fees
- Damage to your credit score

Here's What To Do

1. **Add up your income and expenses.** Look for ways to cut costs. If you can't find enough to pay your minimum payment, decide how much you can afford to pay.

2. **Call your credit card company.**
   - Be sure to clearly explain:
   - Why you can't pay the minimum.
   - How much you can afford to pay.
   - When you could restart your normal payments.

3. **Consider credit counseling**

If you need more help, nonprofit credit counseling organizations can teach you more about handling your money.

No Easy Fixes

Some for-profit debt-relief companies say they can pay off your debts "for pennies on the dollar." But many times, these promises don't measure up. Watch out for any debt-relief organization that:

- Charges fees before it settles your debts.
- Guarantees it can make your unsecured debt go away.
- Tells you to stop communicating with creditors.

Chapter 37

Understanding The Extra Cost Of Minimum Payments

Keep Credit Card Use Under Control

Whether you shop online, by telephone, or by mail, a credit card can make buying things much easier. But when you use a credit card, it's important to keep track of your spending. Incidental and impulse purchases add up. When the bill comes, you have to pay what you owe. Owing more than you can afford to repay can damage your credit rating. Keeping good records can prevent a lot of headaches, especially if there are inaccuracies on your monthly statement. If you notice a problem, report it immediately to the company that issued the card. Usually the instructions for disputing a charge are on your monthly statement. If you use your credit card to order online, by telephone, or by mail, keep copies and printouts with details about the transaction.

These details should include the company's name, address, and telephone number; the date of your order; a copy of the order form you sent to the company or a list of the stock codes of the items you ordered; the order confirmation code; the ad or catalog from which you ordered (if applicable); any applicable warranties; and the return and refund policies.

Real World Examples

Suppose when you're 18, you charge $1,500 worth of clothes and DVDs on a credit card with a 19 percent interest rate.

About This Chapter: This chapter includes text excerpted from "Paying Down Credit Card Debt," Federal Trade Commission (FTC), August 2012.

If you repay only the minimum amount each month, and your minimum is 4 percent of the outstanding balance (the lowest amount permitted by some issuers), you'll start with a $60 payment. You'll be more than 26 years old by the time you pay off the debt. That's 106 payments, and you will have paid more than $889 extra in interest. And that's if you charge nothing else on the card, and no other fees are imposed (for example, late charges).

If your minimum payment is based on 2.5 percent of the outstanding balance, you'll start with a $37.50 payment. You'll be over 35 years old when you pay off the debt. That's 208 payments, and you will have paid more than $2,138 in interest, even if you charge nothing else on the account and have no other fees.

Chapter 38

How To Rebuild Your Credit Score

Your Rights

No one can legally remove accurate and timely negative information from a credit report. You can ask for an investigation—at no charge to you—of information in your file that you dispute as inaccurate or incomplete. Some people hire a company to investigate for them, but anything a credit repair company can do legally, you can do for yourself at little or no cost. By law:

- You're entitled to a free credit report if a company takes "adverse action" against you, like denying your application for credit, insurance, or employment. You have to ask for your report within 60 days of receiving notice of the action. The notice includes the name, address, and phone number of the consumer reporting company. You're also entitled to one free report a year if you're unemployed and plan to look for a job within 60 days; if you're on welfare; or if your report is inaccurate because of fraud, including identity theft.

- Each of the nationwide credit reporting companies—Equifax, Experian, and TransUnion—is required to provide you with a free copy of your credit report once every 12 months, if you ask for it. To order, visit annualcreditreport.com, or call 877-322-8228. You may order reports from each of the three credit reporting companies at the same time, or you can stagger your requests throughout the year.

About This Chapter: Text beginning with the heading "Your Rights" is excerpted from "Credit Repair: How To Help Yourself," Federal Trade Commission (FTC), November 2012; Text under the heading "Five Tips To Help Rebound From A Bad Credit History" is excerpted from "5 Tips To Help Rebound From A Bad Credit History," Federal Deposit Insurance Corporation (FDIC), August 21, 2014; Text under the heading "Changes Could Help Boost Credit Scores" is excerpted from "Changes Could Help Boost Credit Scores," Federal Deposit Insurance Corporation (FDIC), June 10, 2015.

- It doesn't cost anything to dispute mistakes or outdated items on your credit report. Both the credit reporting company and the information provider (the person, company, or organization that provides information about you to a credit reporting company) are responsible for correcting inaccurate or incomplete information in your report. To take advantage of all your rights, contact both the credit reporting company and the information provider.

Do It Yourself (DIY)

Step 1: Tell the credit reporting company, in writing, what information you think is inaccurate. In addition to including your complete name and address, your letter should identify each item in your report that you dispute; state the facts and the reasons you dispute the information, and ask that it be removed or corrected. You may want to enclose a copy of your report, and circle the items in question. Send your letter by certified mail, "return receipt requested," so you can document that the credit reporting company got it. Keep copies of your dispute letter and enclosures.

Credit reporting companies must investigate the items you question within 30 days—unless they consider your dispute frivolous. They also must forward all the relevant data you provide about the inaccuracy to the organization that provided the information. After the information provider gets notice of a dispute from the credit reporting company, it must investigate, review the relevant information, and report the results back to the credit reporting company. If the investigation reveals that the disputed information is inaccurate, the information provider has to notify the nationwide credit reporting companies so they can correct it in your file.

When the investigation is complete, the credit reporting company must give you the results in writing, too, and a free copy of your report if the dispute results in a change. If an item is changed or deleted, the credit reporting company cannot put the disputed information back in your file unless the information provider verifies that it's accurate and complete. The credit reporting company also must send you written notice that includes the name, address, and phone number of the information provider. If you ask, the credit reporting company must send notices of any correction to anyone who got your report in the past six months. You also can ask that a corrected copy of your report be sent to anyone who got a copy during the past two years for employment purposes.

If an investigation doesn't resolve your dispute with the credit reporting company, you can ask that a statement of the dispute be included in your file and in future reports. You also can ask the credit reporting company to give your statement to anyone who got a copy of your report in the recent past. You'll probably have to pay for this service.

Step 2: Tell the creditor or other information provider, in writing, that you dispute an item. Include copies (NOT originals) of documents that support your position. Many providers specify an address for disputes. If the provider reports the item to a consumer reporting company, it must include a notice of your dispute. And if the information is found to be inaccurate, the provider may not report it again.

> If you pay with a credit card, pay your balance off every month You'll build credit by using your credit card and paying on time, every time. Pay off your balances in full each month to avoid paying finance charges. Paying off your balance each month can also build better credit than carrying a balance.
>
> *(Source: "How To Rebuild Your Credit," Consumer Financial Protection Bureau (CFPB).)*

Reporting Accurate Negative Information

When negative information in your report is accurate, only time can make it go away. A credit reporting company can report most accurate negative information for seven years and bankruptcy information for 10 years. Information about an unpaid judgment against you can be reported for seven years or until the statute of limitations runs out, whichever is longer. The seven-year reporting period starts from the date the event took place. There is no time limit on reporting information about criminal convictions; information reported in response to your application for a job that pays more than $75,000 a year; and information reported because you've applied for more than $150,000 worth of credit or life insurance.

The Credit Repair Organizations Act

The Credit Repair Organization Act (CROA) makes it illegal for credit repair companies to lie about what they can do for you, and to charge you before they've performed their services. The CROA is enforced by the Federal Trade Commission (FTC) and requires credit repair companies to explain:

- your legal rights in a written contract that also details the services they'll perform

- your three day right to cancel without any charge

- how long it will take to get results

- the total cost you will pay

- any guarantees

What if a credit repair company you hired doesn't live up to its promises? You have some options. You can:

- sue them in federal court for your actual losses or for what you paid them, whichever is more

- seek punitive damages—money to punish the company for violating the law

- join other people in a class action lawsuit against the company, and if you win, the company has to pay your attorney's fees

Report Credit Repair Fraud

State Attorneys General

Many states also have laws regulating credit repair companies. If you have a problem with a credit repair company, report it to your local consumer affairs office or to your state attorney general (AG).

Federal Trade Commission (FTC)

You also can file a complaint with the Federal Trade Commission. Although the FTC can't resolve individual credit disputes, it can take action against a company if there's a pattern of possible law violations. File your complaint online at ftc.gov/complaint or call 877-FTC-HELP (877-382-4357).

Where To Get Legitimate Help

Just because you have a poor credit history doesn't mean you can't get credit. Creditors set their own standards, and not all look at your credit history the same way. Some may look only at recent years to evaluate you for credit, and they may give you credit if your bill-paying history has improved. It may be worthwhile to contact creditors informally to discuss their credit standards.

If you're not disciplined enough to create a budget and stick to it, to work out a repayment plan with your creditors, or to keep track of your mounting bills, you might consider contacting a credit counseling organization. Many are nonprofit and work with you to solve your financial problems. But remember that "nonprofit" status doesn't guarantee free, affordable, or even legitimate services. In fact, some credit counseling organizations—even some that claim nonprofit status—may charge high fees or hide their fees by pressuring people to make "voluntary" contributions that only cause more debt.

Most credit counselors offer services through local offices, online, or on the phone. If possible, find an organization that offers in-person counseling. Many universities, military bases, credit unions, housing authorities, and branches of the U.S. Cooperative Extension Service (CES) operate nonprofit credit counseling programs. Your financial institution, local consumer protection agency, and friends and family also may be good sources of information and referrals.

If you're thinking about filing for bankruptcy, be aware that bankruptcy laws require that you get credit counseling from a government-approved organization within six months before you file for bankruptcy relief. You can find a state-by-state list of government-approved organizations at www.usdoj.gov/ust, the website of the U.S. Trustee Program. That's the organization within the U.S. Department of Justice (DOJ) that supervises bankruptcy cases and trustees. Be wary of credit counseling organizations that say they are government-approved, but don't appear on the list of approved organizations.

Reputable credit counseling organizations can advise you on managing your money and debts, help you develop a budget, and offer free educational materials and workshops. Their counselors are certified and trained in the areas of consumer credit, money and debt management, and budgeting. Counselors discuss your entire financial situation with you, and can help you develop a personalized plan to solve your money problems. An initial counseling session typically lasts an hour, with an offer of follow-up sessions.

Five Tips To Help Rebound From A Bad Credit History

1. **Order your free credit reports and look for errors.** Credit reporting companies, often referred to as "credit bureaus," maintain reports that show how an individual handles certain aspects of his or her finances. Your credit report includes information on how much credit you have available, how much credit you are using, whether you pay loans and other bills on time, your payment history on closed accounts, and any debt collections or bankruptcy filings. Credit bureaus and other companies use the information in your credit report to generate a credit score to predict, for example, how likely you are to repay your debts or how reliable you may be as a tenant.

   Federal law requires credit reporting companies to provide consumers with a free copy of their credit report once every 12 months, if requested. You can easily obtain your free credit reports from each of the three major credit bureaus (Equifax, Experian, and TransUnion) or by calling 877-322-8228. Under other circumstances, such as being denied a loan or employment based on your credit report or if you believe you may be a fraud victim, you are also entitled to a free copy directly from the credit bureau that provided the initial report. Be cautious of costly subscriptions to additional credit-related services that you may be offered while requesting your credit report.

Because mistakes can happen, closely review your credit report(s) when you receive it. According to a study from the Federal Trade Commission (FTC), more than 25 percent of consumers surveyed identified errors on their credit reports that might affect their credit scores. "It is important to dispute inaccurate information, in writing, with both the credit reporting company as well as with the original source of the information so that the error does not show up again," said Jennifer Dice, a Federal Deposit Insurance Corporation (FDIC) Supervisory Consumer Affairs Specialist.

If you have a complaint about a credit reporting company, you can contact the Consumer Financial Protection Bureau (CFPB) or by calling 855-411-2372.

2. **Improve your credit history by paying your bills on time.** Paying on time is one of the biggest contributors to your credit score. If you have a history of paying bills late, find out if your bank will send you an e-mail or text message reminding you when a payment is due. You may also consider having your payments for loans or other bills automatically debited from your bank account.

Once you become current on payments, stay current. "The more you pay your bills on time after being late, the more your credit score should increase," Dice added. "The impact of past credit problems on your credit score fades as time passes and as your current timeliness in paying bills is reflected on your credit report."

3. **Reduce the amounts you owe.** You can get on track toward a better score by paying down balances owed.

It takes some discipline, so start by getting organized. Make a list of all of your accounts and debts (perhaps using your credit report, if it's accurate, and recent statements) to determine how much you owe and the interest rate you are being charged. You may be able to reduce your interest costs by paying off the debts with the highest interest rate first, while still making the minimum payments (if not more) on your other accounts.

Also consider how to limit your use of credit cards in favor of cash, checks or a debit card. "While regular, responsible use of your credit card may help your credit score, it is best to keep your balance low enough so that you can pay the account balance in full, on time, every month," suggested Heather St. Germain, an FDIC Senior Consumer Affairs Specialist.

4. **Consider free or low-cost help from reputable sources.** Counseling services are available to help consumers budget money, pay bills, and develop a plan to improve their credit report. Be cautious of counseling services that advise you to stop making payments to your creditors or to pay the counselors instead (so they can negotiate on your behalf with the lender). These programs can be costly and may result in your credit score becoming even worse.

5. **Beware of credit repair scams.** Con artists lure innocent victims in with false promises to "erase" a bad credit history in a short amount of time, but there are no quick ways to remove credit problems on your record that are legitimate. "You'll also know you've encountered credit repair fraud if the company insists you pay upfront before it does any work on your behalf or it encourages you to give false information on your credit applications," said St. Germain. In general, before doing business with a for-profit credit repair company, learn how you can improve your own credit history at little or no cost.

Changes Could Help Boost Credit Scores

Your credit score, which is mainly based on your history of repaying loans, can determine your ability to borrow money and how much you will pay for it. Here is good news for some consumers: Your score may improve as a result of changes in how credit reports and scores are compiled.

In one development, Fair Isaac Corporation (FICO), a company that provides software used to produce many consumer credit scores, announced that unpaid medical debt will not have as big an impact on the new version of its most popular credit score.

The Consumer Financial Protection Bureau (CFPB) announced that it will require the major consumer reporting agencies to provide regular accuracy reports to the Bureau on how disputes from consumers are being handled. The CFPB said medical debt in particular is a source of numerous complaints because the billing process can be complicated and confusing to consumers. The CFPB noted that the accuracy reports will help it hold credit reporting companies accountable for ensuring that erroneous information does not damage a consumer's credit score.

Separately, as part of an agreement with the New York Attorney General's Office, the nation's three major credit reporting agencies—Equifax, Experian, and TransUnion—are taking steps that could help some consumers raise their scores. For example, they committed to conduct a more thorough review of documents provided by a consumer who is disputing information in a credit report. Also, they are clarifying how consumers can appeal the decision that the credit reporting company makes. In addition, medical debts will not appear on credit reports until they are at least 180 days past due.

These changes may help raise some consumers' credit scores and reduce their borrowing costs. In general, though, to build or maintain a good credit score, consumers need to manage their money carefully, and that includes using caution when taking on additional debt.

These Four Things Don't Help Rebuild Your Credit

1. Using a debit card or paying cash. These transactions don't help you prove you can repay debts.

2. Using a prepaid card. A prepaid card is your own money, loaded on to the card in advance.

3. Taking out a payday loan. Even making on-time repayments might not help your credit.

4. Taking an auto loan from a "buy here, pay here" car lot, unless they promise in writing to report your on-time payments.

(Source: "How To Rebuild Your Credit," Consumer Financial Protection Bureau (CFPB).)

Chapter 39

Protecting Your Plastic: Don't Be A Victim

How To Help Keep Your Credit And Debit Cards Safe

While many consumers still like to use paper money and coins, more and more people are pulling out credit or debit cards to make purchases. And, as the popularity of payment cards has grown, so has the number of criminals trying to steal very valuable details, including the cardholder's name and the card's account number and expiration date, which are printed on the card itself as well as encoded (for machine readability) in the magnetic stripe or a computer chip.

"No matter how your card information is stored, it is in high demand by criminals who would like to retrieve that data to create a counterfeit version of your card or use the information to make purchases online or over the phone," said Michael Benardo, manager of the Federal Deposit Insurance Corporation's (FDIC) Cyber Fraud and Financial Crimes Section.

If you're ever the victim or target of credit or debit card theft or fraud, catching it fast and reporting it to your card issuer are key to resolving the situation. And while federal laws and industry practices protect consumers in these situations, there are important differences depending on the type of card.

In general, under the Truth in Lending Act, your cap for liability for unauthorized charges on a credit card is $50. But under the Electronic Fund Transfer Act (EFTA), if your debit card or automated teller machine (ATM) card is lost or stolen or you notice an unauthorized purchase or

About This Chapter: This chapter includes text excerpted from "Protecting Your Plastic From High-Tech Criminals," Federal Deposit Insurance Corporation (FDIC), June 14, 2014.

other transfer using your checking or savings account, your maximum liability is limited to $50 only if you notify your bank within two business days. If you wait more than two business days, your debit/ATM card losses under the law could go up to $500, or perhaps much more. With either card, though, industry practices may further limit your losses, so check with your card issuer.

What else can you do to keep thieves away from your cards...and your money?

Never give out your payment card numbers in response to an unsolicited e-mail, text message or phone call, no matter who the source supposedly is. An "urgent" e-mail or phone call appearing to be from a well-known organization is likely a scam attempting to trick you into divulging your card information. It's called "phishing," a high-tech variation of the concept of "fishing" for account information. If they get confidential details, the criminals can use the information to make counterfeit cards and run up charges on your accounts.

Take precautions at the checkout counter, ATM, and gas pump. "Be on the lookout for credit and debit card reading devices that look suspicious, such as a plastic sleeve inside a card slot," Benardo said. "Crooks are getting very good at attaching their own devices over legitimate card readers and gathering account information from the cards that consumers swipe through those readers."

Also be alert when you hand your payment card to an employee at a restaurant or retail establishment. For example, if he or she swipes your card through two devices instead of one, that second device could be recording your account information to make a fraudulent card. Report that situation to a manager and your card issuer.

To help combat payment card fraud, many card issuers have turned to the technology known as radio frequency identification (RFID). This uses wireless radio signals to identify people or objects from a distance. It is also being used with items such as highway toll passes, subway fare cards and pay-at-the-pump cards to add convenience and speed up many routine transactions. While some news reports indicate that payment cards with RFID chips may be more vulnerable to fraud than traditional cards with magnetic stripes on the back, Benardo said that's not the case.

"Today an RFID card is nearly impossible to breach because the chip in it creates an encrypted signal that is extremely difficult to hack or compromise," he said. "If you have questions or concerns about a payment card that is RFID-enabled, ask your bank about the precautions it takes to safeguard your card information."

Closely monitor your bank statements and credit card bills. "Look at your account statements as soon as they arrive in your mailbox or electronic inbox and report a discrepancy or anything suspicious, such as an unauthorized withdrawal," advised FDIC attorney Richard M. Schwartz. "While federal and state laws limit your losses if you're a victim of fraud or theft, your protections may be stronger the quicker you report the problem.

Also, don't assume that a small unauthorized transaction isn't worth reporting to your bank. Some thieves are making low-dollar withdrawals or charges in hopes those will go unnoticed by the account holders. In one recent example, a federal court temporarily halted an operation that allegedly debited hundreds of thousands of consumers' bank accounts and billed their credit cards for more than $25 million—in small charges—without their consent.

And, contact your institution if your bank statement or credit card bill doesn't arrive when you normally expect it because that could be a sign that an identity thief has stolen your mail and/or account information to commit fraud in your name.

Periodically review your credit reports for warning signs of fraudulent activity. Credit reports, which are prepared by companies called credit bureaus (or consumer reporting agencies), summarize a consumer's history of paying debts and other bills. But if a credit report shows a credit card, loan or lease you never signed up for, this could indicate you are a victim of ID theft.

You are entitled to at least one free credit report every 12 months from each of the nation's three major credit bureaus. To maximize your protection against fraud, some experts suggest spreading out your requests throughout the year, such as by getting one free report every four months instead of all three at the same time. To request your free report, go to www.AnnualCreditReport.com or call toll-free 877-322-8228.

Tips For Avoiding Credit Card Fraud

- Don't give out your credit card number online unless the site is secure and reputable. Sometimes a tiny icon of a padlock appears to symbolize a higher level of security to transmit data. This icon is not a guarantee of a secure site, but provides some assurance.

- Don't trust a site just because it claims to be secure.

- Before using the site, check out the security/encryption software it uses.

- Make sure you are purchasing merchandise from a reputable source.

- Do your homework on the individual or company to ensure that they are legitimate.

- Obtain a physical address rather than simply a post office box and a telephone number, and call the seller to see if the telephone number is correct and working.

(Source: "Credit Card Basics," Federal Deposit Insurance Corporation (FDIC).)

Part Five
Identifying And Resolving
Debt-Related Problems

Chapter 40

Federal Consumer-Rights Laws

Fair And Accurate Credit Transactions Act Of 2003

This Act, amending the Fair Credit Reporting Act (FCRA), adds provisions designed to improve the accuracy of consumers' credit-related records. It gives consumers the right to one free credit report a year from the credit reporting agencies, and consumers may also purchase, for a reasonable fee, a credit score along with information about how the credit score is calculated. The Act also requires the provision of "risk-based-pricing" notices and credit scores to consumers in connection with denials or less favorable offers of credit. The Act also adds provisions designed to prevent and mitigate identity theft, including a section that enables consumers to place fraud alerts in their credit files, as well as other enhancements to the FCRA. Certain provisions related to data security ("red flags" of possible identity theft) were amended by the Red Flag Program Clarification Act (RFPCA) of 2010, Pub. L. 111-319, 124 Stat. 3457, to clarify and narrow the meaning of "creditor" for purposes of those provisions. The Dodd-Frank Act transferred most rulemaking and one ongoing study requirement under this Act to the Consumer Financial Protection Bureau, but the Commission retains responsibility for two data security rules ("red flags" and "disposal") as well as all rulemaking under the Act relating to certain motor vehicle dealers.

About This Chapter: Text under the heading "Fair And Accurate Credit Transactions Act Of 2003" is excerpted from "Fair And Accurate Credit Transactions Act Of 2003," Federal Trade Commission (FTC), 2003; Text under the heading "Fair Credit Reporting Act" is excerpted from "Fair Credit Reporting Act," Federal Trade Commission (FTC), February 1, 2001; Text under the heading "Equal Credit Opportunity Act (ECOA)" is excerpted from "V. Lending-Equal Credit Opportunity Act," Federal Deposit Insurance Corporation (FDIC), September 2015; Text under the heading "The Credit Repair Organizations Act" is excerpted from "H.R.458—100th Congress (1987-1988)," Congress.gov, U.S. Library of Congress (LOC), November 9, 2016.

Fair Credit Reporting Act

The Act (Title VI of the Consumer Credit Protection Act (CCPA)) protects information collected by consumer reporting agencies such as credit bureaus, medical information companies, and tenant screening services. Information in a consumer report cannot be provided to anyone who does not have a purpose specified in the Act. Companies that provide information to consumer reporting agencies also have specific legal obligations, including the duty to investigate disputed information. In addition, users of the information for credit, insurance, or employment purposes must notify the consumer when an adverse action is taken on the basis of such reports. The Fair and Accurate Credit Transactions Act added many provisions to this Act primarily relating to record accuracy and identity theft. The Dodd-Frank Act transferred to the Consumer Financial Protection Bureau (CFPB) most of the rulemaking responsibilities added to this Act by the Fair and Accurate Credit Transactions Act (FACTA) and the Credit CARD Act, but the Commission retains all its enforcement authority.

Equal Credit Opportunity Act (ECOA)

The Equal Credit Opportunity Act (ECOA) prohibits discrimination in any aspect of a credit transaction. It applies to any extension of credit, including extensions of credit to small businesses, corporations, partnerships, and trusts.

The ECOA prohibits discrimination based on:

- Race or color,
- Religion,
- National origin,
- Sex,
- Marital status,
- Age (provided the applicant has the capacity to contract),
- The applicant's receipt of income derived from any public assistance program, or
- The applicant's exercise, in good faith, of any right under the CCPA.

The CFPB's Regulation B, found at 12 CFR Part 1002, implements ECOA. Regulation B describes lending acts and practices that are specifically prohibited, permitted, or required. Official staff interpretations of the regulation are found in Supplement I to 12 CFR Part 1002.

The Consumer Financial Protection Bureau (CFPB) helps consumers by providing educational materials and accepting complaints. It supervises banks, lenders, and large nonbank entities, such as credit reporting agencies and debt collection companies. The Bureau also works to make credit card, mortgage, and other loan disclosures clearer, so consumers can understand their rights and responsibilities.

(Source: "Consumer Financial Protection Bureau," USA.gov)

The Credit Repair Organizations Act

Credit Repair Organizations Act (CROA)—Amends the Consumer Credit Protection Act to prohibit any credit repair organization (any person who provides a service for the purpose of improving a consumer's credit record) from: (1) charging or receiving any money prior to the completion of its services (unless it has obtained a $50,000 surety bond); (2) charging or receiving money solely for the referral of a customer to a retailer if the credit which may be extended to the buyer is upon substantially the same terms as those available to the general public; (3) advising any client to make an untrue or misleading statement; and (4) using any untrue or misleading statement.

Requires the organization to provide the consumer with a written disclosure statement which includes a description of: (1) the consumer's rights; (2) the services to be provided by the organization; and (3) the total amount the consumer will be charged. Sets forth contract requirements and the rights of the consumer with regard to cancellation of such contract.

Subjects any organization which fails to comply with any provision of this Act to civil liability. Grants any appropriate U.S. district court jurisdiction in such actions (without regard to the amount in controversy). Provides a two year statute of limitations for such actions (unless the defendant has willfully misrepresented any information required under this Act).

Provides for the administrative enforcement of this Act by the Federal Trade Commission (FTC), as provided in the Federal Trade Commission Act.

Chapter 41

Knee Deep In Debt

What Is Debt?

Debt is money you have borrowed from a person or a business. When you owe someone money, you have a liability. When you owe money, you have to pay it back, sometimes in the form of scheduled payments. Often you use money from your future income to make those payments. While borrowing money may give you access to something today, you may have monthly payments for months or years going forward. This obligation may decrease your options in the future.

Debt is different from credit. Credit is the ability to borrow money. Debt results from using credit. You can have credit without having debt. For example, you may have a credit card but no outstanding balance on it.

Good Debt, Bad Debt?

Sometimes people label debt as good debt or bad debt. Some debt can help you reach your goals or build assets for the future. People will often say that borrowing for your education, for a reliable car, to start a business, or to buy a home can be a good use of debt.

But it's not always that simple. For example, borrowing to further your education may be a good use of debt because earning a certification or a degree may lead to a better paying job and more job security. But if you take on the debt and don't earn the certificate or degree, this student debt has set you back instead of helping you reach your goals.

About This Chapter: This chapter includes text excerpted from "Your Money, Your Goals—A Financial Empowerment Toolkit for Social Services Programs," Consumer Financial Protection Bureau (CFPB), April 15, 2015.

Taking out a loan for a reliable car to get to and from your job can help you stay on track to meet your goals. However, if you borrow 100 percent of the car's value, you may end up owing more than the car is worth. Or if you buy a more expensive car than you need, you'll have less money for other bills each month. While it may get you to work, it might keep you from getting to your financial goals.

Borrowing money to start a business may help create income for yourself and others. If the business fails, however, you may end up owing money and not having any income you can use to make the payments.

Finally, taking out a loan to buy a home of your own may be a way to reach your personal goals. But if you are unable to keep up with the payments or you end up owing more than your home is worth, that debt may set you back for a long time.

This information is not meant to scare you. It's simply meant to show you that even debt that many people consider "good" should be approached with caution.

Secured debt is debt that has an asset attached to it. When debt is secured, a lender can collect that asset if you do not pay. Here are examples of secured debt:

- A home loan. The debt is secured with the home you are buying. If you do not pay your loan, the lender can foreclose on your home, sell it, and use the money from the sale to cover your loan.

- An auto loan. The debt is secured with your car. If you do not pay your loan, the lender can repossess (repo) your car and sell it to cover the loan.

- A pawn loan. The debt is secured with the item you have pawned. If you do not make payment when it is due, the pawned item is eventually sold.

- A secured credit card. The debt you incur is secured by funds you deposit at a bank or credit union. Your credit limit will generally equal your deposit. For example, if you deposit $300, your credit limit will be $300.

Unsecured debt does not have an asset attached to it. Here are examples of unsecured debt:

- Credit card debt from an unsecured card

- Department store charge card debt

- Signature loans

- Medical debt

- Student loan debt

If these loans are not paid as agreed, they often go to collections.

Some people consider loans such as credit card debt, short-term loans, and pawn loans "bad" debt. This is because they carry fees and interest, and when they have been used for things you consume (like meals out, gifts, or a vacation) they do not help build assets. But, these sources of debt can help cover a gap in your cash flow if you have a way to repay them. So, there is no one type of debt that is "good" or "bad." That's why it's important to first understand your goal or your need. Then you can shop for the credit you need, especially for purchases like a car or a home, before you make your final decision on your purchase. Another way to understand debt is whether it is secured or unsecured.

How Much Debt Is Too Much Debt?

One way to know if you have too much debt is based on how much stress your debt causes you. If you are worried about your debt, you likely have too much. A more objective way to measure debt is the debt-to-income ratio. The debt-to-income ratio compares the amount of money you pay out each month for debt payments to your income before taxes and other deductions. The resulting number, a percentage, shows you how much of your income is dedicated to debt—your debt load. The higher the percentage, the less financially secure you may be, because you have less left over to cover everything else. Everything else is all of the other needs, wants, and obligations you pay each month that are not debt.

These include:

- Rent

- Savings

- Taxes

- Insurance

- Utilities

- Food

- Clothing

- Child care

- Healthcare (that has not turned into debt)

- Child support and other court-ordered obligations

- Charitable contributions and gifts

- Other family expenses

Avoiding Debt Traps

If you are considering loan products that meet an immediate need, it's important to avoid debt traps on your path to your goals. A debt trap is a situation where people take a loan and have to take new loans to make the payment on the first loan. It is called a trap because for many people, it becomes difficult to escape the cycle of borrowing and taking on more debt to cover the loan payment and still be able to pay for other expenses like food, rent, and transportation.

A debt trap can happen when people use short-term loans that have to be paid back in just a couple of payments such as payday loans. Signature loans and deposit advance loans are other examples of short-term loans.

These loans have many things in common. They:

- Are small dollar loans—generally under $500

- Must be repaid quickly—14 days is the median term of payday loans

- Require the borrower to give creditors access to repayment through an authorization to present a check or debit a borrower's deposit account

Common Misunderstandings About Payday Loans And Deposit Advance Products

If you are considering these products, it's important to be aware of common misunderstandings and the facts about payday and deposit advance loans.

1. The money is borrowed for emergencies.

   Fact: Most borrowers do not use their first loans for emergency expenses. The Pew Charitable Trusts' Payday Lending in America found that 69 percent of first-time borrowers use the loan to pay for regular bills, while only 16 percent use them for emergencies such as a car repair.

2. The borrowers can pay back the loan.

   Fact: While they may pay it back on time, many borrowers have to either immediately take a new loan or take another one in the same pay-period. A Consumer Financial Protection Bureau (CFPB) study found that payday borrowers are in debt for a median of 199 days (nearly seven months) of the year and pay a median of $458 in fees (not including the principal). The Pew Charitable Trust found similar results—that on average, borrowers are in debt for five months out of the year and pay an average of $520 in fees on top of the money they have borrowed.

How Do Payday Loans Work?

Here is an example of how a 14-day payday loan generally works:

- Borrower visits a storefront payday lender and completes an application (there is generally no credit check or ability to repay the loan; the borrower only needs a deposit account so he can write a postdated check). Loans also be taken out online.

- Borrower gets loan (the median loan amount is $350) and pays $10–$20 per $100 borrowed ($15 per $100 is the median fee).

- The borrower provides the lender with 14-day postdated check for the amount of the loan + the fee or $350 + $52.50 = $402.50 or authorization to present a debit against the borrower's account.

- In 14 days, the loan is due. Often, the borrower does not have $402.50 to satisfy the debt. Instead he will pay the fee ($52.50) and renew the loan for another 14 days. (**Note:** 14 days is used for example purposes only. Repayment may fall on the next payday or another minimum period as specified by state law.)

- Every 14 days, the borrower must pay the full amount or renew the debt for $52.50. The average borrower has 10 transactions a year. Applied to this loan, that would mean a fee of $525 to borrow $350.

Alternatives To High-Cost Credit

There are ways to avoid a debt trap if you're in a situation where you need money quickly.

If you are short on cash, consider other alternatives, including:

- Using your own emergency savings.

- Using lower-cost short-term loan alternatives from a credit union or bank.

- Borrowing from a friend or family member.

- Using a credit card—while it will increase your monthly card payment, it may prove cheaper in the long run.

- Negotiating for more time to pay if the loan is for a bill that is due.

- Bartering for part or all of what you are borrowing the money to cover.

- Determining whether the item or circumstance you are borrowing the money for is a need, an obligation, or a want. If it's a want, consider whether it's possible to spend less money for it or not purchasing it.

The Cost Of High-Cost Credit

Here is an example scenario using different options for taking care of emergency expenses. The example examines the costs of paying for an unexpected expense with emergency savings, a credit card, or a payday loan.

Cost To Replace Spark Plugs In Your Automobile = $350

Table 41.1. Cost Of High-Cost Credit

	Emergency Savings	Credit Card	Payday Loan
Amount	$350	$350	$350
APR		21.99 percent annual percentage rate (APR)	$15 for every $100 borrowed for 14 days. This means a 391 percent annual percentage rate (APR)
Payment		Must pay at least a certain amount each month. (For the purposes of the example, the individual is choosing a fixed monthly payment of $50.)	Must pay back loan amount ($350) plus fee ($52.50) within 14 days. If entire loan cannot be paid within 14 days, it can be rolled over (or extended) for another 14 days for an additional fee of ($52.50).
Total cost and time to repay	$0	You would pay $28.11 in interest in addition to the principal borrowed. It will take just over eight months32 to pay back the full amount.	The total cost depends on how long it takes you to save up to pay back the entire loan. If you renew or roll over this loan seven times, you would be in debt for 14 additional weeks and could pay up to $367.50 in fees.

Chapter 42

Consolidating Credit Card Debt

When you consolidate your credit card debt, you are taking out a new loan. You have to repay the new loan just like any other loan. If you get a consolidation loan and keep making more purchases with credit, you probably won't succeed in paying down your debt. If you're having trouble with credit, consider contacting a credit counselor first.

Consolidation means that your various debts, whether they are credit card bills or loan payments, are rolled into one monthly payment. If you have multiple credit card accounts or loans, consolidation may be a way to simplify or lower payments. But, a debt consolidation loan does not erase your debt. You might also end up paying more by consolidating debt into another type of loan.

Before you use a consolidation loan:

- **Take a look at your spending.** It's important to understand why you are in debt. If you have accrued a lot of debt because you are spending more than you are earning, a debt consolidation loan probably won't help you get out of debt unless you reduce your spending or increase your income.

- **Make a budget.** Figure out if you can pay off your existing debt by adjusting the way you spend for a period of time.

- Try **reaching out to your individual creditors to see if they will agree to lower your payments.** Some creditors might be willing to accept lower minimum monthly payments, waive certain fees, reduce your interest rate, or change your monthly due date to match up better to when you get paid, to help you pay back your debt.

About This Chapter: This chapter includes text excerpted from "What Do I Need To Know If I'm Thinking About Consolidating My Credit Card Debt?" Consumer Financial Protection Bureau (CFPB), June 7, 2017.

Here's what you need to know if you are considering loan consolidation:

Credit Card Balance Transfers

Many credit card companies offer zero-percent or low-interest balance transfers to invite you to consolidate your debt on one credit card.

What you should know:

- The promotional interest rate for most balance transfers lasts for a limited time. After that, the interest rate on your new credit card may rise, increasing your payment amount.

- If you're more than 60 days late on a payment, the credit card company can increase your interest rate on all balances, including the transferred balance.

- You probably have to pay a "balance transfer fee." The fee is usually a certain percentage of the amount you transfer or a fixed amount, whichever is more.

- If you use the same credit card to make purchases, you won't get a grace period for those purchases and you will have to pay interest until you pay the entire balance off in full (including the transferred balance).

Debt Consolidation Loan

Banks, credit unions, and installment loan lenders may offer debt consolidation loans. These loans collect many of your debts into one loan payment. This simplifies how many payments you have to make. These offers also might be for lower interest rates than you are currently paying.

What you should know:

- Many of the low interest rates for debt consolidation loans may be "teaser rates" that only last for a certain time. After that, your lender may increase the rate you have to pay.

- The loan may also include fees or costs that you would not have to pay if you continued making your other payments.

- Although your monthly payment might be lower, it may be because you're paying over a longer time. This could mean that you will pay a lot more overall.

Home Equity Loan

With a home equity loan, you are borrowing against the equity in your home. When used for debt consolidation, you use the loan to pay off existing creditors. Then you have to pay back the home equity loan.

What you should know:

- Using a home equity loan to consolidate credit card debt is risky. If you don't pay back the loan, you could lose your home in foreclosure.

- Home equity loans may offer lower interest rates than other types of loans.

- You may have to pay closing costs with a home equity loan. Closing costs can be hundreds or thousands of dollars.

- If you use your home equity to consolidate your credit card debt, it may not be available in an emergency, or for expenses like home renovations or repairs.

- Using your equity for a loan could put you at risk for being "underwater" on your home if your home value falls. This could make it harder to sell or refinance.

Things To Consider Before Debt Consolidation

If you want to consolidate your debt, there are a few things you should think about:

- Taking on new debt to pay off old debt may just be kicking the can down the road. Many people don't succeed in paying off their debt by taking on more debt, unless they lower their spending.

- The loans you take out to consolidate your debt may end up costing you more in costs, fees, and rising interest rates than if you had just paid your previous debt payments.

- If problems with debt have affected your credit score, you probably won't be able to get low interest rates on the balance transfer, debt consolidation loan or home equity loan.

- A nonprofit credit counselor can help you weigh your choices and help you to decide how you want to use credit in the future so that any problems that are leading you to consider debt consolidation do not come back later.

Chapter 43

Student Loan Consolidation

A Direct Consolidation Loan allows you to consolidate (combine) multiple federal education loans into one loan. The result is a single monthly payment instead of multiple payments. Loan consolidation can also give you access to additional loan repayment plans and forgiveness programs.

There is no application fee to consolidate your federal education loans into a Direct Consolidation Loan. You may be contacted by private companies that offer to help you apply for a Direct Consolidation Loan, for a fee. These companies have no affiliation with the U.S. Department of Education (ED) or its consolidation loan servicers. There's no need to pay anyone for assistance in getting a Direct Consolidation Loan. The application process is easy and free.

Should I Consolidate My Loans?

The answer depends on your individual circumstances.

Pros

- If you currently have federal student loans that are with different loan servicers, consolidation can greatly simplify loan repayment by giving you a single loan with just one monthly bill.

- Consolidation can lower your monthly payment by giving you a longer period of time (up to 30 years) to repay your loans.

About This Chapter: This chapter includes text excerpted from "Loan Consolidation," Federal Student Aid, U.S. Department of Education (ED), April 25, 2017.

- If you consolidate loans other than Direct Loans, it may give you access to additional income-driven repayment plan options and Public Service Loan Forgiveness (PSLF). (Direct Loans are from the William D. Ford Federal Direct Loan Program.)

- You'll be able to switch any variable-rate loans you have to a fixed interest rate.

Cons

- Because consolidation usually increases the period of time you have to repay your loans, you might make more payments and pay more in interest than would be the case if you don't consolidate.

- Consolidation may also cause you to lose certain borrower benefits—such as interest rate discounts, principal rebates, or some loan cancellation benefits—that are associated with your current loans.

- If you're paying your current loans under an income-driven repayment plan, or if you've made qualifying payments toward PSLF, consolidating your current loans will cause you to lose credit for any payments made toward income-driven repayment plan forgiveness or PSLF.

If you want to lower your monthly payment amount but are concerned about the impact of loan consolidation, you might want to consider deferment or forbearance as options for short-term payment relief, or consider switching to an income-driven repayment plan.

Once your loans are combined into a Direct Consolidation Loan, they cannot be removed. The loans that were consolidated are paid off and no longer exist.

What Types Of Loans Can Be Consolidated?

Most federal student loans, including the following, are eligible for consolidation:

- Subsidized Federal Stafford Loans

- Unsubsidized Federal Stafford Loans

- Parent Loan for Undergraduate Students (PLUS) loans from the Federal Family Education Loan (FFEL) Program

- Supplemental Loans for Students

- Federal Perkins Loans

- Nursing Student Loans

- Nurse Faculty Loans

- Health Education Assistance Loans

- Health Professions Student Loans

- Loans for Disadvantaged Students

- Direct Subsidized Loans

- Direct Unsubsidized Loans

- Direct PLUS Loans

- FFEL Consolidation Loans and Direct Consolidation Loans (only under certain conditions)

Private education loans are not eligible for consolidation, but for some Direct Consolidation Loan repayment plans, the total amount of your education loan debt—including any private education loans—determines how long you have to repay your Direct Consolidation Loan.

Direct PLUS Loans received by parents to help pay for a dependent student's education cannot be consolidated together with federal student loans that the student received.

When Can I Consolidate My Loans?

Generally, you are eligible to consolidate after you graduate, leave school, or drop below half-time enrollment.

What Are The Requirements To Consolidate A Loan?

Here are some of the eligibility requirements for receiving a Direct Consolidation Loan:

- The loans you consolidate must be in repayment or in the grace period.

- Generally, you cannot consolidate an existing consolidation loan unless you include an additional eligible loan in the consolidation.

- Under certain circumstances, you may reconsolidate an existing FFEL Consolidation Loan without including any additional loans. These circumstances are explained in the Federal Direct Consolidation Loan Application and Promissory Note.

- If you want to consolidate a defaulted loan, you must either make satisfactory repayment arrangements (defined as three consecutive monthly payments) on the loan before you consolidate, or you must agree to repay your new Direct Consolidation Loan under the:
  - Income-Based Repayment Plan,
  - Pay As You Earn Repayment Plan,
  - Revised Pay As You Earn Repayment Plan, or
  - Income-Contingent Repayment Plan.
- If you want to consolidate a defaulted loan that is being collected through garnishment of your wages, or that is being collected in accordance with a court order after a judgment was obtained against you, you cannot consolidate the loan unless the wage garnishment order has been lifted or the judgment has been vacated.

What Is The Interest Rate On A Consolidation Loan?

A Direct Consolidation Loan has a fixed interest rate for the life of the loan. The fixed rate is the weighted average of the interest rates on the loans being consolidated, rounded up to the nearest one-eighth of one percent. There is no cap on the interest rate of a Direct Consolidation Loan.

When Do I Begin Repayment?

Repayment of a Direct Consolidation Loan will begin within 60 days after the loan is disbursed (paid out). Your loan servicer will let you know when the first payment is due.

If any of the loans you want to consolidate are still in the grace period, you have the option of indicating on your Direct Consolidation Loan application that you want the servicer that is processing your application to delay the consolidation of your loans until closer to the grace period end date. If you select this option, you won't have to begin making payments on your new Direct Consolidation Loan until closer to the end of the grace period on your current loans.

Are There Different Repayment Plans?

Borrowers have different needs, so there are several repayment plans—including income-driven repayment plans, which base your monthly payment amount on your income and family size. You'll select a repayment plan when you apply for a Direct Consolidation Loan.

How Do I Apply For A Direct Consolidation Loan?

You apply for a Direct Consolidation Loan through StudentLoans.gov. You can complete and submit the application online, or you can download and print a paper application from StudentLoans.gov for submission by U.S. mail.

After you submit your application electronically at StudentLoans.gov or by mailing a paper application, the consolidation servicer you selected will complete the actions required to consolidate your eligible loans. The consolidation servicer will be your point of contact for any questions you may have related to your consolidation application.

Unless the loans you want to consolidate are in a deferment, forbearance, or grace period, it's important for you to continue making payments on those loans until your consolidation servicer tells you that they have been paid off by your new Direct Consolidation Loan.

Whom Do I Contact If I Have Questions About Consolidation?

This depends on where you are in the consolidation process.

To ask questions about consolidating your loans before you apply for a Direct Consolidation Loan, contact the Loan Consolidation Information Call Center at 800-557-7392.

To request technical assistance while you are signed in and completing the *Federal Direct Consolidation Loan Application and Promissory Note* online, select the "Contact Us" tab in the top menu bar of StudentLoans.gov. From there, you can either complete and submit the feedback form or select "Additional Information" and contact the Student Loan Support Center at the phone number provided.

To ask questions after you have submitted your *Federal Direct Consolidation Loan Application and Promissory Note*, contact the servicer for your new Direct Consolidation Loan. If you submitted your application online, your consolidation servicer's contact information was provided at the end of the online process. If you submitted a paper application by U.S. mail, your consolidation servicer's contact information was available when you downloaded or printed the paper application.

Chapter 44

Repaying Your Loans

Understanding how to repay your federal student loans can save you a lot of time and money. This chapter will help you manage repayment and answer any questions you have along the way.

Finding The Right Repayment Plan For You

There are several repayment plans available, providing the flexibility you need. Here are some things you should know:

- You'll be asked to choose a plan. If you don't choose one, you will be placed on the Standard Repayment Plan, which will have your loans paid off in ten years.

- You can switch to a different plan at any time to suit your needs and goals.

- Your monthly payment can be based on how much you make.

How To Make A Payment

Your loan servicer handles all billing regarding your student loan, so you'll need to make payments directly to your servicer. Each servicer has its own payment process and can work with you if you need help making payments.

About This Chapter: This chapter includes text excerpted from "How To Repay Your Loans," Federal Student Aid, U.S. Department of Education (ED), May 1, 2015.

> ## Never Miss A Payment
> Got a Direct Loan? Sign up for automatic debit through your loan servicer, and your payments will be automatically taken from your bank account each month. As an added bonus, you get a 0.25 percent interest rate deduction when you enroll!

What To Do If You Can't Afford Your Payments

If you're having trouble making payments, don't ignore your loans. There are several options that can help keep your loans in good standing, even if your finances are tight.

Three Ways You Can Keep On Track With Loan Payments

1. **Change your payment due date.** Do you get paid after your student loan payment is due each month? If so, contact your loan servicer and ask whether you'd be able to switch the date your student loan payment is due.

2. **Change your repayment plan.** What you ultimately pay depends on the plan you choose and when you borrowed. If you need lower monthly payments, consider an income-driven repayment plan that'll base your monthly payment amount on how much you make.

3. **Consolidate your loans.** If you have multiple student loans, simplify the repayment process with a Direct Consolidation Loan—allowing you to combine all your federal student loans into one loan for one monthly payment.

If the options above don't work for you and you simply can't make any payments right now, you might be eligible to postpone your payments through a deferment or forbearance. However, depending on the type of loan you have, interest may still accrue (accumulate) on your loan during the time you're not making payments.

Student Loan Forgiveness, Cancellation, And Discharge

There are some circumstances that may result in your no longer having to repay your federal student loan. For instance, some or all of your loan could be forgiven in exchange for your performing certain types of service such as teaching or public service. Or the obligation to make further payments on your loan might be discharged based on specific factors such as your school closing or you're becoming totally and permanently disabled.

Chapter 45

Facts About Credit Repair And Debt Relief Services

If you've maxed out your credit cards and are getting deeper in debt, chances are you're feeling overwhelmed. How are you ever going to pay down the debt? Now imagine hearing about a company that promises to reduce—or even erase—your debt for pennies on the dollar. Sounds like the answer to your problems, right?

The Federal Trade Commission (FTC), the nation's consumer protection agency, says slow down, and consider how you can get out of the red without spending a whole lot of green.

Debt Settlement Companies

Debt settlement programs typically are offered by for-profit companies, and involve the company negotiating with your creditors to allow you to pay a "settlement" to resolve your debt. The settlement is another word for a lump sum that's less than the full amount you owe. To make that lump sum payment, the program asks that you set aside a specific amount of money every month in savings. Debt settlement companies usually ask that you transfer this amount every month into an escrow-like account to accumulate enough savings to pay off a settlement that is reached eventually. Further, these programs often encourage or instruct their clients to stop making any monthly payments to their creditors.

About This Chapter: Text in this chapter begins with excerpts from "Settling Credit Card Debt," Federal Trade Commission (FTC), November 2012; Text under the heading "Debt Settlement And Debt Relief Services" is excerpted from "What Are Debt Settlement/Debt Relief Services And Should I Use Them?" Consumer Financial Protection Bureau (CFPB), February 15, 2017.

Debt Settlement Has Risks

Although a debt settlement company may be able to settle one or more of your debts, consider the risks associated with these programs before you sign up:

1. These programs often require that you deposit money in a special savings account for 36 months or more before all your debts will be settled. Many people have trouble making these payments long enough to get all (or even some) of their debts settled. They drop out the programs as a result. Before you sign up for a debt settlement program, review your budget carefully to make sure you are financially capable of setting aside the required monthly amounts for the full length of the program.

2. Your creditors have no obligation to agree to negotiate a settlement of the amount you owe. So there is a chance that your debt settlement company will not be able to settle some of your debts—even if you set aside the monthly amounts the program requires. Debt settlement companies also often try to negotiate smaller debts first, leaving interest and fees on large debts to grow.

3. Because debt settlement programs often ask—or encourage—you to stop sending payments directly to your creditors, they may have a negative impact on your credit report and other consequences. For example, your debts may continue to accrue late fees and penalties that can put you further in the hole. You also may get calls from your creditors or debt collectors requesting repayment. You could even be sued for repayment. In some instances, when creditors win a lawsuit, they have the right to garnish your wages or put a lien on your home.

Beware Of Debt Settlement Scams

Some companies offering debt settlement programs may engage in deception and fail to deliver on the promises they make—for example, promises or "guarantees" to settle all your credit card debts for, say, 30–60 percent of the amount you owe. Other companies may try to collect their own fees from you before they have settled any of your debts—a practice prohibited under the FTC's Telemarketing Sales Rule (TSR) for companies engaged in telemarketing these services. Some fail to explain the risks associated with their programs: for example, that many (or most) consumers drop out without settling their debts, that consumers' credit reports may suffer, or that debt collectors may continue to call you.

Avoid doing business with any company that promises to settle your debt if the company:

• charges any fees before it settles your debts

- touts a "new government program" to bail out personal credit card debt

- guarantees it can make your unsecured debt go away

- tells you to stop communicating with your creditors, but doesn't explain the serious consequences

- tells you it can stop all debt collection calls and lawsuits

- guarantees that your unsecured debts can be paid off for pennies on the dollar

Researching Debt Settlement Companies

Before you enroll in a debt settlement program, do your homework. You're making a big decision that involves spending a lot of your money—money that could go toward paying down your debt. Check out the company with your state Attorney General and local consumer protection agency. They can tell you if any consumer complaints are on file about the firm you're considering doing business with. Ask your state Attorney General if the company is required to be licensed to work in your state and, if so, whether it is.

Enter the name of the company name with the word "complaints" into a search engine. Read what others have said about the companies you're considering, including news about any lawsuits with state or federal regulators for engaging in deceptive or unfair practices.

Fees

If you do business with a debt settlement company, you may have to put money in a dedicated bank account, which will be administered by an independent third party. The funds are yours and you are entitled to the interest that accrues. The account administrator may charge you a reasonable fee for account maintenance, and is responsible for transferring funds from your account to pay your creditors and the debt settlement company when settlements occur.

A company can charge you only a portion of its full fee for each debt it settles. For example, say you owe money to five creditors. The company successfully negotiates a settlement with one of your creditors. The company can charge you only a portion of its full fee at this time because it still needs to successfully negotiate with four other creditors. Each time the debt settlement company successfully settles a debt with one of your creditors, the company can charge you another portion of its full fee. If the company's fees are based on a percentage of the amount you save through the settlement, it must tell you both the percentage it charges and the estimated dollar amount it represents. This may be called a "contingency" fee.

Disclosure Requirements

Before you sign up for the service, the debt relief company must give you information about the program:

- The price and terms: The company must explain its fees and any conditions on its services.

- Results: The company must tell you how long it will take to get results—how many months or years before it will make an offer to each creditor for a settlement.

- Offers: The company must tell you how much money or the percentage of each outstanding debt you must save before it will make an offer to each creditor on your behalf.

- Nonpayment: If the company asks you to stop making payments to your creditors—or if the program relies on you to not make payments—it must tell you about the possible negative consequences of your action, including damage to your credit report and credit score; that your creditors may sue you or continue with the collections process; and that your credit card companies may charge you additional fees and interest, which will increase the amount you owe.

The debt relief company also must tell you that:

- the funds are yours and you are entitled to the interest earned;

- the account administrator is not affiliated with the debt relief provider and doesn't get referral fees; and

- you may withdraw your money any time without penalty.

Tax Consequences

Depending on your financial condition, any savings you get from debt relief services can be considered income and taxable. Credit card companies and others may report settled debt to the IRS, which the IRS considers income, unless you are "insolvent." Insolvency is when your total debts are more than the fair market value of your total assets. Insolvency can be complex to determine. Talk to a tax professional if you are not sure whether you qualify for this exception.

Other Debt Relief Options

Working with a debt settlement company is just one option for dealing with your debt. You also could: negotiate directly with your credit card company, work with a credit counselor, or consider bankruptcy.

Talk with your credit card company, even if you have been turned down before. Rather than pay a company to talk to your creditor on your behalf, remember that you can do it yourself for free. You can find the telephone number on your card or your statement. Be persistent and polite. Keep good records of your debts, so that when you do reach the credit card company, you can explain your situation. Your goal is to work out a modified payment plan that reduces your payments to a level you can manage.

If you don't pay on your debt for 180 days, your creditor will write your debt off as a loss; your credit score will take a big hit, and you still will owe the debt. Creditors often are willing to negotiate with you even after they write your debt off as a loss.

Contact a credit counselor. Reputable credit counseling organizations can advise you on managing your money and debts, help you develop a budget, and offer free educational materials and workshops. Their counselors are certified and trained in consumer credit, money and debt management, and budgeting. Counselors discuss your entire financial situation with you, and help you develop a personalized plan to solve your money problems. An initial counseling session typically lasts an hour, with an offer of follow-up sessions.

Most reputable credit counselors are nonprofits and offer services through local offices, online, or on the phone. If possible, find an organization that offers in-person counseling. Many universities, military bases, credit unions, housing authorities, and branches of the U.S. Cooperative Extension Service operate nonprofit credit counseling programs. Credit card issuers must include a toll-free number on their statements that gives cardholders information about finding nonprofit counseling organizations. The U.S. Trustee Program—the organization within the U.S. Department of Justice (DOJ) that supervises bankruptcy cases and trustees—also maintains a list of government-approved organizations. If a credit counseling organization says it's government-approved, check the U.S. Trustee's list of approved organizations to be sure. Your financial institution, local consumer protection agency, and friends and family also may be good sources of information and referrals.

But be aware that "nonprofit" status doesn't guarantee that services are free, affordable, or even legitimate. In fact, some credit counseling organizations charge high fees, which they made hide, or urge their clients to make "voluntary" contributions that can cause more debt.

Bankruptcy. Declaring bankruptcy has serious consequences, including lowering your credit score, but credit counselors and other experts say that in some cases, it may make the most sense. Filing for bankruptcy under Chapter 13 allows people with a steady income to keep property, like a mortgaged house or a car, that they might otherwise lose through the Chapter 7 bankruptcy process. In Chapter 13, the court approves a repayment plan that allows you to pay off your debts over three to five years, without surrendering any property. After you have made all the payments under the plan, your debts are discharged. As part of the Chapter 13 process, you will have to pay a lawyer, and you must get credit counseling from a government-approved organization within six months before you file for any bankruptcy relief.

You must get credit counseling from a government-approved organization within six months before you file for any bankruptcy relief. You can find a state-by-state list of government-approved organizations at the U.S. Trustee Program. Before you file a Chapter 7 bankruptcy case, you must satisfy a "means test." This test requires you to confirm that your income does not exceed a certain amount. The amount varies by state and is publicized by the U.S. Trustee Program.

Filing fees are several hundred dollars. Attorney fees are extra and vary.

Debt Settlement And Debt Relief Services

Debt settlement companies are companies that say they can renegotiate, settle, or in some way change the terms of a person's debt to a creditor or debt collector. Dealing with debt settlement companies can be risky.

Debt settlement companies, also sometimes called "debt relief" or "debt adjusting" companies, often claim they can negotiate with your creditors to reduce the amount you owe. Consider all of your options, including working with a nonprofit credit counselor, and negotiating directly with the creditor or debt collector yourself. Before agreeing to work with a debt settlement company, there are risks that you should consider:

- Debt settlement companies often charge expensive fees.

- Debt settlement companies typically encourage you to stop paying your credit card bills. If you stop paying your bills, you will usually incur late fees, penalty interest, and other charges, and creditors will likely step up their collection efforts against you.

- Some of your creditors may refuse to work with the company you choose.

- In many cases, the debt settlement company will be unable to settle all of your debts.

- If you do business with a debt settlement company, the company may tell you to put money in a dedicated bank account, which will be managed by a third party. You may be charged fees for using this account.

- Working with a debt settlement company may lead to a creditor filing a debt collection lawsuit against you.

- Unless the debt settlement company settles all or most of your debts, the built up penalties and fees on the unsettled debts may wipe out any savings the debt settlement company achieves on the debts it settles.

- Using debt settlement services can have a negative impact on your credit scores and your ability to get credit in the future.

Avoid doing business with any company that promises to settle your debt if the company:

- Charges any fees before it settles your debts

- Represents that it can settle all of your debt for a promised percentage reduction

- Touts a "new government program" to bail out personal credit card debt

- Guarantees it can make your debt go away

- Tells you to stop communicating with your creditors

- Tells you it can stop all debt collection calls and lawsuits

- Guarantees that your unsecured debts can be paid off for pennies on the dollar

Chapter 46

How To Dispute Credit Report Errors

Your credit report contains information about where you live, how you pay your bills, and whether you've been sued or arrested, or have filed for bankruptcy. Credit reporting companies sell the information in your report to creditors, insurers, employers, and other businesses that use it to evaluate your applications for credit, insurance, employment, or renting a home. The federal Fair Credit Reporting Act (FCRA) promotes the accuracy and privacy of information in the files of the nation's credit reporting companies.

Some financial advisors and consumer advocates suggest that you review your credit report periodically. Why?

- Because the information it contains affects whether you can get a loan—and how much you will have to pay to borrow money.

- To make sure the information is accurate, complete, and up-to-date before you apply for a loan for a major purchase like a house or car, buy insurance, or apply for a job.

- To help guard against identity theft. That's when someone uses your personal information—like your name, your Social Security number (SSN), or your credit card number—to commit fraud. Identity thieves may use your information to open a new credit card account in your name. Then, when they don't pay the bills, the delinquent account is reported on your credit report. Inaccurate information like that could affect your ability to get credit, insurance, or even a job.

About This Chapter: This chapter includes text excerpted from "Disputing Errors On Credit Reports," Federal Trade Commission (FTC), February 2017.

> ## What Are Common Credit Report Errors That I Should Look For On My Credit Report?
>
> When reviewing your credit report, check that it contains only items about you. Be sure to look for information that is inaccurate or incomplete.
>
> - Identity errors
> - Incorrect reporting of account status
> - Data management errors
> - Balance errors
>
> *(Source: "What Are Common Credit Report Errors That I Should Look For On My Credit Report?" Consumer Financial Protection Bureau (CFPB).)*

How To Order Your Free Report

An amendment to the FCRA requires each of the nationwide credit reporting companies—Equifax, Experian, and TransUnion—to provide you with a free copy of your credit report, at your request, once every 12 months.

The three nationwide credit reporting companies have set up one website, toll-free telephone number, and mailing address through which you can order your free annual report. To order, visit annualcreditreport.com, call 877-322-8228, or complete the Annual Credit Report Request Form and mail it to:

Annual Credit Report Request Service

P.O. Box 105281

Atlanta, GA 30348-5281

Do not contact the three nationwide credit reporting companies individually.

You may order your reports from each of the three nationwide credit reporting companies at the same time, or you can order from only one or two. The FCRA allows you to order one free copy from each of the nationwide credit reporting companies every 12 months.

You need to provide your name, address, Social Security number, and date of birth. If you have moved in the last two years, you may have to provide your previous address. To maintain the security of your file, each nationwide credit reporting company may ask you for some information that only you would know, like the amount of your monthly mortgage payment.

Each company may ask you for different information because the information each has in your file may come from different sources.

Other Situations Where You Might Be Eligible For A Free Report

You're also entitled to a free report if a company takes adverse action against you, such as denying your application for credit, insurance, or employment, based on information in your report. You must ask for your report within 60 days of receiving notice of the action. The notice will give you the name, address, and phone number of the credit reporting company.

You're also entitled to one free report a year if you're unemployed and plan to look for a job within 60 days; if you're on welfare; or if your report is inaccurate because of fraud, including identity theft.

Otherwise, a credit reporting company may charge you a reasonable amount for another copy of your report within a 12-month period. To buy a copy of your report, contact the three credit report companies:

Experian-888-397-3742

www.experian.com

TransUnion-800-916-8800

www.transunion.com

Equifax-800-685-1111

www.equifax.com

Correcting Errors

Under the FCRA, both the credit reporting company and the information provider (that is, the person, company, or organization that provides information about you to a credit reporting company) are responsible for correcting inaccurate or incomplete information in your report. To take advantage of all your rights under this law, contact the credit reporting company and the information provider.

Step One

Tell the credit reporting company, in writing, what information you think is inaccurate. Include copies (NOT originals) of documents that support your position. In addition to providing your complete name and address, your letter should clearly identify each item in your report you dispute, state the facts and explain why you dispute the information, and request that it be removed or corrected. You may want to enclose a copy of your report with the items in question circled. Send your letter by certified mail, "return receipt requested," so you can document what the credit reporting company received. Keep copies of your dispute letter and enclosures.

Credit reporting companies must investigate the items in question—usually within 30 days—unless they consider your dispute frivolous. They also must forward all the relevant data you provide about the inaccuracy to the organization that provided the information. After the information provider receives notice of a dispute from the credit reporting company, it must investigate, review the relevant information, and report the results back to the credit reporting company. If the information provider finds the disputed information is inaccurate, it must notify all three nationwide credit reporting companies so they can correct the information in your file.

When the investigation is complete, the credit reporting company must give you the results in writing and a free copy of your report if the dispute results in a change. This free report does not count as your annual free report. If an item is changed or deleted, the credit reporting company cannot put the disputed information back in your file unless the information provider verifies that it is accurate and complete. The credit reporting company also must send you written notice that includes the name, address, and phone number of the information provider.

If you ask, the credit reporting company must send notices of any corrections to anyone who received your report in the past six months. You can have a corrected copy of your report sent to anyone who received a copy during the past two years for employment purposes.

If an investigation doesn't resolve your dispute with the credit reporting company, you can ask that a statement of the dispute be included in your file and in future reports. You also can ask the credit reporting company to provide your statement to anyone who received a copy of your report in the recent past. You can expect to pay a fee for this service.

Step Two

Tell the information provider (that is, the person, company, or organization that provides information about you to a credit reporting company), in writing, that you dispute an item in your credit report. If the provider listed an address on your credit report, send your letter to that address. If no address is listed, contact the provider and ask for the correct address to send your letter. If the information provider does not give you an address, you can send your letter to any business address for that provider.

If the provider continues to report the item you disputed to a credit reporting company, it must let the credit reporting company know about your dispute. And if you are correct—that is, if the information you dispute is found to be inaccurate or incomplete—the information provider must tell the credit reporting company to update or delete the item.

About Your File

Your credit file may not reflect all your credit accounts. Although most national department store and all-purpose bank credit card accounts will be included in your file, not all creditors supply information to credit reporting companies: some local retailers, credit unions, travel, entertainment, and gasoline card companies are among the creditors that don't.

When negative information in your report is accurate, only the passage of time can assure its removal.

Chapter 47

Dealing With A Debt Collector

Often people find out they have a debt in collection when they receive a letter or phone call from a debt collection agency. Sometimes, they don't remember owing a debt, so they are surprised when they're told a debt has gone to collections.

Debt collectors use persuasive techniques to get you to send in money to pay your debt.

Before you send in money, you should confirm that:

- You actually owe the debt.

- The collection isn't fraudulent and is legitimate.

You may be able to confirm this information during an initial or follow-up discussion with the debt collector, but be careful of fraudulent debt collectors. You should ensure that you recognize the debt and know that you owe it and have not paid it before.

When The Phone Rings...

Sometimes it's hard to know if a caller is really a debt collector. To avoid falling victim to a scam, ask for the name, number, and address for the debt collector and request information about the debt in writing. Be wary of sharing your personal information by phone. If a stranger asks for your Social Security number, date of birth, or bank account information, this can be a "red flag."

About This Chapter: Text in this chapter begins with excerpts from "Your Money, Your Goals: A Financial Empowerment Toolkit For Community Volunteers," Consumer Financial Protection Bureau (CFPB), April 2015; Text under the heading "When Debt Collectors Call" is excerpted from "Debt Collection," Federal Trade Commission (FTC), May 2015.

Many people know they do owe the debt and are able to confirm that the collector is the right person to pay when they receive the first phone call or letter. Paying right away can benefit you because it allows you to resolve the matter and take advantage of a settlement offer if one has been made. If you pay the debt, it's important to request confirmation of payment or a payment receipt so that you have a record of it.

If you are uncertain that the debt is yours or that the collector has the authority to collect it, you can ask the debt collection agency to verify the debt. You can do this by sending a letter within 30 days of the debt collector's providing you with certain information regarding the debt. That information includes the name of the creditor, the amount owed, and statements concerning how to dispute and seek verification of the debt.

Your Rights In Debt Collection

The Fair Debt Collection Practices Act (FDCPA) says what debt collectors can and cannot do. This law covers businesses or individuals that collect the debt of other businesses. These are often called "third party debt collectors." This law does not apply to businesses trying to collect their own debts.

The law states that debt collectors may not harass, oppress, or abuse you or any other people they contact. Some examples of harassment are:

- Repeated phone calls that are intended to annoy, abuse, or harass you or any person answering the phone.
- Obscene or profane language.
- Threats of violence or harm.
- Publishing lists of people who refuse to pay their debts (this does not include reporting information to a credit reporting company).
- Calling you without telling you who they are

The law also says debt collectors cannot use false, deceptive, or misleading practices. This includes misrepresentations about the debt, including the amount owed, that the person is an attorney if they are not, threats to have you arrested if you cannot be, threats to do things that cannot legally be done, or threats to do things that the debt collector has no intention of doing.

Keep a file of all letters or documents a debt collector sends you and copies of anything you send to them. Also, write down dates and times of conversations along with notes about what you discussed. These records can help you if you have a dispute with a debt collector, meet with a lawyer, or go to court.

Even if the debt may be yours, you have the right under the Fair Debt Collection Practices Act (FDCPA) to ask the debt collector to stop contacting you. Once you make this request, they can contact you to tell you that they won't contact you again. Or they may notify you that they or the creditor could take other action (for example, filing a lawsuit against you). Otherwise they must stop contacting you.

Stopping them from contacting you does not cancel the debt. You still might be sued or have debt reported to the credit reporting agencies (Equifax, Experian, and TransUnion). You can ask a debt collector to stop contacting you at any time, so keep in mind that you could ask them for more information before deciding whether to tell them to stop contacting you.

When Debt Collectors Call

If you're behind in paying your bills, or a creditor's records mistakenly make it appear that you are, a debt collector may be contacting you.

The Federal Trade Commission (FTC), the nation's consumer protection agency, enforces the Fair Debt Collection Practices Act (FDCPA), which prohibits debt collectors from using abusive, unfair, or deceptive practices to collect from you.

Under the FDCPA, a debt collector is someone who regularly collects debts owed to others. This includes collection agencies, lawyers who collect debts on a regular basis, and companies that buy delinquent debts and then try to collect them.

Reason Why Debt Collectors May Contact You

A debt collector may be trying to contact you because:

- A creditor believes you are past due on a debt. Creditors may use their own in-house debt collectors or may refer or sell your debt to an outside debt collector.

- A debt collector also may be calling you to locate someone you know, as long as the collector does not reveal that they are collecting a debt.

- A debt buyer has bought the debt and is now collecting that debt or is hiring collectors.

- If the debt collector is contacting you for payment on a debt and you have concerns about the debt, the amount they are claiming, or the company contacting you, you might want to speak to an attorney or a credit counseling organization. Before speaking with a debt collector, consider working up a plan. You might be able to set up a payment plan or negotiate with them to resolve the debt.

(Source: "What Is A Debt Collector And Why Are They Contacting Me?" Consumer Financial Protection Bureau (CFPB).)

Here are some questions and answers about your rights under the Act.

What Types Of Debts Are Covered?

The Act covers personal, family, and household debts, including money you owe on a personal credit card account, an auto loan, a medical bill, and your mortgage. The FDCPA doesn't cover debts you incurred to run a business.

Can A Debt Collector Contact Me Anytime Or Anyplace?

No. A debt collector may not contact you at inconvenient times or places, such as before 8 in the morning or after 9 at night, unless you agree to it. And collectors may not contact you at work if they're told (orally or in writing) that you're not allowed to get calls there.

Debt collectors can contact you by phone, letter, e-mail or text message to collect a debt, as long as they follow the rules and disclose that they are debt collectors. No matter how they communicate with you, it's against the law for a debt collector to pretend to be someone else—like an attorney or government agency—or to harass, threaten or deceive you.

How Can I Stop A Debt Collector From Contacting Me?

If a collector contacts you about a debt, you may want to talk to them at least once to see if you can resolve the matter—even if you don't think you owe the debt, can't repay it immediately, or think that the collector is contacting you by mistake. If you decide after contacting the debt collector that you don't want the collector to contact you again, tell the collector—in writing—to stop contacting you. Here's how to do that:

Make a copy of your letter. Send the original by certified mail, and pay for a "return receipt" so you'll be able to document what the collector received. Once the collector receives your letter, they may not contact you again, with two exceptions: a collector can contact you to tell you there will be no further contact or to let you know that they or the creditor intend to take a specific action, like filing a lawsuit. Sending such a letter to a debt collector you owe money to does not get rid of the debt, but it should stop the contact. The creditor or the debt collector still can sue you to collect the debt.

Can A Debt Collector Contact Anyone Else About My Debt?

If an attorney is representing you about the debt, the debt collector must contact the attorney, rather than you. If you don't have an attorney, a collector may contact other people—but only to find out your address, your home phone number, and where you work. Collectors usually are prohibited from contacting third parties more than once. Other than to obtain this location information about you, a debt collector generally is not permitted to discuss your debt with anyone other than you, your spouse, or your attorney.

What Does The Debt Collector Have To Tell Me About The Debt?

Every collector must send you a written "validation notice" telling you how much money you owe within five days after they first contact you. This notice also must include the name of the creditor to whom you owe the money, and how to proceed if you don't think you owe the money.

Can A Debt Collector Keep Contacting Me If I Don't Think I Owe Any Money?

If you send the debt collector a letter stating that you don't owe any or all of the money, or asking for verification of the debt, that collector must stop contacting you. You have to send that letter within 30 days after you receive the validation notice. But a collector can begin contacting you again if it sends you written verification of the debt, like a copy of a bill for the amount you owe.

What Practices Are Off Limits For Debt Collectors?

Harassment. Debt collectors may not harass, oppress, or abuse you or any third parties they contact. For example, they may not:

- use threats of violence or harm;

- publish a list of names of people who refuse to pay their debts (but they can give this information to the credit reporting companies);

- use obscene or profane language; or

- repeatedly use the phone to annoy someone.

False statements. Debt collectors may not lie when they are trying to collect a debt. For example, they may not:

- falsely claim that they are attorneys or government representatives;

- falsely claim that you have committed a crime;

- falsely represent that they operate or work for a credit reporting company;

- misrepresent the amount you owe;

293

- indicate that papers they send you are legal forms if they aren't; or

- indicate that papers they send to you aren't legal forms if they are.

Debt collectors also are prohibited from saying that:

- you will be arrested if you don't pay your debt;

- they'll seize, garnish, attach, or sell your property or wages unless they are permitted by law to take the action and intend to do so; or

- legal action will be taken against you, if doing so would be illegal or if they don't intend to take the action.

Debt collectors may not:

- give false credit information about you to anyone, including a credit reporting company;

- send you anything that looks like an official document from a court or government agency if it isn't; or

- use a false company name.

Unfair practices. Debt collectors may not engage in unfair practices when they try to collect a debt. For example, they may not:

- try to collect any interest, fee, or other charge on top of the amount you owe unless the contract that created your debt—or your state law—allows the charge;

- deposit a post-dated check early;

- take or threaten to take your property unless it can be done legally; or

- contact you by postcard.

Can I Control Which Debts My Payments Apply To?

Yes. If a debt collector is trying to collect more than one debt from you, the collector must apply any payment you make to the debt you select. Equally important, a debt collector may not apply a payment to a debt you don't think you owe.

Can A Debt Collector Garnish My Bank Account Or My Wages?

If you don't pay a debt, a creditor or its debt collector generally can sue you to collect. If they win, the court will enter a judgment against you. The judgment states the amount of money you owe, and allows the creditor or collector to get a garnishment order against you, directing a third party, like your bank, to turn over funds from your account to pay the debt.

Wage garnishment happens when your employer withholds part of your compensation to pay your debts. Your wages usually can be garnished only as the result of a court order. Don't ignore a lawsuit summons. If you do, you lose the opportunity to fight a wage garnishment.

Can Federal Benefits Be Garnished?

Many federal benefits are exempt from garnishment, including:

- Social Security Benefits
- Supplemental Security Income (SSI) Benefits
- Veterans' Benefits
- Civil Service and Federal Retirement and Disability Benefits
- Military Annuities and Survivors' Benefits
- Federal Emergency Management Agency (FEMA) Federal Disaster Assistance

Federal benefits may be garnished under certain circumstances, including to pay delinquent taxes, alimony, child support, or student loans.

Do I Have Any Recourse If I Think A Debt Collector Has Violated The Law?

You have the right to sue a collector in a state or federal court within one year from the date the law was violated. If you win, the judge can require the collector to pay you for any damages you can prove you suffered because of the illegal collection practices, like lost wages and medical bills. The judge can require the debt collector to pay you up to $1,000, even if you can't prove that you suffered actual damages. You also can be reimbursed for your attorney's fees and court costs. A group of people also may sue a debt collector as part of a class action lawsuit and recover money for damages up to $500,000, or one percent of the collector's net worth, whichever amount is lower. Even if a debt collector violates the FDCPA in trying to collect a debt, the debt does not go away if you owe it.

What Should I Do If A Debt Collector Sues Me?

If a debt collector files a lawsuit against you to collect a debt, respond to the lawsuit, either personally or through your lawyer, by the date specified in the court papers to preserve your rights.

Where Do I Report A Debt Collector For An Alleged Violation?

Report any problems you have with a debt collector to your state Attorney General's office, the Federal Trade Commission (FTC), and the Consumer Financial Protection Bureau (CFPB). Many states have their own debt collection laws that are different from the federal Fair Debt Collection Practices Act. Your Attorney General's office can help you determine your rights under your state's law.

Chapter 48

Vehicle Repossession

If you miss payments, the dealership or finance company you lease your vehicle from, known as the "lessor," may be entitled to repossess the vehicle.

Your lease agreement will state what constitutes a default of the lease as well as if there is any "grace period" in making lease payments. Not making a contractually required monthly payment will normally be a breach of the lease and the lessor can then repossess the vehicle from you. You should contact your lender if you are unable to make your monthly payment on its due date. Service members may have additional protections under the Service member's Civil Relief Act (SCRA). You should contact your local judge advocate general (JAG) to find out if these protections apply.

You may have a right to "cure" or reinstate the lease. Your lease contract, as well as your state law, may provide for a right to cure or reinstate the lease after a missed payment. If you have this right, it allows you to make up your missed lease payments before the vehicle is repossessed. You would generally receive a notice after a missed payment and one to two weeks to make up the missed payment. While only a minority of states provide for a right to cure before repossession, even fewer states provide for a right to cure after repossession. Check with your state attorney general or consumer protection office for more information on your state law.

Your lessor cannot "breach the peace." Your vehicle can only be repossessed if it can be done without breaching the peace. The definition of "breach of the peace" varies depending on

About This Chapter: Text in this chapter begins with excerpts from "What Happens If I Don't Make The Payments On My Auto Lease?" Consumer Financial Protection Bureau (CFPB), September 22, 2016; Text under the heading "Repossessing Vehicles" is excerpted from "Vehicle Repossession," Federal Trade Commission (FTC), November 2008.

your state law. Typically, it includes things like threatening or using physical force, removing a vehicle from a closed garage without permission, or continuing with repossession after you have resisted or refused to allow the repossession.

Repossession methods. Besides physically removing the vehicle, a lessor may also use a starter interrupt device (SID) in place of repossession or to help facilitate repossession. A SID is a device that allows a lessor to remotely deactivate a vehicle's ignition system if a borrower/lessee misses payments or defaults. The shut-down can be temporary, until a payment is made, or it can be done to make repossession easier. The rules on SIDs vary from state to state so ask your lessor before signing the contract if your vehicle is equipped with a SID. If it is, you should ask if there are any warnings given before the vehicle is shut down. You may also want to ask if there is a way for the vehicle to be re-activated in case of an emergency.

You may be liable for early termination fees. Defaulting on a lease or voluntarily returning your vehicle to the lessor can trigger a substantial early termination fee. Check your lease agreement. Under the federal Consumer Leasing Act (CLA), the method for calculating the early termination fee must be disclosed in the lease. The early termination fee is generally the difference between the early termination payoff and the amount credited to you for the vehicle. Suppose, for example, that your early termination payoff amount is $16,000 and the amount credited for the vehicle is $14,000. The early termination charge would be $16,000 minus $14,000, or $2,000. The earlier your lease is terminated, the greater this charge is likely to be. If you are unable to pay the early termination fee, and default, the lessor can report the amount of delinquent fees to the credit bureau.

If you are charged an early termination fee, be sure you understand how it is being calculated and consult an attorney if you think it has been done incorrectly.

Repossessing Vehicles

Chances are you rely on your vehicle to get you where you need to go—and when you need to go—whether it's to work, school, the grocery store, or the soccer field. But if you're late with your car payments, or in some states, if you don't have adequate auto insurance, your vehicle could be taken away from you.

Seizing The Vehicle

In many states, your creditor can seize your vehicle as soon as you default on your loan or lease. Your contract should state what constitutes a default, but failure to make a payment on time is a typical example.

Creditor's Rights

When you finance or lease a vehicle, your creditor or lessor has important rights that end once you've paid off your loan or lease obligation. These rights are established by the contract you signed and the law of your state. For example, if you don't make timely payments on the vehicle, your creditor may have the right to "repossess"—or take back your car without going to court or warning you in advance. Your creditor also may be able to sell your contract to a third party, called an assignee, who may have the same right to seize the car as the original creditor.

The Federal Trade Commission (FTC), the nation's consumer protection agency, wants you to know that your creditor's rights may be limited. Some states impose rules about how your creditor may repossess the vehicle and resell it to reduce or eliminate your debt. Creditors that violate any rules may lose other rights against you, or have to pay you damages.

However, if your creditor agrees to change your payment date, the terms of your original contract may not apply any longer. If your creditor agrees to such a change, make sure you have it in writing. Oral agreements are difficult to prove.

Once you are in default, the laws of most states permit the creditor to repossess your car at any time, without notice, and to come onto your property to do so. But when seizing the vehicle, your creditor may not commit a "breach of the peace." In some states, that means using physical force, threats of force, or even removing your car from a closed garage without your permission.

Should there be a breach of the peace in seizing your car, your creditor may be required to pay a penalty or to compensate you if any harm is done to you or your property. A breach of peace also may give you a legal defense if your creditor sues you to collect a "deficiency judgment"—that is, the difference between what you owe on the contract (plus repossession and sale expenses) and what your creditor gets from the resale of your vehicle.

Selling The Vehicle

Once your vehicle has been repossessed, your creditor may decide to either keep it as compensation for your debt or resell it in a public or private sale. In some states, your creditor must let you know what will happen to the car. For example, if the car will be sold at public auction, state law may require that the creditor tell you the time and place of the sale so that you can attend and participate in the bidding. If the vehicle will be sold privately, you may have a right to know the date of the sale.

In any of these circumstances, you may be entitled to "redeem"—or buy back—the vehicle by paying the full amount you owe (usually, that includes your past due payments and the entire remaining debt), in addition to the expenses connected with the repossession, like storage, preparation for sale, and attorney fees. Or you could try to buy back the vehicle by bidding on it at the repossession sale.

Some states have consumer protection laws that allow you to "reinstate" your loan. This means you can reclaim your car by paying the amount you are behind on your loan, together with your creditor's repossession expenses. Of course, if you reclaim your car, your future payments must be made on time, and you must meet the terms of your reinstated contract to avoid another repossession.

Any resale of a repossessed vehicle must be conducted in a "commercially reasonable manner." Your creditor doesn't have to get the highest possible price for the vehicle—or even a good price. But a resale price that is below fair market value may indicate that the sale was not commercially reasonable. "Commercially reasonable" may depend on the standard sales practices in your area. A creditor's failure to resell your car in a commercially reasonable manner may give you a claim against that creditor for damages or a defense against a deficiency judgment.

Personal Property In The Vehicle

Regardless of the method used to dispose of a repossessed car, a creditor may not keep or sell any personal property found inside. In some states, your creditor must tell you what personal items were found in your car and how you can retrieve them. Your creditor also may be required to use reasonable care to prevent anyone else from removing your property from the car. If your creditor can't account for articles left in your vehicle, you may want to speak to an attorney about your right to compensation.

Paying The Deficiency

Any difference between what you owe on your contract (plus certain expenses) and what your creditor gets for reselling the vehicle is called a "deficiency." For example, if you owe $10,000 on the car and your creditor sells it for $7,500, the deficiency is $2,500 plus any other fees you owe under the contract. Those might include fees related to the repossession and early termination of your lease or early payoff of your financing. In most states, your creditor is allowed to sue you for a deficiency judgment to collect the remaining amount owed as long as it followed the proper procedures for repossession and sale. Similarly, your creditor must pay you if there are surplus funds after the sale proceeds are applied to the outstanding contract obligation and related expenses, but this situation is less common.

You may have a legal defense against a deficiency judgment if, for example, your creditor breached the peace when seizing the vehicle, failed to sell the car in a commercially reasonable manner, or waited too long before suing you. An attorney will be able to tell you whether you have grounds to contest a deficiency judgment.

Electronic Disabling Devices

Some creditors might not provide you with financing unless you agree to the installation of an electronic device that prevents your car from starting if you do not make your payments on time. Depending on your contract with the lender and your state's laws, using that sort of device may be considered the same as a repossession or a breach of the peace. How your state treats the use of these devices could affect your rights. Contact your state consumer protection agency or an attorney if you have questions about the use of these devices in your state.

Talking With Your Creditor Or Lessor

It's easier to try to prevent a vehicle repossession from taking place than to dispute it after the fact. Contact your creditor as soon as you realize you will be late with a payment. Many creditors work with consumers they believe will be able to pay soon, even if slightly late. You may be able to negotiate a delay in your payment or a revised schedule of payments. If you can reach an agreement to change your original contract, get it in writing to avoid questions later.

However, your creditor or lessor may refuse to accept late payments or make other changes in your contract—and may demand that you return the car. If you agree to a "voluntary repossession," you may reduce your creditor's expenses, which you would be responsible for paying. But even if you return the car voluntarily, you still are responsible for paying any deficiency on your contract, and your creditor still may enter the late payments or repossession on your credit report.

Finally, if you are facing, or already in, bankruptcy, ask an attorney for information about your rights to the vehicle during that process.

Chapter 49

Bankruptcy: A Last Resort

Debt Relief Or Bankruptcy?

Debt got you down? You're not alone. Consumer debt is at an all-time high. Whether your debt dilemma is the result of an illness, unemployment, or simply overspending, it can seem overwhelming. In your effort to get solvent, be on the alert for advertisements that offer seemingly quick fixes. And although bankruptcy is one option to deal with financial problems, it's generally considered the option of last resort. The reason: its long-term negative impact on your creditworthiness. Bankruptcy information (both the date of your filing and the later date of discharge) stays on your credit report for 10 years, and can hinder your ability to get credit, a job, insurance, or even a place to live.

Read Between The Lines

The Federal Trade Commission (FTC) cautions consumers to read between the lines when faced with ads in newspapers, magazines, or even telephone directories that say:

- "Consolidate your bills into one monthly payment without borrowing."
- "STOP credit harassment, foreclosures, repossessions, tax levies, and garnishments."
- "Keep your property."
- "Wipe out your debts! Consolidate your bills! How? By using the protection and assistance provided by federal law. For once, let the law work for you!"

About This Chapter: Text under the heading "Debt Relief Or Bankruptcy?" is excerpted from "Debt Relief Or Bankruptcy?" Federal Trade Commission (FTC), May 2008; Text under the heading "Filing For Bankruptcy" is excerpted from "Filing For Bankruptcy: What To Know," Federal Trade Commission (FTC), August 2012.

You'll find out later that such phrases often involve filing for bankruptcy relief, which can hurt your credit and cost you attorneys' fees.

If you're having trouble paying your bills, consider these possibilities before considering filing for bankruptcy:

- Talk with your creditors. They may be willing to work out a modified payment plan.

- Contact a credit counseling service. These organizations work with you and your creditors to develop debt repayment plans. Such plans require you to deposit money each month with the counseling service. The service then pays your creditors. Some nonprofit organizations charge little or nothing for their services.

- Carefully consider all your options before you take out a second mortgage or home equity line of credit. While these loans may allow you to consolidate your debt, they also require your home as collateral.

If none of these options is possible, bankruptcy may be the likely alternative. There are two primary types of personal bankruptcy: Chapter 13 and Chapter 7. Each must be filed in federal bankruptcy court. Filing fees are several hundred dollars.

The consequences of bankruptcy are significant and require careful consideration. Other factors to think about: Effective October 2005, Congress made sweeping changes to the bankruptcy laws. The net effect of these changes is to give consumers more incentive to seek bankruptcy relief under Chapter 13 rather than Chapter 7. Chapter 13 allows you, if you have a steady income, to keep property, such as a mortgaged house or car, that you might otherwise lose. In Chapter 13, the court approves a repayment plan that allows you to use your future income to pay off your debts during a 3- to 5-year period, rather than surrender any property. After you have made all the payments under the plan, you receive a discharge of your debts.

Chapter 7, known as straight bankruptcy, involves the sale of all assets that are not exempt. Exempt property may include cars, work-related tools, and basic household furnishings. Some of your property may be sold by a court-appointed official—a trustee—or turned over to your creditors. The new bankruptcy laws have changed the time period during which you can receive a discharge through Chapter 7. You now must wait eight years after receiving a discharge in Chapter 7 before you can file again under that chapter. The Chapter 13 waiting period is much shorter and can be as little as two years between filings.

Both types of bankruptcy may get rid of unsecured debts and stop foreclosures, repossessions, garnishments and utility shut-offs, and debt collection activities. Both also provide exemptions that allow you to keep certain assets, although exemption amounts vary by state. Personal bankruptcy usually does not erase child support, alimony, fines, taxes, and some student loan obligations. Also, unless you have an acceptable plan to catch up on your debt under Chapter 13, bankruptcy usually does not allow you to keep property when your creditor has an unpaid mortgage or security lien on it.

Another major change to the bankruptcy laws involves certain hurdles that you must clear before even filing for bankruptcy, no matter what the chapter. You must get credit counseling from a government-approved organization within six months before you file for any bankruptcy relief. You can find a state-by-state list of government-approved organizations at www.usdoj.gov/ust. That is the website of the U.S. Trustee Program, the organization within the U.S. Department of Justice (DOJ) that supervises bankruptcy cases and trustees. Also, before you file a Chapter 7 bankruptcy case, you must satisfy a "means test." This test requires you to confirm that your income does not exceed a certain amount. The amount varies by state and is publicized by the U.S. Trustee Program at www.usdoj.gov/ust.

Filing For Bankruptcy

> If you plan to file for bankruptcy protection, you must get credit counseling from a government-approved organization within 180 days before you file. You also have to complete a debtor education course before your debts can be discharged.

Approved Credit Counselors And Debtor Educators

The U.S. Department of Justice's (DOJ) U.S. Trustee Program approves organizations to provide the credit counseling and debtor education required for anyone filing for personal bankruptcy. Only the counselors and educators that appear on the U.S. Trustee Program's lists can advertise that they are approved to provide the required counseling and debtor education. By law, the U.S. Trustee Program does not operate in Alabama and North Carolina; in these states, court officials called Bankruptcy Administrators approve prebankruptcy credit counseling organizations and predischarge debtor education course providers.

Counseling And Education Requirements

Prebankruptcy credit counseling and predischarge debtor education may not be provided at the same time. Credit counseling must take place before you file for bankruptcy; debtor education must take place after you file.

You must file a certificate of credit counseling completion when you file for bankruptcy, and evidence of completion of debtor education after you file for bankruptcy—but before your debts are discharged. Only credit counseling organizations and debtor education course providers that have been approved by the U.S. Trustee Program may issue these certificates. To protect against fraud, the certificates are numbered, and produced through a central automated system.

Prebankruptcy Counseling

A prebankruptcy counseling session with an approved credit counseling organization should include an evaluation of your personal financial situation, a discussion of alternatives to bankruptcy, and a personal budget plan. A typical counseling session should last about 60–90 minutes, and can take place in person, on the phone, or online. The counseling organization is required to provide the counseling for free for people who can't afford to pay. If you can't afford to pay a fee for credit counseling, ask for a fee waiver from the counseling organization before the session begins. Otherwise, you may be charged a fee for the counseling. It will generally is about $50, depending on where you live, and the types of services you receive, among other factors. The counseling organization must discuss any fees with you before you start the counseling session.

Once you complete the required counseling, you must get a certificate as proof. Check the U.S. Trustee's website to be sure that you receive the certificate from a counseling organization that is approved in the judicial district where you are filing bankruptcy. Credit counseling organizations may not charge an extra fee for the certificate.

Postfiling Debtor Education

A debtor education course by an approved provider should include information on developing a budget, managing money, and using credit wisely. Like prefiling counseling, debtor education can take place in person, on the phone, or online. The education session might last longer than the prefiling counseling—about two hours—and the fee is between $50 and $100. As with prefiling counseling, if you can't afford the session fee, ask the debtor education provider to waive it. Check the list of approved debtor education providers (www.justice.gov/ust/list-approved-providers-personal-financial-management-instructional-courses-debtor-education) online or at the bankruptcy clerk's office in your district.

Once you have completed the required debtor education course, you should receive a certificate as proof. This certificate is separate from the certificate you received after completing your prefiling credit counseling. Check the U.S. Trustee's website (www.justice.gov/ust) to be sure that you receive the certificate from a debtor education provider that is approved in the judicial district where you filed for bankruptcy. Unless the debtor education provider told you there's a fee for the certificate before the education session begins, you can't be charged an extra fee for it.

Choosing A Credit Counselor

If you're looking for credit counseling to fulfill the bankruptcy law requirements, make sure you receive services only from approved providers for your judicial district. Check the list of approved credit counseling providers online or at the bankruptcy clerk's office for the district where you will file. Once you have the list of approved organizations, call several to gather information before you pick one. Some key questions to ask are:

- What services do you offer?

- Will you help me develop a plan for avoiding problems in the future?

- What are your fees?

- What if I can't afford your fees?

- What qualifications do your counselors have? Are they accredited or certified by an outside organization? What training do they receive?

- How do you keep information about me (including my address, phone number, and financial information) confidential and secure?

- How are your employees paid? Are they paid more if I sign up for certain services, if I pay a fee, or if I make a contribution to your organization?

Part Six
If You Need More Information

Chapter 50

Interactive Tools, Online Calculators, And Other Web-Based Resources

Mobile Apps

Bankaroo

Bankaroo is a virtual bank for kids. It will teach kids about the value of money in a simple and fun way.

Website: play.google.com/store/apps/details?id=com.rimmer.android.bankaroo&hl=en

CheckoutSmart

CheckoutSmart is a fun and easy way to make your supermarket shopping more rewarding—whether you shop instore or online. You can earn cashback when you shop at the supermarket—save money with great grocery deals and try new products for free!

Website: play.google.com/store/apps/details?id=com.checkoutsmart.checkoutsmart&hl=en

Debt Payoff Planner

Debt Payoff Planner helps tracking customization by highest debt, interest, or balance. It helps you to plan to pay off your debts. It can design a project of when the debt will be paid off given the details of the repayment plan and interest rates.

Website: play.google.com/store/apps/details?id=com.oxbowsoft.debtplanner&hl=en

---

About This Chapter: The mobile apps listed in this chapter were compiled from several sources deemed reliable. Inclusion does not constitute endorsement, and there is no implication associated with omission. All website information was verified and updated in February 2018.

Financial Calculators

For phone and tablet, Financial Calculators application includes the complete package of financial calculators. The app allows you to edit and prioritize the list of calculators for easy access.
Website: play.google.com/store/apps/details?id=com.financial.calculator

Goodbudget

Goodbudget is a money manager and expense tracker suitable for home budget planning. Built for easy, real-time tracking, and sync across Android, iPhone, and the web, to share your budget with your budgeting partners.
Website: play.google.com/store/apps/details?id=com.dayspringtech.envelopes

iAllowance

iAllowance is a money-tracking app. It creates a platform for parents/guardians and teens to work together on money management habits and applications.
Website: itunes.apple.com/in/app/iallowance/id398299456?mt=8

idealo

The idealo app lets you compare more than 107.2 million offers from over 21,300 online shops, such as Amazon, eBay, John Lewis, Currys, and Argos. Find cheapest prices from top-rated shops with the help of intuitive search suggestions and a wide range of filters to narrow your search or discover niche shops specializing in the products you are looking for.
Website: play.google.com/store/apps/details?id=de.idealo.android&hl=en

Left for Spending

Left for Spending app takes an approach to budget management that is entirely different from all other budgeting apps. Instead of overloading you with features and options, the app cuts to the core of the task and gives you an immediate and intuitive overview of your current financial situation.
Website: play.google.com/store/apps/details?id=com.halilibrahim.lefttospend&hl=en

Mint

Mint is a free money manager and financial tracker app. It brings together your bank accounts, credit cards, bills, and investments so you know where you stand.
Website: play.google.com/store/apps/details?id=com.mint&hl=en

Money Manager

Money Manager makes managing personal finances as easy as pie! Now easily record your personal and business financial transactions, generate spending reports, review your daily, weekly, and monthly financial data and manage your assets with Money Manager's spending tracker and budget planner.
Website: play.google.com/store/apps/details?id=com.realbyteapps.moneymanagerfree

Monefy

Monefy is a simple budget app. The app tries to set itself up in a way that makes adding new data quickly and easily. Alongside that, you'll get various currency support, a built-in calculator, passcode protection, Dropbox integration, widgets, and more.
Website: play.google.com/store/apps/details?id=com.monefy.app.lite

Payfriendz

Payfriendz is a payment app that makes payments with friends simple and free. Real time balance and search activity 100 percent free to use, no fees for anything, ever.
Website: play.google.com/store/apps/details?id=com.payango.payfriendz&hl=en

PiggyBot

PiggyBot has neat features, such as the ability to post photos of things your children want and a screen to show off the things they've purchased, giving them an idea of their goals and rewards. The app's developer says it reinforces principles of saving.
Website: itunes.apple.com/us/app/piggybot/id844151884?mt=8

PocketGuard

PocketGuard is a personal finance app in the United States and Canada. This handy tool can finally make money management and budgeting trouble-free. Paying bills, managing multiple accounts, staying on top of your spending habits—all of this is now available in one place.
Website: play.google.com/store/apps/details?id=com.pocketguard.android.app&hl=en

Simple

Simple is an online bank that includes a bunch of money management tools to help you plan your spending and figure out how to keep within your means.
Website: play.google.com/store/apps/details?id=com.banksimple&hl=en

Spendee

With Spendee, you can track your spending and budget so that you can save more money. You can connect Spendee to your bank account to track all your expenses, you can create a shared account with your family, and it supports multiple currencies.
Website: play.google.com/store/apps/details?id=com.cleevio.spendee&hl=en

Toshl Finance

Toshl Finance app helps setting a monthly budget and track every expense. It tracks all your credit cards, bank accounts, and cash in one place.
Website: play.google.com/store/apps/details?id=com.thirdframestudios.android.expensoor&hl=en

313

USAA Mobile

USAA Mobile gives you immediate and secure account access from your mobile device. Manage your finances, investments, insurance, and much more—all from one convenient app. Website: play.google.com/store/apps/details?id=com.usaa.mobile.android.usaa&hl=en

Wallet

Wallet is all about keeping track of and getting a handle on your spending. It works across multiple currencies and banks. You can use this app to plan your financial future and keep track of all your expenses and income. The app is free, and it doesn't require you to make any payments or enter any credit card information.
Website: play.google.com/store/apps/details?id=com.droid4you.application.wallet&hl=en

Yuby

Yuby is a free app designed to help your child learn how to manage money. Three core features teach kids the relationship between earning, spending, and saving to help them understand the value of money.
Website: play.google.com/store/apps/details?id=com.yuby.yuby&hl=en

Web-Based Financial Sources And Tools

Alliance for Investor Education (AIE)

The Alliance for Investor Education is dedicated to facilitating greater understanding of investing, investments, and the financial markets among current and prospective investors of all ages.
Savings Calculator: www.investoreducation.org/cindex2.cfm
Savings Game: www.investoreducation.org/savings_game.cfm

Bankrate.com

Bankrate helps you maximize your money and master life's financial journey. It also helps you find and compare rates on financial products like mortgages, credit cards, car loans, savings accounts, certificates of deposit, checking and ATM fees, home equity loans, and banking fees.
Financial calculators: www.bankrate.com/calculators.aspx Debt management calculators: www.bankrate.com/calculators/index-of-debt-management-calculators.aspx

Bureau of Consumer Protection

The Federal Trade Commission's Bureau of Consumer Protection stops unfair, deceptive, and fraudulent business practices by collecting complaints and conducting investigations, suing companies and people that break the law, developing rules to maintain a fair marketplace, and educating consumers and businesses about their rights and responsibilities.
Facts about fraud, deception, and unfair business practices: www.ftc.gov/bcp/index.shtml
"Focus on Finances—Preparing for Your Future": www.ftc.gov/bcp/edu/pubs/consumer/general/gen18.pdf

Bureau of the Fiscal Service

The Bureau of the Fiscal Service is an agency of the U.S. federal government that promotes the financial integrity and operational efficiency of the U.S. government through exceptional accounting, financing, collections, payments, and shared services. They help transform financial management and delivery of shared services in the federal government and also collaborate with and help other government organizations raise the level of their performance.

Website: www.fiscal.treasury.gov

Choose to Save®

The Choose to Save® national public education and outreach program is dedicated to raising awareness about the need to plan and save for long-term personal financial security.

Loan, budget, college, savings, and other calculators: www.choosetosave.org/calculators

Federal Student Aid

U.S. Department of Education's Federal Student Aid is responsible for managing the student financial assistance programs authorized under Title IV of the Higher Education Act of 1965. These programs provide grants, loans, and work-study funds to students attending college or career school.

Federal Student Aid Gateway: studentaid.ed.gov/sa/redirects/federal-student-aid-ed-gov

FinAid!

FinAid, The SmartStudent Guide to Financial Aid, is a free resource for objective and unbiased information, advice, and tools about student financial aid, college scholarships, and education loans.

College cost and savings calculators: www.finaid.org/calculators

Financial Industry Regulatory Authority, Inc. (FINRA)

FINRA is dedicated to investor protection and market integrity through effective and efficient regulation of broker-dealers. Its regulations play a critical role in America's financial system—by enforcing high ethical standards, bringing the necessary resources, and expertise to regulation and enhancing investor safeguards and market integrity—all at no cost to taxpayers.

Research tools, financial calculators, and simulation games: www.finra.org/investors/tools

HelpWithMyBank.gov

Office of the Comptroller of the Currency's Helpwithmybank.gov helps you find answers to your questions regarding national banks and federal savings associations.

Answers to national banking questions: www.helpwithmybank.gov

Managing Money

Managing Money is a financial literacy clearinghouse featuring Consumer Action's award-winning multilingual educational materials, headline news on personal finance topics, and recommended publications created by other organizations and government agencies. It focuses on financial services, sound financial planning and debt management, saving for emergencies and retirement, and how to avoid frauds and scams.

Interactive financial education: www.managing-money.org/articles/moneywie_offers_online_financial_education_courses

Money Matters to Me

Money Matters to Me can help you to understand financial matters that are relevant to you and to take control of your money on a day to day basis.

Financial calculators and other tools: www.moneymatterstome.co.uk/Interactive-Tools

The Motley Fool

The Motley Fool is a multimedia financial-services company that provides financial advice for investors through various stock, investing, and personal finance services.

Resources for teens: www.fool.com/shop/books/index.htm

MyBankTracker

MyBankTracker is an independent resource that helps consumers make smarter banking and money decisions.

APY calculator: www.mybanktracker.com/apy-calculator

MyMoney.gov

Financial Literacy and Education Commission's MyMoney.gov offers a variety of tools including calculators, budgeting worksheets, and checklists to assist consumers with making more financial decisions.

Website: mymoney.gov

National Foundation for Credit Counseling (NFCC)

NFCC promotes financially responsible behavior and delivers the highest-quality financial education and counseling services.

Budget worksheet: www.nfcc.org/financial-education

Practical Money Skills

Practical Money Matters column delivers expert personal finance tips to consumers of all ages. Personal finance resources: www.practicalmoneyskills.com/learnFinancial calculators: www.practicalmoneyskills.com/calculators

TeenAnalyst.com

TeenAnalyst.com has been teaching the basics of investing for about a decade.
Website: www.teenanalyst.com

TeenBusiness.com

TeenBusiness.com provides in-depth information about investing, starting your own business, the stock market, and the economy.
Website: www.teenbusiness.com

Wells Fargo Advisors

Wells Fargo Advisors is a financial services firm, serving investors nationwide through more than 14,500 financial advisors. It helps its clients succeed financially with investment planning and advice for helping them achieve their life needs and financial goals.
Website: www.wellsfargoadvisors.com

What's My Score.org

What's My Score.org helps you test your speed, agility, and endurance in the field of money management.
Downloadable resources: www.whatsmyscore.org/downloads

YoungBiz

YoungBiz is a financial and business education company for youths, young adults, and educators. It is committed to delivering game-changing training, providing effective e-learning tools, and providing published content that turns classrooms into real-life entrepreneurial experiences.
Website: youngbiz.com

Chapter 51

Additional Resources For Learning More About Money

America Saves Campaign

The Consumer Federation of America (CFA)
1620 Eye St. N.W., Ste. 200
Washington, DC 20006
Phone: 202-387-6121
Fax: 202-265-7989
Website: www.americasaves.org
E-mail: save@americasaves.org

American Bankers Association (ABA)

1120 Connecticut Ave. N.W.
Washington, DC 20036
Toll-Free: 800-BANKERS (800-226-5377)
Website: www.aba.com
E-mail: custserv@aba.com

American Financial Services Education Foundation (AFSAEF)

919 18th St. N.W.
Ste. 300
Washington, DC 20006-5517
Toll-Free: 888-400-7577
Fax: 202-223-0321
Website: www.afsaef.org
E-mail: info@afsaef.org

About This Chapter: Resources in this chapter were compiled from several sources deemed reliable; all contact information was verified and updated in February 2018

American Institute of Certified Public Accountants (AICPA)
1455 Pennsylvania Ave. N.W.
Washington, DC 20004-1081
Toll-Free: 888-777-7077
Phone: 202-737-6600
Toll-Free Fax: 800-362-5066
Fax: 202-638-4512
Website: www.aicpa.org
E-mail: service@aicpa.org

Canadian Foundation for Economic Education (CFEE)
110 Eglinton Ave. W.
Ste. 201
Toronto, ON M4R 1A3
Toll-Free: 888-570-7610
Phone: 416-968-2236
Fax: 416-968-0488
Website: www.cfee.org
E-mail: mail@cfee.org

Center for Responsible Lending (CRL)
302 W. Main St.
Durham, NC 27701
Phone: 919-313-8500
Website: www.responsiblelending.org

Certified Financial Planner (CFP) Board of Standards
1425 K St. N.W.
Ste. 800
Washington, DC 20005
Toll-Free: 800-487-1497
Phone: 202-379-2200
Fax: 202-379-2299
Website: www.cfp.net
E-mail: mail@cfpboard.org

Choose to Save

Employee Benefit Research Institute (EBRI)
1100 13th St. N.W., Ste. 878
Washington, DC 20005
Phone: 202-659-0670
Fax: 202-775-6312
Website: www.choosetosave.org
E-mail: info@choosetosave.org

Consumer Financial Protection Bureau (CFPB)

1700 G St. N.W.
Washington, D.C. 20552
Toll-Free: 855-411-CFPB (855-411-2372)
Toll Free TTY/TDD: 855-729-CFPB (855-729-2372)
Website: www.consumerfinance.gov

Council for Economic Education (CEE)

122 E. 42nd St., Ste. 2600
New York, NY 10168
Toll-Free: 800-338-1192
Phone: 212-730-7007
Fax: 212-730-1793
Website: www.councilforeconed.org

Credit Union National Association (CUNA)

601 Pennsylvania Ave. N.W.
S. Bldg, Ste. 600
Washington, DC 20004
Toll-Free: 800-356-9655
Fax: 202-638-7734
Website: www.cuna.org
E-mail: hello@cuna.coop

Debtors Anonymous

1116 Great Plain Ave.
P.O. Box 920888
Needham, MA 02492-0009
Toll-Free: 800-421-2383
Phone: 781-453-2743
Fax: 781-453-2745
Website: www.debtorsanonymous.org
E-mail: new@debtorsanonymous.org

Equifax, Inc.
1550 Peachtree St. N.W.
Atlanta, GA 30309
Toll-Free: 800-685-5000
Website: www.equifax.com
E-mail: cust.serv@equifax.com

Experian
475 Anton Blvd.
Costa Mesa, CA 92626
Toll-Free: 888-EXPERIAN (888-397-3742)
Phone: 714-830-7000
Website: www.experian.com

Federal Deposit Insurance Corporation (FDIC)
1776 F St. N.W.
Washington, DC 20006
Toll-Free: 877-ASK-FDIC (877-275-3342)
Toll-Free TDD: 800-925-4618
Website: www.fdic.gov

Federal Reserve Bank of Boston
600 Atlantic Ave.
Boston, MA 02210-2204
Phone: 617-973-3000
Website: www.bostonfed.org
E-mail: inquiries@bos.frb.org

Federal Reserve Bank of Cleveland
1455 E. Sixth St.
Cleveland, OH 44114
Toll-Free: 877-372-2457
Phone: 216-579-2000
Website: www.clevelandfed.org

Federal Reserve Bank of Dallas
2200 N. Pearl St.
Dallas, TX 75201
Toll-Free: 800-333-4460
Phone: 214-922-6000
Website: www.dallasfed.org

Federal Reserve Bank of Philadelphia

10 Independence Mall
Philadelphia, PA 19106-1574
Phone: 215-574-6000
Website: www.philadelphiafed.org

Federal Reserve Bank of San Francisco (FRBSF)

101 Market St.
San Francisco, CA 94105
Phone: 415-974-2000
Website: www.frbsf.org

Federal Reserve System

Board of Governors
20th St. and Constitution Ave. N.W.
Washington, DC 20551
Phone: 202-452-3000
TDD: 202-263-4869
Website: www.federalreserve.gov

Federal Student Aid Information Center

P.O. Box 84
Washington, DC 20044-0084
Toll-Free: 800-4-FED-AID (800-433-3243)
Phone: 319-337-5665
Toll-Free TTY: 800-730-8913
Website: studentaid.ed.gov

Federal Trade Commission (FTC)

600 Pennsylvania Ave. N.W.
Washington, DC 20580
Phone: 202-326-2222
Website: www.ftc.gov

Financial Consumer Agency of Canada (FCAC)
427 Laurier Ave. W.
Sixth Fl.
Ottawa, ON K1R 1B9
Toll-Free: 866-461-FCAC (866-461-3222)
Phone: 613-996-5454
Toll-Free TTY: 866-914-6097
TTY: 613-947-7771
Toll-Free Fax: 866-814-2224
Fax: 613-941-1436
Website: www.canada.ca

Financial Planning Association (FPA)
7535 E. Hampden Ave., Ste. 600
Denver, CO 80231
Toll-Free: 800-322-4237
Phone: 303-759-4900
Website: www.onefpa.org

Fincert
Institute for Financial Literacy (IFL)
P.O. Box 1842
Portland, ME 04104
Toll-Free: 855-436-2039
Phone: 207-873-0043
Fax: 207-873-0118
Website: www.fincert.org
E-mail: certifications@financiallit.org

InCharge Education Foundation
5750 Major Blvd.
Ste. 300
Orlando, FL 32819
Toll-Free: 800-565-8953
Website: www.incharge.org/foundation

Junior Achievement USA
One Education Way
Colorado Springs, CO 80906
Phone: 719-540-8000
Website: www.juniorachievement.org/web/ja-usa/home

National Association of Personal Financial Advisors (NAPFA)
8700 W. Bryn Mawr Ave.
Ste. 700N
Chicago IL 60631
Toll-Free: 888-FEE-ONLY (888-333-6659)
Phone: 847-483-5400
Fax: 847-483-5415
Website: www.napfa.org
E-mail: info@napfa.org

National Consumers League (NCL)
1701 K St. N.W., Ste. 1200
Washington, DC 20006
Phone: 202-835-3323
Fax: 202-835-0747
Website: www.nclnet.org
E-mail: info@nclnet.org

National Credit Union Administration (NCUA)
1775 Duke St.
Alexandria, VA 22314-3428
Toll-Free: 800-827-9650
Phone: 703-518-6540
Website: www.ncua.gov
E-mail: ogcmail@ncua.gov

National Endowment for Financial Education (NEFE)
1331 17th St.
Ste. 1200
Denver, CO 80202
Phone: 303-741-6333
Fax: 303-220-0838
Website: www.nefe.org

National Foundation for Credit Counseling (NFCC)
2000 M St. N.W., Ste. 505
Washington, DC 20036
Phone: 202-677-4300
Fax: 202-677-4333
Website: www.nfcc.org
E-mail: info@nfcc.org

Northwestern Mutual Foundation
720 E. Wisconsin Ave.
Milwaukee, WI 53202
Toll-Free: 866-950-4644
Phone: 414-271-1444
Website: www.northwesternmutual.com

Office of the Comptroller of the Currency (OCC)
U.S. Department of Treasury (USDT)
400 Seventh St. S.W.
Washington, DC 20219
Toll-Free: 800-613-6743
Phone: 202-649-6800
Toll-Free TTY: 800-877-8339
TDD: 713-658-0340
Website: www.occ.treas.gov

Securities Industry and Financial Markets Association (SIFMA)
1101 New York Ave. N.W.
Eighth Fl.
Washington, DC 20005
Phone: 202-962-7300
Website: www.sifma.org
E-mail: inquiry@sifma.org

Society of Financial Service Professionals (FSP)
3803 W. Chester Pike
Ste. 225
Newtown Square, PA 19073-2334
Phone: 610-526-2500
Fax: 610-359-8115
Website: www.financialpro.org
E-mail: Info@SocietyofFSP.org

TransUnion
1510 Chester Pike
Crum Lynne, PA 19022
Toll-Free: 800-888-4213
Fax: 610-546-4771
Website: www.transunion.com

The USAA Educational Foundation

9800 Fredericksburg Rd.
San Antonio, TX 78288-0026
Website: www.usaaedfoundation.org
E-mail: edfoundation_info@usaa.com

U.S. Bureau of Engraving and Printing (BEP)

14th and C Streets, S.W.
Washington, DC 20228
Toll Free: 877-874-4114
Phone: 202-874-4000
Website: www.moneyfactory.gov
E-mail: moneyfactory.info@bep.gov

U.S. Department of the Treasury (USDT)

1500 Pennsylvania Ave. N.W.
Washington, DC 20220
Phone: 202-622-2000
Fax: 202-622-6415
Website: www.treasury.gov

U.S. Mint

801 Ninth St. N.W.
Washington, DC 20220-0012
Toll-Free: 800-USA-MINT (800-872-6468)
Phone: 202-756-6468
Toll-Free TTY: 888-321-MINT (888-321-6468)
Website: www.usmint.gov

U.S. Securities and Exchange Commission (SEC)

100 F St. N.E.
Washington, DC 20549
Toll-Free: 800-SEC-0330 (800-732-0330)
Phone: 202-942-8088
Fax: 202-772-9295
Website: www.sec.gov

Index

Index

Page numbers that appear in *Italics* refer to tables or illustrations. Page numbers that have a small 'n' after the page number refer to citation information shown as Notes. Page numbers that appear in **Bold** refer to information contained in boxes within the chapters.